Come Hell on High Water

Come Hell on High Water

A

Really

Sullen

Memoir

Gregory Jaynes

North Point Press

A division of Farrar, Straus and Giroux

New York

North Point Press
A division of Farrar, Straus and Giroux
19 Union Square West, New York 10003

Copyright © 1997 by Gregory Jaynes
All rights reserved
Distributed in Canada by Douglas & McIntyre Ltd.
Printed in the United States of America
Designed by Jonathan D. Lippincott
First edition, 1997

Library of Congress Cataloging-in-Publication Data
Jaynes, Gregory.
    Come hell on high water / Gregory Jaynes. — 1st ed.
        p.   cm.
    ISBN 0-86547-522-9 (cloth : alk. paper)
    1. Jaynes, Gregory.   2. Voyages around the world.   I. Title.
G440.J36J39   1997
910.4'1—dc21   97-16084

To Bob and Esther Greenleaf
with thanks everlasting
for Madeline

Grownup men of sanguine temperament do cry.

—Leo Tolstoy

Sitting here in my cabin, I feel electrical and buzzy; my testicles hum like a tomcat's.

In organizing these notes for publication, I realize I penciled that tomcat business in my diary right off the bat on December 2, 1995, the morning my ship sailed from Liverpool, commencing her maiden voyage around the world. I did not have the tactile awareness then, there in my first hours aboard, to note that my cabin was vibrating, for it was vibrating at such speed the physical sensation was subliminal, at least in the beginning. I did not know then my cabin would vibrate as long as the big diesel engines were running belowdecks, that I myself would vibrate for more than one hundred days. I was never warned about the maddening effect a tingling assault of near-eternal duration (or at least that's how long it felt like to me) would have on the libido of a man alone. I just thought I was excited to be about to circumnavigate the earth on a freighter, that the commencement of my adventure had me organically aquiver, and that a side effect of my great anticipation seemed to be a nascent and, at the time, easily dismissed case of sexual arousal. I did not know then that you can vibrate a middle-aged man until all his vague yearnings metastasize into a profound and goatish lust, distinguished only by its indiscrimination.

A lust that exceeded garden-variety horniness was but one unpleasant and unanticipated element of my trip. The way the journey played out, desire rose within me just as my humanity—a component of my character I felt I held in great supply—began to drain away. For example, I see, poring over the accounts now, in the first week I introduce my shipmates as sunny enough for old folk. No doubt in those days I was looking at myself romantically, as something of a shepherd. I'd tend to them. They'd cherish me. We'd all be fine. But as it happened there was meanness and sourness among them, and one grande dame was perceived to be the daughter of Lucifer, and gradually I withdrew from their company. This doesn't sound like me.

That john in the sack with the twenty-dollar whore on Western Samoa in January—he doesn't sound like me, either. Nor the poor stiff atremble in Papua New Guinea in February, having himself a good cry in front of the captain. However, the chap jumping ship in Singapore in March, running out on his paid-for berth—given his frame of mind, that's my kind of sailor.

Sorry to say, they are all of those men me. Now that I no longer stand in their boots, I can see them clearly as schizophrenic spirits on the loose, pieces of the whole looking for a home. They're kind of sad.

It's hard, being an honest diarist. The temptation to tinker with the story is powerful. When you have the opportunity to go back and spruce up your life, there is a pull to make yourself prescient ("But there was something dark about that woman . . ."), or at least erudite ("Citing Ludwig Wittgenstein, I was able to blunt the vicar's point . . ."). The proof of truth in a man's diary is in the paucity of times he comes out on top.

On my honor, I haven't rearranged any furniture here—in fact, all I've done to alter these premises is take out the trash, which is to say I've excised the tedium I saw lying around (I didn't go under the sofa or anything), and attempt a polish, which is nothing more than vanity giving the surfaces a lick and a promise.

A diarist, keeping a diary, possesses no natural urge to elaborate; knowing everything, he tends to record no more than gist (to serve, years on, merely as a tickler to his full, rich, satisfying memory of the life he lived). This seems to me what I have done on several occasions in the text. In my defense, I would point out that Voltaire said the secret to becoming a bore was to tell everything. Nonetheless, I offer this primer, for use in transit; break glass in case of ellipsis:

In the summer of 1995, I turned forty-seven years old, and I was disenchanted with the view. I wanted change.

I thought it might help if I slipped into isolation on a cargo ship for a few months. I did not expect growth, depth, development, or serenity so much as I reckoned I might return home a man who had, after serious reflection, reversed a steady buildup of bile and learned to smile with greater ease, though not so much that I could be singled out of a lineup.

I felt free of delusion. I wasn't throwing myself at some Olympian test. I did not anticipate finding anything in myself or my journey worth sanctifying.

No one in my family opposed me. Then again, I did not entertain a show of hands. I simply said I was shipping out. I told this to my wife in New York City, my daughter and my son down in Georgia, my parents in Alabama, my brothers and sisters in Arkansas and Tennessee, and a few friends. To the question "Why?" I was often flip: "Why not?" I let them speculate. It wasn't as though a common blue suit, a pillar of the community, a deacon at Pea Rock Presbyterian was uprooting to farm opium in Tadzhikistan. This was *me*, whose soul was abroad even on days when my shoes were nailed to the kitchen floor. And given that it was me, sailing away shouldn't come as much of a surprise. After all, this was a man who, as a boy, thought the coolest nickname a boy could have was Nighttrain. Nighttrain Jaynes.

For their part, my friends and relations seemed to think that my daughter's being pregnant, and my feeling that becoming a grandfather at this stage was a little premature, might have had something to do with my decision to go on off. True, that may have been a part of it, but leaving was never a clear-cut deal with me. I see by my diary that once in a while I try to sneak up on my reasoning, but somehow I always manage to snap a twig, or sneeze, and I catch but a flash of white tail before my quarry springs out of sight. I do not mean to imply I invested less mental currency in examining "Why am I on this ship?" than the next fellow plows into "Why am I on this earth?" To me this one's a complicated and entirely personal question, and I do the best I can with it, and the journal is shot through with my anemic answers. It doesn't strike me as frivolous to offer that they come down to this: A man's mind does not get to be forty-seven years old without attracting boogers. And this: Who's to say I didn't leave merely because I could, and that I expected to have a little fun?

No, not frivolous—evasive perhaps.

While I am on the subject—evasion—I may as well confront the first question I am asked by anyone who has caught wind of my tale: What was my wife's reaction? It is the hardest question for me to answer. First, this is a report of my journey, not a portrait of my marriage. I won't presume to say how she feels. I can say we are still together, either in spite of or because of my voyage. I can say, as I do more than once in the diary, that my interest in marriage began to wane about ten years ago, but, my behavior to the contrary, I never lost my love or my respect for my wife. Because this journal is my story, not hers, she is as offstage from its content as she was from my life while I was on the ship. I can say that I did not sail away owing to a problem of the heart. I can say I know no one more special than the woman who told me to go ahead if I must.

I contacted a travel agency in California that keeps track of merchant vessels. I learned that most freighters take a dozen passengers (more than twelve and, under some maritime law, the ship would have to employ a full-time medical officer), and that bookings, especially for a lone traveler, were tight. If I could find a berth, the fare would work out to about one hundred dollars a day, room and board.

I was wait-listed for a number of ships, as far ahead as a year. Then, in September, I was offered passage on the shakedown cruise of a Finnish ship a British line had purchased and refitted. Because it was a maiden voyage, reasons for dissatisfaction were anticipated, and I was offered a 12 percent discount, knocking the fare down from nearly thirteen thousand dollars to a little less than eleven. I leaped at it.

I packed Leo Tolstoy's *War and Peace*, aiming once and forever to read a book that is so widely known for its large bones that most people speak of it as though it should be called *Mount War and Peace*.

It turned out I was misinformed about my ship. I would be sailing on a Russian vessel built in Helsinki, not a Finnish vessel. The ship would carry a Russian crew, under the command of British officers. The ship would be an icebreaker, formerly used by the Soviets to supply military installations in the Arctic. A Soviet icebreaker in the torrid South Pacific—it had a certain comic appeal.

Sailing a Russian ship, and taking Tolstoy into the belly of the bear, was sheer coincidence. And coincidentally, *War and Peace* became my touchstone.

As I said, or boasted, I am an honest diarist, but I must confess to name-robbing. I am changing all the names in this document. However, one of the changes is an act of restoration.

I call my ship *Tiksi*, MV *Tiksi* (Motor Vessel *Tiksi*). *Tiksi* is her given name, her Russian name, the name she had, that fit, the name that she wore well, before her new owners, the British, rechristened her, naming her after a river in England. Tiksi is a Russian town in the Arctic. For all my murking of other identities in this book, as well as my theft of people's idiosyncrasies, at least I can claim to have returned to one character something that belongs to her.

G. J./New York City

Come Hell on High Water

I have come to the end of something in my life—the best way I can describe it is to say I feel devalued, like a peso—and I suspect a long sail, and undistracted time to ponder, might be the medicine to see me through. To that purpose, this morning I wrote a check for $10,708 and dropped it into the mail. For my trouble, I secured passage on a cargo ship that is to leave Liverpool, England, on the second of November, and circumnavigate the world, fetching up back in Antwerp, Belgium, early next spring. Tonight, I am out of sorts, wondering if I couldn't have managed to plot a less precipitous course.

This woolgathering is another symptom of some sort of shifting within me. With age I have become aware of a lifelong, nearly unconscious tendency to run when I am bothered. I don't even have to be cornered before I bolt, just mildly unhappy. I see it now as an almost constitutional recklessness. Up to now the unexamined exit has always been worth taking, to me. What's new, now, is the examination. It means I'm unsure of myself; I've lost confidence. Moreover, there are two barrels to this gun, both bearing the same shot. I suspect I am leaving because in my life I have become unsure of myself. And now I am unsure of leaving.

I can make it without brio; I'd be lost without nerve.

This morning I poked about the neighborhood on my way to the post office to send off the fare, stalling. Obviously, it is a lot of money and a substantial voyage, not the sort of thing to hurl yourself into entirely on impulse. The envelope, in an inside jacket pocket, seemed a hot brand against my breast, really. I couldn't stop myself thinking: A bold move or the removal of a fool? An old drunk romantic thing to do? Isn't this a pretty theatrical distance to go just to pout or to sulk or, for pity's sake, to see if my subtraction leaves a hole?

I walked the Upper West Side of Manhattan and read historical plaques I had not paid attention to in years, or never had. According to a sidewalk medallion at Eighty-fourth Street and Broadway, one block from where I live, Edgar Allan Poe wrote "The Raven" there on a chicken farm in 1844. Chicken. Raven. Shrewd substitution. No one expects a chicken at the door in the middle of the night. I turned east on West Eighty-sixth Street, or Isaac Bashevis Singer Boulevard. Singer said that even an idiot is a millionaire in emotion. It bucked me up to be reminded that this area has always sheltered writers, good and bad.

I'm a writer. I got into the trade because, early on, schoolteachers told me I had a knack for it. My own insecurity told me I was deft but dumb. Nevertheless, I became addicted to the praise. I had begun to earn my living as a boy police reporter on the morning paper in Memphis when, one midnight in 1967, I overheard four officers beating the dickens out of a suspect on the other side of the pressroom wall. I wrote this in the paper, and the four officers were suspended. It became a racial issue: cops white; victim black. Later in the year a Civil Service commission reinstated the cops. At the time, the city's Sanitation Department, which is to say the city's Negro garbagemen, was in contract negotiations. Dismissing the police-brutality charges was viewed by union leaders as one more intolerable racial slight on the part of the city. In time, the garbagemen went on strike. Their placards said: I AM A MAN. The Rev. Dr. Martin Luther King, Jr., came to Memphis to lead them in a march.

The power of journalism seduced me evermore. It paid poorly in the minors, but I plugged away, and gradually I was able to move up to the Show: Miami; Atlanta; New York City. *The New York Times. Time. Life.* Africa. Asia. Europe. The Middle East. The Gulf War. The collapsing Soviet Union. Then one day in October 1991 I was taking a shower in Novgorod, Russia, one of those showers so icy they coax involuntary screams out of you, and I took an unexamined exit out of journalism to come back to America to find a better way. In time I gave up drinking, too, because I was brooding more than looking for a better way, and I thought, either way, brooding or looking, I could do it better without the alcohol that had besotted my brain for twenty years. After a year or so clean and sober, I found I had worked through my grief over the loss of liquor, but I was still pathetically hooked on praise. I returned to writing.

I went back to work about the same time George Foreman went back in the ring. (George and I are close in age. One time in Humble, Texas, when George was idle, he told me, "Them licks hurt." I asked him to describe to me what it felt like to be hit by, say, Muhammad Ali. George bent way back around himself and then delivered a haymaker, with a fist about the size of a soccer ball, that stopped just at the tip of my nose. Nothing fell out, but my sphincter shot open all the same.) I went off to Ho Chi Minh City for *Time*. The Great Sweet Potater gained the White House and I flew to Little Rock to prospect for *Esquire*. I was back in the game, but I never seemed to draw a hot hand anymore. And the dealers cut the praise so much with caveat it didn't get me high.

Ten minutes afoot today and I had passed three newsstands where my work was on prominent display. My name appears in a strong red font on the cover of the current *Esquire*. I am also the author of the cover story in this week's *Time*. It pleased me to see my words were still getting around, more or less (*Time* fussed with them, fluffed them, as you would a poodle, for show; *Esquire* whacked them in two, as if advised by Solomon that half a baby would do). But for some time I have felt uncertain about continuing to contribute at all. Time to go.

It feels like time to go for many reasons: shallow; deep; real; imagined; tiresome. I have a dresser drawer full of justifications, one to bolster any frame of mind. I have my ego to consider, for one thing. My ego has been suffering various slights, all of them about the size, and lingering nastiness, of a paper cut. And I'm not sure but my usefulness might be sluing into doubt.

Another concern is that my youth is leaving, and I am finding it painful to say goodbye. I live in fear that I will learn one morning soon that it is not the stair doing the creaking.

And I have snarly things in my head that are making me upset and petulant. Inarticulation about the subject is part of the reason for tearing off to think on it, I think. If I could satisfactorily explain or describe my distress there might be no point in disappearing. Look at it this way: if either of these acts attains the same result, which should a man commit: (1) pay ten grand to a shrink? (2) haul ass to Tahiti?

None but a moron would pick door number one.

I suspect my general symptoms are universal. Most men reach a period in which they have a sense they are faltering, misfiring, a period in which no one wants to toss them out, but no one wants to give them the keys to the store. A period in which their own ways of doing things, personal stamps that once gained them praise, now have to be altered to appease new demands. To accept modifications with stoical good grace gains a man the patronizing reputation of a "pro." To see change as purely arbitrary and protest it is to be categorized as being "too sensitive." The trick is to elude the sad-sack qualities: self-pity, snideness, a tendency to be arch. Either that or find something to do with your hands. But I've had to keep in mind there's not much call for yard work in Manhattan.

When the envelope bearing my check dropped, and the slot closed on the letter box, I seized on the idea of straightening a wire coat hanger and affixing chewing gum to one end, and seeing if I could master a smart retrieval. Much less embarrassing that way than to call up the shipping line and confess to cold feet. The panic passed in the bat of an eye, but it was very real, the panic.

I just shared a roasted chicken, some sweet bananas, and rice and beans with my friend Roy in a Brazilian restaurant on Broadway, and he said he could see a movie in my travel plan if I could put some nudity and some gunfire in it. Roy and I have taken to meeting for lunch occasionally here in the neighborhood, and I had brought the news of my imminent voyage as a centerpiece for our table. Roy's news was that he had successfully gained the sole screenwriting credit for a big-budget Hollywood comedy that will be released in a few months; that he had finished his column for a slick men's magazine on the grand opening of the Rock and Roll Hall of Fame in Cleveland, at which Roy's own band had performed; that he had not yet commenced to write of his recent travels in China; that he had just signed with a prestigious publisher to write a memoir of his childhood; that the son of a martyred President of the United States had asked him, Roy, to write for his, the son's, new magazine, and that Roy had negotiated triumphantly with the scion for a higher fee. My ripping change of life became less a centerpiece than a side salad, or a garnish—a bacon bit.

To the library. My branch, on Amsterdam Avenue between Eighty-first Street and Eighty-second, while my branch and proud of it, was little use to the aspiring sailor in me, except for the inspiring, crayoned poster on the wall that said: One Thing At A Time (You Can Do Everything). The thing I couldn't do at my branch was find any books by middle-aged men who'd chucked their everydayness and run off to sea.

I walked to Fifth Avenue and Forty-second Street, to the New York Public Library, home of the pride. I go here occasionally, like George Peppard in *Breakfast at Tiffany's*, to look myself up. Twenty years ago I published a book every bit as impudent, to say nothing of empty, as my head. It was a time when I believed too much introspection would destroy a man. In those days my idea of words to live by ran along the lines of: Never eat chili in a place called Stinky's. In those days I could hit bull's-eyes without taking aim. I had fathered early, married early. I dragged my young family from pillar to post while I taught myself a trade and chased recognition. By the time the successes amounted to anything, that marriage was over.

At the library today, in my chosen field, I was able to run a finger down the spines of *Five Against the Sea* and *Twenty Years Before the Mast*, down *The Lonely Sea and the Sky* (read it, once glimpsed the *Gypsy Moth* itself, outside the National Maritime Museum in Greenwich), and *Sons of Sinbad*. I had not only read *A Night to Remember*, by Walter Lord, the saga of "the ship that God himself couldn't sink," I had, in 1988, in Boston, interviewed the last living survivors of the *Titanic*. "You're smoking?" I shrieked to a ninety-year-old Englishman in the bar of the Ritz-Carlton. "I survived the *Titanic*," he wheezed, making me feel real small and backward.

More titles: *The Mutiny on the Globe, The Voyage of the Mir-el-lah, The Wreck on the Half-Moon Reef, Collision Course, Altering Course, Nothing Can Go Wrong, Adrift, Posted Missing*, and, praise one's lucky stars, *Reaching Port*. I lingered over a book subtitled *Around the World in a Bad Mood*, but the one that won my crown, though it had absolutely nothing to do with what I was up to, was *Roots Schmoots: Journeys among Jews*. I have not selected it for my sea chest, but I shall always admire the title.

In all the New York library system, there were only two books that addressed the sort of mission I had set myself. One was John McPhee's *Looking for a Ship*, an account I had read of a forty-two-day run on an American cargo vessel down the west coast of South America, and the other was Christopher Buckley's *Steaming to Bamboola*, which I sat down and read on the spot. In *Bamboola*, the author caught a freighter out of Charleston, South Carolina, in 1979, and sailed to Bremerhaven, West Germany, then back to New Orleans. It occurred to me while reading that when Buckley wrote the book he was of an age (twenty-seven) when he could still swash, while I (forty-seven) am merely slinking out of town on old frequent-flier miles. The thought made me sigh, the only exclamation a civilized man should make in a public library.

In my careful (for me) thinking about reading matter to take along, I have decided to pass over *Moby-Dick*. The evidence reveals every writing mariner for the last century has cleaved to Herman Melville. Melville didn't just inform their work, he lent it granite (I was tempted to say "gravitas," but that one is so picked clean it begs to go under the plow). Melvilleans are everywhere. Melville is on the Internet (call it Ish-Mail). Not that Melville is not a siren to me, too; who wouldn't be seduced by the way Herman swans up the gangway? ". . . having little or no money in my purse, and nothing particular to interest me on shore, I thought I would sail about a little and see the watery part of the world."
Laying Melville aside, I will place in my luggage my own conceit. I have decided to pack *War and Peace*. I aim to read it. Indeed, if I accomplish nothing else in all this removal, I will have read *War and Peace*. Jimmy Carter once told me he read *War and Peace* when he was twelve. I felt like saying that if I had been stuck in a one-holer like Plains, Georgia, when I was twelve, I would have read it, too. But that would have been a nervous shot at wit and a lie to boot. I didn't have the discipline to read *War and Peace* when I was twelve. In fact, even as an idle mature man in the middle of the Atlantic, Caribbean, Pacific, Indian, and Mediterranean Oceans, as well as vast stretches of minor waters, I anticipate a struggle finishing *War and Peace*. For most

of my life, I have devoted great sums of energy to avoiding reading *War and Peace*. The only critical area I can think of that may have gotten more of my energy was the ducking of the Jehovah's Witnesses at the door on hung-over Saturday mornings.

September 22, 1995
New York City

I am not examining it very carefully, but I am aware I am waking up these days feeling churlish, a direct manifestation of anxiety. By midmorning I am hoping to outrun the mood, as you would a mugger. Today I was sore about my good memory. It is mostly a burdensome possession. One has to grow very old or enter a coma or die to get shed of having Super Glue for a memory. It is true I do not have to use a bookmark, nor dog-ear a page, but I also remember everything a man needn't. Memory gives me such a short fuse with people who don't bother with it, as most people don't; nor should they. Much of life is trivial and should go behind you unremarked, shit through a goose. Now, that's a refreshing point of view, coming from an aspiring diarist.

September 28, 1995
New York City

Glorious fall days passing now across the American Northeast. Too pretty out for sketches from the interior. A vaulting blue sky above the terrace, here amid heaping salads of summer flowers—impatiens, and salvia and geraniums, their heads held high, shoulders back, in the face of an imminent autumn collapse.

I have a modest apartment on a roof. Living on a roof is like living in a marina. There are other people around living on roofs, but you can't walk over to their house, borrow a cup of the

Glenlivet, say, as you could not walk on water to a neighbor's boat. You see your neighbors, see them doing maintenance, or sunning themselves, and some hot days the air is liquid and there is something very nautical about living on the roofs of New York City. At sundown, though, looking west at the water towers on all the roofs against a sky on fire, it is just like looking west from Midland or Odessa, Texas, and being able to see all the way to La Jolla, California.

I make myself prematurely homesick adoring this so.

They are preparing the Great Lawn in Central Park for the arrival of Pope John Paul next week. I walked my dog, Willie, through the preparations this morning. There were great, Erector-set-like structures going up for a stage and sound system. Unloading some long steel slats off a very long flatbed truck with a crane, a workman on the ground shouted to the man in the truck's cab, "Swing the son of a bitch around!" Given that this labor was in service of the Holy See, how irreverent. But I have seen serious irreverence with this Pope before.

In 1980, John Paul made his first visit to Africa. I was then the *Times* man in Nairobi, and it was my task to follow along. I say I had to follow rather than accompany, because at the last minute papal tape denied me a seat with the Vatican press on the Pope's plane. I had to chase the whole Roman Catholic mob across Africa on commercial airlines, which did not in those days fly east–west with any frequency, meaning that to make a short lateral move, I had to fly vertically all the way to Europe to change planes immediately to head back south, to catch a Mass. That kind of travel is sorry work, even for the Lord.

I glimpsed the Pope when fortune allowed. As it happened, things didn't work all that well for the Pope and his folk in Africa, either, and I took perverse comfort in their discomfort. In Ghana, for example, there was a six-foot-seven-inch cardinal from Illinois who had to sleep in a bed custom-made for a diplomat's twelve-year-old daughter; the big cardinal issued forth next day with the posture of a boomerang.

The mechanicals conspired most woefully in Kinshasa, Zaire. There John Paul celebrated a Mass, and, according to the Associated Press, a million people came. For fifteen years, I've wondered about the person who disseminated that information: a *million* people! Has anyone ever seen a *million* people in one spot? You look out the window and there are a *million* people on the grass! How would you know it was a *million*? There was no computer doing the sums from a satellite, no chopper with a cop working with a grid. There was just some news-agency mathematician there on the banks of the Congo who said, holy shit, looks like a *million* people, and . . . well, *The New York Times* rang my head like a Hong Kong gong. I mean, I'd seen sixty-five thousand people in a football stadium once. But a *million* was hard for me to verify. All right, then, a *million*—the Pope's African microphone still didn't work. The Pope knocked on the microphone with his fist, and nothing. The Zairois fiddled with that microphone all morning, thinking now and again they had it right, and the Pope would get up, knock on it, and sit down again. The throng milled around, as throngs are wont. The Pope sat through it, never looking impatient. He wore no expression. I was on the stage and at one point I held the Pope's gaze and I rolled my eyes, the way you'd do conspiratorially with someone you knew. The Pope had no reaction, though he looked sternly straight at me (we were about eight feet apart), and I was suddenly, overwhelmingly self-conscious. For many days afterward, I expected to go straight to hell.

The physician was an amiable blond man of about forty, in a cluttered second-floor office at Park Avenue and Seventy-ninth Street. He threw me down and looked at me, thumping on me fore and aft, kneading me, tested ball joints, listened for misfires in the motor, and pronounced me fairly fit, considering. He signed a document that said as much (a requirement of the shipping line). I wrote a check for $450 and let my beating heart—106 over 82—out into the late-September light. Celebrities were everywhere.

The artist LeRoy Neiman was having brunch at a French sidewalk café on Madison Avenue, his signature waxed mustaches stiff as a still propeller beneath his nose. LeRoy looked particularly full of himself and I came to find by the afternoon papers he had just this day given six million dollars to Columbia University—he was impressed by the cut of the campus, he said; "I couldn't believe the classic look of it sitting right in the middle of the city"—to create the LeRoy Neiman Center for Print Studies.

The guy coming out of the coffee shop on Fifty-ninth Street between Madison and Fifth Avenues was the guy who always plays Harrison Ford's boss, and Harrison and all the rest of us always think this guy is on our side when Harrison gets into trouble, and when Harrison calls him from a pay phone to gasp for help because death-dealing danger is hot on Harrison's tail, the guy coming out of the coffee shop always betrays Harrison and nearly gets him killed. Yeah, that's the guy. You're always seeing that guy and other guys like him coming out of coffee shops or delicatessens in New York. You never can think of their names.

I had some business in midtown, and then I headed back up the West Side.

At a sidewalk table on Broadway, alone in the autumn at an Italian place across from Lincoln Center, her face turned full south and shimmering coppery in the sun, Joan Baez, accepting compliments graciously from admiring passersby. Thirty years ago I used to fantasize coming home to Joan Baez, I had such a crush. She'd be in a corner of our love nest, softly strumming her guitar, her soprano so light and soft it seemed to sleep on the wind, my woman—kind of quiet and self-assured. Ah, Joan, in your middle-aged matron's silks, the gray streaks in your blackbird's hair.

I collected my springer spaniel and set off for Riverside

Park. Coming my way, walking east on West Eighty-fourth Street: Tom Hayden. Tom's old lawyer, William Kunstler, died here in town a week or so ago. Tom married Jane Fonda. Jane married Ted Turner. Ted Turner sold his show to Time Warner a day or two ago for seven point five billion dollars in stock. Billion. The paper this morning said Time Warner, the media colossus that has been driven so far into debt by its fat-cat stewards even Benetton doesn't have a shade for the red, will pay Ted, for serving as a vice-chairman, a salary of fifteen million dollars a year. *Million*. Tom Hayden on Eighty-fourth Street alone. Joan Baez on Broadway, alone in her silks. When my check to the doctor clears the bank, my account will be down to stems and seeds, to use an expression Tom and Joan would remember.

$$\approx\approx\approx$$

October 6, 1995
New York City

Stepped out the kitchen door and heard Pope John Paul singing a Polish children's song, over in the park. The sky was low and damp; on the roof here I had the sensation I could snatch a handful of it, roll it up, and have a cloud-ball fight. They were saying there were one hundred and twenty thousand people on the Great Lawn, one hundred thousand spread out around the perimeter. A security helicopter roaring back and forth over my roof drowned out the amplified Pope from time to time, but I had him inside on the television as well. On the TV, a crippled fellow in a wheelchair, who met the Pope before the Mass, said, "Evil doesn't stand a chance with me anymore!"

With one foot in my apartment, the other on my terrace, I had the real Pope in one ear (three blocks away), the televised Pope in the other (over there in the corner of the living room). The Pope said man at the end of the twentieth century is afraid.

In the mail, a letter from my doctor, computer printouts of various findings, an electrocardiogram, and a laboratory bill big enough to kill a man if the conclusion in the envelope had gone the other way. "You are in excellent health," my doctor writes. "Keep up the good work!" On the one hand, I feel I've gotten away with something—reckless living on my part without penalty, so far. On the other hand, the precocious curmudgeon in me wants to complain that there goes poor health as a good excuse.

Graham Greene is back in the morning paper, as a local correspondent has gained Sierra Leone. Thank God for Greene, who wrote of everywhere. In Port-au-Prince earlier this year, I shared a van with two Canadian television gents who could speak of no one else. "Yes, a very Greeney place," one kept saying, thumbing his copy of *The Comedians*. No journalist goes to Vietnam without a copy of *The Quiet American*. In Sierra Leone, it is *The Heart of the Matter*. Literature from writers who penned through in better times is a cornerstone of Third World correspondency. One can show the glory, and then bring all the sad developments up to date.

"At the City Hotel," writes Howard French from Freetown, "the place Graham Greene made his home for two years in the 1940s, the old round-keyed cash register at the bar is frozen with rust and the ceiling sags from leaking rain. In the absence of a kitchen, the squatters who live there now prepare food in a smoky courtyard, with pots balanced on stones, where women can be seen bending over to fan fires underneath."

When I was in West Africa, I used to lean on Greene (*A Burnt-Out Case* was a particular favorite). In East Africa, in ad-

dition to Karen Blixen and Elspeth Huxley, there was always
Winston Churchill. You will read that Winston Churchill called
Uganda "the pearl of Africa" in every correspondent's first dispatch from Kampala. Then the writer is free to knock the country down. (Churchill, incidentally, got around as much as
Greene; I saw him in a dispatch from Sarajevo just the other day.
"Churchill said the trouble with the Balkans was it produces
more history than it can consume," a journalist on the spot in-
formed me.)

You have to send young people to write about these shallow-
grave countries. They have to have hope and enthusiasm and
exuberance to write seriously of insecure governments standing
frailly on ridiculously thin intelligence, and inhumanity without
end. It is only when you detect between the lines of their text
that what they really wanted to say was "As I should have pointed
out the last time I was forced to visit this cruel shithole . . ." that
you know the young correspondents have had enough, that they
have washed their hands of sorrow, and they have booked passage
back to somewhere people rarely starve ignominiously to death.

October 11, 1995
New York City

Gore Vidal gave a talk in the big bookshop across the street
tonight. The crowd overflowed the corner of the store reserved
for the lecture. There must have been three or four hundred of
us shoulder to shoulder in the aisles. Initially I was squeezed
between *First Guitar Riffs* and *The Complete Illustrated Atlas of
Reptiles and Amphibians for the Terrarium*, and I couldn't even see
Vidal, though I kept hearing a fat man's chuckle through the
cheap amplifier. Everyone took to his naughty wit right away.
He called Jack Kennedy "the President-Erect" and chuckled.

Directly, I insinuated myself between a prunish old couple in the nude-photography stacks and caught a glimpse of Gore, rotund and perspiring but enjoying himself. With relish, he got onto the subject of war and peace. He said this country's biggest problem is its failure, in forty-five years, to shift from a wartime to a peacetime economy—and here we are five trillion dollars in debt later. He said it wasn't the generals' fault; said West Pointers hate war. "You lose a lot of bed sheets and pillowcases," Gore said. "War is messy." He said it's the guys from the seminaries who get elected to Congress who want us in these dicey places where we don't belong.

Gore said, "Sissies are warmongers."

A woman in a hurry fell in stride alongside me for a few steps today, then proceeded to move in front of me, as a faster car overtakes a slower one from the passing lane. Blond, expensively tousled hair. The burgundy silk back of a suede vest over a chambray work shirt (sleeves rolled up like a laborer's, not even an infinitesimal wrinkle on the spare flesh of the elbows; I could tell because I was sporting my best spectacles). A denim skirt faded the heat-drained blue of an August afternoon. Split up the rear to afford ample room for active, milky calves in supple brown leather boots. This sylph from the Ponderosa (on West Eighty-first Street, across from the Museum of Natural History; even a feeble imagination could work with that) trailed a bosky fragrance. I had my shoulder to the task of elevating the thinking inner me, but as I followed the whip of cotton, the flash of alabaster calf, I thought: I'm going to miss this. I lost sight of her in a herd crossing Columbus Avenue. I had yellow fever and cholera shots to attend to, inoculations against everything but love.

Running this morning, two women ahead of me either were the most indiscreet young, physically flawless runners in Central Park or thought everyone else laying down laps was deaf.

"He like couldn't do anything," said one.

The other laughed, and then they both laughed.

"I mean I had fun," said the first, "but we—well, don't tell anybody except maybe Kathy and Martha and"—bursts of laughter here, and me, from two paces behind, involuntarily slowed and turned slightly by the information, as a following boat is by the wake of a water hog off the bow—"and, oh, you know. He'd just die if he knew I said anything. He's so sensitive."

I've noticed women seem to be leaving men for other women a lot lately, surrendering to their own side, as it were. I have had to counsel an older male friend whose mate has gone over. My friend's generation tends to see any sapphic happiness as a poor showing on the part of all mankind. I have told him that in times of an epidemic it is no loss of face when the plague knocks at the family door.

I get around some. I hear things. Now they're saying young women you'd think the least likely are taking a run at prostitution. They see it as a political statement. Use your power to soak the bastard. To me, this doesn't track. To me, the bastard still gets the bargain. He still leaves the woman a monetary token for her time, and an organic down payment on her self-esteem, the world's oldest leveraged buyout.

The heebie-jeebies again. A natural resistance to write. The reality of leaving is all over the house and out on the terrace as I
try to tidy up my affairs.

I have said nothing of the Million Man March on Washington two days ago. A *million* men. The National Park Service,
which takes aerial photographs of crowds, superimposes grids,
and counts noses, says there were four hundred thousand participants in the Million Man March. Organizers of the march
say there were a million participants. By comparison, the Pope,
who drew a million in Zaire (my career was nearly derailed
over this), only pulled about one hundred and twenty thousand
(the official police count) onto the Great Lawn of Central Park
a couple of weeks ago. The Great Lawn is thirteen acres, large
enough to accommodate ten football fields (about half again
the size of the site of the Pope's Mass in Kinshasa). The most
people ever gathered on the Great Lawn was six hundred
thousand in 1991 (filling it to the brim), to hear Paul Simon
sing. My dog and I were on the Great Lawn today. It's bald
and brown as a lion. They've closed it for two years to bring
back grass (the *Great* Lawn). A million people. Not here. Not
in Washington. And not fifteen years ago in Africa, I say. But
who listens to me? Come to think of it, isn't this the point
of keeping a diary? It's a thing for pissing and moaning into,
isn't it?

Yes.

But what folly to use a forum like this to kid myself. So some

crowd arithmetic is wrong, so what? Does this really arouse me?
Am I not using this to distract? What's really eating me?
Uncertainty.

Pope to Man:
Scaredy-Cat!

Pulled away from Liverpool at ten of seven this morning, one month to the day behind schedule and six weeks or better since I made jot one in this journal. My writing hand has been stayed by frustration with the sailing delays and the embarrassment of accepting warm parting wishes from friends and faux friends only to be spotted in the street again a day or two later shopping for provender, or a funny periodical to pass the time. The lesson here is, if you want to leave in a huff, don't book a freighter. It's like leaping into ankle-deep water with suicide on your mind, or, similarly disposed, flinging yourself from a ladderback chair with a thirty-foot rope affixed to your noose.

My worldview now is through a porthole I would reckon is eighteen inches wide by thirty inches deep. It is all gray as a trout out there over the gray, flat sea with once in a while a break in the cottony fog and a glimpse of Welsh headlands. There's no roll, no pitch, no yaw to the ship, but I can hear a faint drone from the engines, and my body hair is standing and kind of dancing, modern dancing, and my skin fairly tingles. Sitting here in my cabin, I feel electrical and buzzy; my testicles hum like a tomcat's.

The size of my cabin is 10.7 square meters—about 116 square feet. It has a single bunk, also a steel frame with a piece of upholstered foam rubber that serves as a sofa, a writing desk and chair, three drawers for storage, a two-door wardrobe, a shower, sink, shaving mirror, and toilet, a half fridge, television with built-in videocassette player, shortwave radio, and an electric teakettle. It is all so North Country fair, Scandiwegian blond, except for the blue industrial carpet. On the desk are canisters of instant coffee, tea bags, and sugar, and a bowl spilling over with dyed, but not artificial, carnations, daisies, and goldenrod. On the wall above my bunk is a framed print of a Gauguin oil of two naked brown Tahitian women cutting their eyes at me; they follow me round my quarters no matter what corner I hold. A man by himself with two nudes on the wall, I don't know.

My cabin is on deck five, just below the bridge. Sometimes I think I hear the captain pacing above.

My ship is twelve years old, built in Finland for Russians. She has a Russian crew still. She was designed to defeat ice in the polar cap on runs from Northern Europe to Japan (one of the officers said yesterday she can break through ice a meter thick), and so she has had to be retooled, refitted for the business her new British owners have in mind. That would be the business of trading in the South Pacific, where I'm told by the skipper there is still a pretty penny to be made. Basically, you take the islanders everything this side of fruit, coconuts, and sunshine, since they manufacture practically nothing themselves ("The French, of course, want all the cheeses, the brandies, the liqueurs," the captain explained). And you bring back palm oil and copra, would be my guess.

I don't have all of the story yet because in the first days of any long voyage sailors have their hands full, but as best I can piece it together this ship was purchased, and made over, for about a quarter of what a new ship of her sort would cost, which is to say one-fourth of fifty-eight million dollars. The poor Russians, caught in calamitous political and economic circumstances and starved for hard currency, sold off seventeen vessels like this one in all, fetching for themselves little more than scrap-iron prices, and the shipping line I am patronizing bought four. All the Brits had to do was adjust the picture so that this great bargain in Arctic navigational hardware worked efficiently down where the waters have never known ice, let alone a ship designed to break it.

The Liverpool shipyard that won the contract to make the

necessary modifications went about modifying at a somewhat languorous pace (with consequences extending all the way to Broadway, where one could hear me saying, "Goodbye, Judy"; "Oh, hullo, Judy—no, I should be gone indeed, but as you can see . . ."). You break ice with a ship by going over the top of it, and crashing down and through, I am told. By design, then, this vessel was broad of beam but featured a scissors-like, ice-cracking bow configuration; she raked back sharply and then reversed herself, like this: <. To make her more fuel-conservative going around the world under her first frost-free mandate, she has been given the opposite of a plastic surgeon's bread-and-butter work: they have built upon her face a bulbous nose. The thing juts out in front of us like the knob one grips on a carpenter's plane, or, if that's an unfamiliar image, the knob on the heel of a fine shoe tree. A knob: unnatural, removing all grace from her figure, but, as long as business is good and we are loaded to the gills, a knob that stays out of sight below the waterline.

Theoretically, the bulbous bow—that's what they call it—displaces the ocean in such a way that it does not immediately close back in along her zaftig flanks and create the resistance that accompanies the parting of the waters by sleeker ships. No, the water rejoins itself in "eddies," the captain told me, using his bare hands to make eddies. And the ship burns less fuel, if you are going around the world with yourself spread a little too wide. I asked the captain how far out he had sailed to test her and he said not at all. He said a model of her had been tested in a tub. In any event, I should not run on about the ship so early when I know so little about her. We have been at sea but five hours.

I have been in England seventy-two. I spent late October and all of November making and canceling flight reservations out of New York while Liverpudlians with acetylene torches shot sparks across the Mersey, cutting away my ship's Communist past, and others with paint guns sprayed over her old Russian name. I asked a Russian third mate this morning what the ship had been called when she was Russian, and he said she *is* Russian and that her name was something that sounded, to me, like "Dixie." This made no sense, but, since I was born in Alabama, my soul commenced a jig. I asked him if he could spell it in my alphabet. He said, "Tango. India. Kilo. Sierra. India." *Tiksi.* To my ear, the name sounded airy; it seemed to want to sail a lighter craft, not this massive pile of steel (about twenty thousand tons), but I liked it all the same. *Tiksi.*

Ninety-six hours ago I received word from London that I might seriously consider coming over at once. I flew to Heathrow, caught a taxi to Euston Station, and then took a train to Liverpool. Through Milton Keynes, Nuneaton, Stafford, Crewe, and Runcorn, I rolled drably across the Midlands—sheep, hedges, hogs, and all. Everywhere lining pastures were lombardy poplars, planted as windbreaks, leafless and all stick this time of year, and leaking breezes badly under nacreous skies.

In Liverpool Lime Street Station, wrangling five months' worth of reading material (*War and Peace* alone demands a block and tackle), toothbrush, lucky horseshoe, and spare pair of boxers, I lost a tussle for the last baggage trolley to a thewy Briton, strong in every aspect but her chin. Evidently she snagged the cart to ease her burden, a compact overnight cosmetics case. Her entire load weighed about as much as a chihuahua, and she left me in a clatter of hard, nasty heels. Looking on the bright side, my eye caught the slithery promise of shin-high hose starting to slip down and ruck up on her ankles.

By the time I reached a cab, there were loud bursts in my ears that I took for the sound of my heart exploding. I didn't feel myself again physically until my driver and I were out of town a ways and my chest calmed down. Directly we made a turn by a self-effacing barbershop that had a sign in the window that reassured patrons: "It'll look fine after a wash."

In my lumpy-bedded room in the Blundellsands, the inn I had been directed to by my shipping line, BBC television played those black-and-white American movies Victor Mature distinguished so. Red tinsel hung from the heavily plastered ceiling of the inn's dining room, and a lit Christmas fir winked in the corner. Starched maroon napkins rolled into cones stood at attention like stiff linen megaphones on a fleet of unoccupied tables. A boy in a white shirt and a crimson bow tie, hunched over the spinet, got a little wedge of finger fat caught between the sharps and flats on occasion, but otherwise, as a gap-toothed nymph sawed on the English roast beef done in its English way— "chef's special"—until dust poured from the kerf her knife left in the meat, the music came on, from "Vincent" to "Cracklin' Rosie," and my first jet-lagged gloaming back in there'll-always-be-an-England I closed my eyes over a trifle but rejected prayer, after a struggle.

The next morning there was another postponement of sailing and a change of hotels. A young man with a ring in his nose was nailing up a plywood reindeer outside my second-floor window as I pulled away in a cab. At my new lodging I purchased a London paper, *The Times*, and learned that Bill and Hillary Clinton had apparently followed me across the Atlantic. The Washington couple had spent the preceding day with John and Norma Major. Mrs. Major, according to the fashion cop who wrote the dispatch I read, "sported a cream silk, double-breasted jacket and charcoal skirt. Mrs. Clinton, obviously wary of the British winter, had chosen to wrap herself in what looked like an old car blanket." There was no sartorial word on the trencherman from the White House, the Great Sweet Potater.

BBC radio said it would be "mainly dry" today except for some "drizzly spells in Merseyside." We were supposed to sail at five o'clock but we didn't. We sailed at ten of seven, an hour or better before you could see anything. Daybreak in December in the north of England arrives between eight and nine and is just a lighter shade of dark. I feel now I should leave off accounting for a while until my mood lifts, to say nothing of the fog, and my inner clock adjusts to the Old World.

I gave five deutsche marks to a tenor singing a cappella in the streets of Hamburg today. He looked like Oliver Hardy, and sang like a fat celestial person. I did not recognize his song, but it was so cold out you almost expected his breath to draft the notes upon the air so you could read along. He acknowledged my contribution with a crinkle of powder-blue eyes. I put the money in an upturned hat at his feet. It was just a man's hat, not a bowler, nor a Stetson, nor anything strange with a feather in the band. It was my only transaction on my only day in Germany.

Barry, our purser, who is Irish, arranged for a minivan to meet the ship at the quay and take eight of us into town. We stopped at a bank and changed some money and, just here, I thought I perceived the first faintest strain on our overall relations. A little black cloud materialized in our hired vehicle, I think, because not all of us needed to stop and change money, but the running meter made no exceptions for the passengers who came prepared. Those of us who did not have to change money (I had to change, or thought I did) would have to pay their share of the fare at the end of the line all the same. The tension was faint, as I say, but before bedtime I would hear "and we waited a frightfully long time at the bank" more than once in the retelling of the day.

An angelic-looking little white-haired woman named Agatha, from the Lake District of England, seemed to complain most heartily, but it was hard to take it as a whine, there was such warmth in her voice. I have learned Agatha is a retired nurse (a whole career dressed in scary white, making us do or swallow things we didn't want to; hence the unction in her delivery, I suppose). Her new husband, Dick, who wears muttonchops like a truck driver—perhaps to compensate for a hairline that has receded over the pole—is a pensioner who was a laboratory assistant. Dick's speech is "typical Lancashire," I'm told, meaning his words run backwards off his tongue and down his esophagus, and I can't understand him. He and Agatha have a double cabin next door to me. Dick rapped at my door yesterday afternoon to tell me I could see the coast.

"What coast?" I said.

"The Dootch," said Dick.

The single cabin on the other side of me is occupied by Peter. The fussbudget among us seems to be Peter, an American from upstate New York, quite near Canada. I'm given to believe he is a retired chemist. He's a slight fellow—though a little heavy in the hind, like one of those dolls that won't stay down when knocked over—who wears large eyeglasses and sweeps a swatch of long, salt-and-pepper side hairs over a grassless pate. Some days, either intentionally or swept by the wind, it seems a Caesar style, or the way actors playing Caesar wear their hair, laurel-crown fashion, but in Peter's case it swoops over the high bald brow like a molting pigeon's wing.

Peter struck me at first as being a little draggy on the beat of life, but I think he is just careful, wants to make sure he is clear on everything and everyone is clear with him. He spent a good deal of time making sure the driver understood where he was to pick up the eight of us at the hour we had agreed—in advance, by vote; Peter made us do this—we would all be finished with Hamburg, where exactly the ship's berth was, and whether everyone agreed that if you weren't at the meeting spot at the appointed minute, and the hired van driver was there to bear you home, you were on your own (meter running and time being money, you see). We agreed, and Peter set off in the company of Ernie, who is a big old Tennessean who favors suspenders and unhurried speech and movement, a man who lumbers unyoked and a compliment, in a way, to Peter's birdy pecking at the ordinary details of muddling through.

Tennessee Ernie has a great moon face of surprising opacity. He is a talker, to the point of garrulousness, but his face is actually stolid—a voluble stone. I first heard Ernie's Smoky Mountain voice at the front desk of the second hotel I patronized in Liverpool. "Would you be needing a porter, sir?" a receptionist asked as Ernie and his wife, May, were checking in.

"Not if you've got a buggy," Ernie said. The choice of words and the flat drawl in which they rode pricked up my ears, and I introduced myself.

They were from Knoxville, or New Market, they said, which is just outside Knoxville. "We been in Ireland," Ernie explained. "We pretty much looked at that place from end to end." Then they went to Wales and exhausted all its vistas as well. Ernie had been a government man with the soil conservation service, telling farmers they had better plow around those hills, not up and down them. He and May had always wanted to travel, but they had to wait until their parents were dead. When they buried May's daddy six or eight years ago, they cut loose. They've been posing as vagabonds ever since. May isn't as ambulatory as her husband, or as trim (I suspect her weight has something to do with "that knee" and "that hip," as Ernie gravely refers to May's infirmities, and I suspect that both "that knee" and "that hip" are recent plastic additions to May's anatomy, a new hinge and a new swivel), but Ernie seems to look after her with great gentleness, and with Ernie's steady hand, they are able to keep on exploring.

Another thing about May and Ernie: in the way of many couples married nearly all their lives, they validate one another inconsequentially throughout their conversations, especially when someone else is present. "I fell asleep, what was it, about two?"

"About two."

"We were there, how long, about three weeks?"

"About three weeks."

I've only been listening to him a couple of days, but Ernie

seems to be taken with the natural world as well as what man has wrought with it and how things work, a curiosity I share but sometimes fail to exercise. This morning, I heard him lecturing on the properties of limestone, sandstone, and shale, as well as the effect of acid rain on marble tombstones, and then he said the smoky perspiration the trees put off in his part of Appalachia is what got the mountains named the Great Smokies. A little later, I heard him tell Peter that at Okinawa during World War II "I saw fifty kamikazes in one day. One in ten hit a ship. They filled the pilots full of sake, for one thing, and the planes they gave 'em to crash was the worst they had, for another. And if I was goin' at it like they was, knowin' I was goin' to blow up, too, I just might miss a whole ship like most of them did. One in four ships they hit went down."

In the van taking us back to the port in Hamburg today, Ernie was telling Peter, "Look at the purty cirrus up there. It's just ice crystals is all it is. Means a cold front's movin' in, although it's already here. They'll go up sixty thousand feet high. One-hundred-mile-an-hour winds sweep it at one end up there to what they call a mare's tail."

"A what?" said Peter.

"Mare. M-A-R-E. Look at that bridge over yonder. It's got that new way of spreadin' out the load. They got one in St. Petersburg, Florida. Had a pretty bitter debate on it. Engineers said it'd never hold, but it seems to be holdin' all right. You think this ride'll run us as much as this morning? Seems like it took less time gettin' back."

As I sat in the seat behind Ernie while he lectured Peter, it occurred to me that this big Tennessean has the self-confident bearing of a successful and Godlike physician, either that or an extraordinarily secure idiot; for most of my life I've been incapable of telling the two apart.

At supper tonight, Ernie said, "Believe I've got all of it off there that'll come off." He meant lamb off a chop bone. He laid down his knife. "You, May?"

"Me May what?"

"You got all the meat off yours?"

"Believe I have, Ernie."

When May and Ernie say "believe," a word they use prefatorially with great frequency, they do not pronounce the first "e" and they make it one syllable—"blieve"—and they give it as much force and authority as the issue of a shotgun: BLAM! So when Ernie, at table, wads up his napkin and says, "BLIEVE! I've had enough" you see people who are new to the experience reflexively diving for the carpet. We are all inured now after three nights, and keep our seats. Tonight the after-dinner talk turned to movies. Ernie told us:

"In the shows it seems like they always give us a feller we like, and they build him up so likable like, when he comes to get threatened with somethin' bad happenin' to him we just can't wait to see how he's gonna figure his way out of it. Last night May put on this video, *Beethoven*, 'bout a cute little puppy. Anyways the bad guys needed a dog with a big head to test with a bullet: see what kind of damage it did to that head; and I just went on to sleep."

I said, "You mean you didn't want to see how the dog figured his way out?"

"No," Ernie said. "I couldn't take the trauma. I can't stand cruelty."

We are all attended to by three Russian stewardesses, Galena, Nadezhda, and Olga, whose combined weight I would estimate at forty-two pounds less than the Chrysler Building. I noticed this morning, while the three of them were Hoovering on the starboard, my cabin on the port lifted four and a half feet. I do not mean to disparage them; it is just they are so large they take getting used to. Then, too, there's their temperament: in just this short time, I have learned that when they are cheerful, they are very, very cheerful, but when they are foul, the three of them could take Cuba, or any other country with a standing army about the size of Cuba's.

We are lucky all three seem naturally sunny. I would give the award for most infectious smile among them to Olga, the youngest (I've heard it said she is twenty-eight). Agatha of the Lakes says Olga cuts her eyes at me during supper. Agatha said tonight, "You'll be gettin' a cuddle by Christmas, Gregory, there's no doubt."

It's a suffocating prospect.

December 7, 1995
Antwerp, Belgium

I was up on Monkey Island, the roof of the wheelhouse, when we negotiated a lock into Antwerp this afternoon. Gray day. Gray water. Northern Europe. Like living under a gray blanket. A bridge rose up on one end of itself, like a horse rearing, to let us through. From behind me a voice I wasn't prepared to entertain said, "That's pretty ingenious the way they got that bridge counterbalanced with that great big chunk of concrete." I turned and said, "Hey, Ernie." The Tennessean swept me into his day.

"Look at that tug," Ernie said. Below us, the tugboat on our stern seemed to move in on us, away from us, out from us impatiently, as an adolescent practices dancing with a door. "They're easy to maneuver. You just run your fanger around that wheel. They got power steering. They got a variable pitch propeller. They got about six thousand horsepower. Some of 'em got bow thrusters. After I got out of the Navy I was in the Reserve for, oh, near about thirty years. They used to send me to Roanoke, Virginia, two weeks a year to run tug. They got a deep keel. Got a 'leven-foot propeller. You wouldn't know it to look at it. They'll back up straight. You can make 'em go sideways."

I looked at the tug, looked back at Ernie, and saw then that something else entirely had captured his sense of narrative. "Look at that *Bayer* on that smokestack. You think they mean the aspirin? Wouldn't think it'd take such a big factory to make such a itty-bitty pill. They used to advertise, 'A penny a pill.' I remember when they used to say that. Now they'll sell you two hundred in a jar for fifty-nine cents. Do you know what they make aspirin out of? It must of started with a plant. They tell me it's one of the world's oldest medicines. Aspirin has got to be two or three thousand years old. It dudn't do me much good. I can get a headache and take two of them and it dudn't do me much good at all. They hep some people but I can't feel nothin'. Doctor has me taking two baby aspirin a day to keep from clottin'. S'posed to be some kind of anticoagulant." Ernie lifted his eyes and took a breath. He needed a breath.

"I counted fifteen ships over there a while ago. There's a Oriental one there. Got some kind of Oriental writing on her." He looked down at the lock we were rising in. "Looks like she's up to the waterline here. I think it's a half pound of pressure a vertical foot, I think that's what it is. The arithmetic may have gotten away from me, not using it. Is that a refinery over there? BLIEVE! it is. In Fiji . . ."

We were a while clearing Belgian customs tonight, and as the docks customarily occupy the aesthetically impoverished quarter of every town, everyone elected to stay aboard until daylight. At the cocktail hour, Barry the Purser appeared in the passengers' lounge with a small, blond Englishwoman he introduced as June, our eleventh passenger. With the help of a cane, she settled herself onto a sofa, and Barry the Purser gave her a tall glass of a restorative he seemed to mix with serious intent. It was brown as the Mississippi, indicating, to me, it had strength enough to stun.

June set about learning our names. The first thing one noticed about her (all right, the first thing I noticed about her) was that she had one of those broad-as-the-Channel accents people mostly parody nowadays. Clearly, a gerontocrat had come into my crowd. Scarcely a dozen words had been exchanged when all of a sudden there was a palpable shift in the mood of the room (I could swear I heard something that sounded exactly like bonhomie being sucked away). Then there was a physical change.

The women's body language switched to defense; they whipped themselves back, as though someone had thrown a serpent on the coffee table. The men rearranged themselves swiftly along the far side of the salon, as though a list to starboard had flung them.

June turned to Little Peter and demanded, "Why aren't you drinking?" Peter said he had already refreshed himself, said he had had a modest splash of wine. "I can't drink wine," June said. Cahn't. "Whiskey, gin, or vodka is fine with my doctor. But no wine of any description." She batted some assessing eyelids at Peter, as though marking down a floor model. Quickly Peter blurted, for no reason at all other than to escape the harsh light, "Greg's a writer." He might as well have added, "Pick on him."

Snake eyes. No lids. Up and down me. "Poetry, I'd say, from the look of him." I think she was saying I was shabbily gotten up.

"No, no poetry," I said.

"In your soul, then."

My new friend Leicester, inching backwardly toward the door, cleared his throat nervously. Leicester of Devon. Leicester is pronounced Lester. Leicester of Devon is a retired solicitor. "Just a country solicitor," he likes to say. "A quiet, family practice it was. I still see to the grandchildren of some of the clients I had in the beginning." Leicester gave me a look of distress. "Dining, Greg?" We beat it down five decks to the dining room, Leicester leading me by half a flight of stairs and thirty-six years. "I can't stand bossy women," he called back.

By the end of supper, June had alienated the lot of them. I think I saw her taking devilish pleasure. She seemed to want to share some conspiratorial look with me from time to time, or she may have been flirting, or simply nearsighted. It was obvious, though, she thought she had a confederate: as we left the table she leaned to me and said, "Wasn't that appalling, darling?"

I've been listening to some hymns (Charlie Haden and Hank Jones; their *Steal Away* album) on my Walkman here in my cabin as the clock strikes a ruminative midnight, and I've been thinking I'm on a passenger list of souls nearing the end of their temporal lives, while I signed on merely because I felt near the end of my metaphorical rope. I'm afraid I'm already casually being arch with my shipmates here in my accounting, and that, while this is all very well for my private amusement, I should be careful not to go about the ship being snotty and offend them. What reason have I to feel superior anyway?

My only legitimate complaint, and thus the only one I think I should be allowed to insert into the record, would concern the paucity of humor around these parts, or at least my brand. Most of my shipmates don't seem to have a very highly evolved sense of humor. Either I am right or they use humor as sparingly as one does the silver and the good china—either that or some time ago they found that wit took too much out of them and they stuck it away for good, put it way back in that closet where their stationary bicycles collect cobwebs.

For example, at lunch today, fruit came up. I'm keen on fruit, and the galley seems stingy with it, and I aim to pry more fruit loose. Peter, giving me a wink from beneath that pigeon's wing of hair across his forehead, as though he and I were in on some sort of misbehavior pact, leaned my way and said, "We don't want to get, heh-heh, *scurvy*." He said it like a boy saying "pee-pee" in church.

I acknowledged Little Peter's point and segued into an anecdote custom-tailored for this table. I said I was reminded of an incurious man I used to know, a sophisticated but timid Arkansan, a finicky soul who clung to the familiar whenever possible and despised surprise, a journalist whose newspaper in Chicago assigned him to Rome. This man was single at the time, unadventurous to a fault, and once he found a place to live he found a trattoria downstairs and never offered his patronage to another. Not only that, but after he discovered the first meal he ordered was entirely satisfactory, he never ordered anything else. Less than a year into his assignment, his gums were bleeding badly. Worse, he was mortified to find that, with the touch of a toothbrush, he could rock his molars in their sockets. He went to a dentist. The dentist was appalled. The dentist asked him what he had been eating. My friend said, *"Fettucine alfredo."* The dentist asked what else. My friend said, "That's all, just *fettucine alfredo*." The dentist said, "Good God, man, you have scurvy!"

"I have a companion story to the one you just described," Little Peter said in a rushing way. If anyone was amused by my true recollection, Peter did not give them a second to show it. Instead, Peter offered the table a piece I first heard in third grade, the one about the Italian immigrant in New York, the laborer whose only English was "Apple a'pie and coffee." Thus, that was all he ever ate. By and by a cousin told him his diet was boring. The kinsman taught the newcomer to say, "Ham sandwich." The man tried it out when he went to order his next meal. The waitress asked, "Rye bread or white?" This totally flummoxed the Italian, who gushed (here Peter pulled a goofy face), "Apple a'pie and coffee."

The crowd gave Peter a bunch of old chuckles and appreciative sighs, and then fell to talking about Christmas cards and the price of stamps. Tennessee Ernie said, "I always buy my stamps at the cheapest place."

No one paid him any mind.

A mulish look came on Ernie's face then. "They were raising the price of stamps back home again the other day," he said, "and we went out and bought all the cheap ones we could find."

"That's very funny, Ernie," Ernie's wife, May, said.

"Well, I thought it was," Ernie said.

In a letter home tonight, I wrote: I sense a test of tolerance and humility coming on, a long exam indeed.

~~~~~

In the lightening gray of the Belgian dawn the stevedores on the quay built a fire in an oil drum with kindling from a busted-up wooden pallet. From my porthole, I watched them hugging themselves. I was anxious to go ashore and concerned a little about the anxiety. If I wanted to break with my environment and my companions this early, it was a bad sign. I had told myself since September to be prepared for physical restriction, and to be prepared to be restricted with a generation a furlong closer to heaven than my own. Being borderline rueful within one week at sea meant I might have overestimated my inner resourcefulness. The idea stayed with me through breakfast and a shared taxi ride to a central bank in town. I changed fifty bucks into Belgian francs and bolted from the pack.

At the moment, this very one, I am lighthearted, and what passes for happy, but I think I'm on the verge of being at odds with myself. Guilt, no bigger than a hummingbird, hovers about my head. Protectively, I think I have just resolved to let guilt grow and fatten before I let it get me down. After all, there are less fortunate brethren out there, people who pay big bucks for seminars where they learn, primarily, not to sweat the small shit.

The waiter brings me a bowl of mussels steaming in a garlicky, onion-tomato affair, and bread. I am out of doors, in a square of sunlight, at a café on a plaza with a cathedral on one side and a statue in the center (which pinpoints my location in Europe about as precisely as saying, in Persia, I could be found between sand and sky). A fairer clue, perhaps: yonder stands the Flemish painter Peter Paul Rubens on his plinth, pigeon droppings in his copper hair. In a corner to my right, a stooped old man, wearing a white mustache you could mop a galley with, is playing an accordion. It seems to be a medley including "Silver Bells" and

"Amazing Grace." It works for me. Mulled wine in glass mugs is everywhere to be found. Couples stroll and drink among the Christmas trees for sale (*zilver kerstbomen met wortels en in de pot geplant*). There is the smell of sausage. Smoke from braziers. A woman at a wooden booth just down from me is selling shots of Cutty Sark. A young man approaches me and offers, for a small sum of francs, to swallow fire. On the opposite side of the plaza I notice a Hard Rock Café is scheduled to open between a Hilton Hotel and Chicago-style Pizza any day now.

After lunch I walked away the afternoon. Lots of hubs in the layout of old Antwerp, and tiny streets for spokes, lined with smart shops and pretty food. My practical side dragged me down a flight of stairs to a subterranean supermarket where I bought a coffee cup for my cabin and a packet of cheap onionskin airmail envelopes for my correspondence. It was Bing Crosby and "White Christmas" at street level, but down below in the cut-rate Belgian vegetables Engelbert Humperdinck and his perfumed tonsils were dispatching a tune to all the girls he'd loved before who'd traveled in and out his door.

Toward the end of the shopping day I ran across Agatha and Dick of the Lake District of England, married a year now, my shipmates. Dick had been a widower five years, Agatha a widow twelve, when friends in Canada convinced them, go on, in Agatha's words, tie the knot. Until then she hadn't really fancied marriage, though her daughter had pointed out she wasn't setting much of an example for the grandchildren. But she had her flat and Dick had his bungalow with a nice little garden. They had their routines. Dick woke up in his own bed, for one. "Mind you," Agatha says, "I think he got a bit cheesed off having to drive himself home at one o'clock in the morning."

So they were wed, and here they were a year later, honeymooning, and inviting me into an Antwerp tearoom. We were joined at the last moment by Little Peter, who was dropped at the door by Leicester of Devon, who set off in search of apples, having consumed the "four jolly fine russets" he had brought aboard at Liverpool. Leicester has joined me in my dissatisfaction with the galley's fruit rationing, and has taken to subsidizing on his own. "They'll not parcel apples to me one at a time," he declared, going forth to find a bushel.

Peter had coffee and noted for us that this tearoom was the third establishment today that had failed to offer him a napkin. But, Little Peter said, the men's room at the café where he and Leicester had lunch was worth the trip to Antwerp. "The water comes on automatically for you to wash your hands, activated by a light sensor," Peter said. "That way you don't have to touch any germs on the taps."

Dick brought up a fond memory: a men's urinal in Austria that flushed when you walked away, whether you had used it or not. "We had to send the ladies in to prove it," Dick said. He snickered.

I was seated tonight at dinner between Toxic June and Leicester of Devon. Nadezhda, one of the three vast stewardesses, asked June if she wanted milk. "Heavens!" June exclaimed. "Never!"

Over the course of the meal June brought me into her confidence. The food was "appalling." The ship was "claustrophobic and overheated." She did not care for anything else she had seen in her twenty-four hours aboard, either, including "this crowd." She was thinking of pulling out, but the thing was, "I'm lame." With her degree of arthritis, the English winter (she has a flat in London, a house on one of the Channel Islands) all but paralyzes her. Then, too, she did not want to "disorganize the family's skiing holiday." About here, smarmy Agatha of the Lake District moved in on her own cane and said, "What's upsetting you, dear?" Agatha was a nurse, I think I've noted. On my other side, Leicester of Devon said, "Do you feel like shoving off yet? Do you feel replete?"

In the stairwell, Leicester called June "highfalutin." He said she comes from "a notorious tax-dodging island."

Agatha of the Lake District, in the companionway outside my cabin, told the captain and me, "June was quite naughty with her language. She said the money didn't matter an F-U-C-K with her. I'm not a prude, but it wasn't very English of her to be so vulgar with a stranger, practically speaking."

At dinner, June, ablaze in red—lips, nails, the frames of her spectacles, her disposition—kept the room in high ferment. I ate every morsel before me—sclerotic lamb chops, potatoes, a rice pudding that was presented to us in a hard gob, a compact disc denser than a burned fudge brownie—as June pronounced it "inedible." Afterward, to me alone, in the staircase ascending to bed, Leicester of Devon was very rough with June. "Directly I heard her voice, I thought: 'Hullo, there you are.' She's ex-Army, they tell me. Needs a load of Bangladeshis to boss around."

June tells me she may leave us in Dunkirk.

My unreliable shortwave picked up the BBC just now. They say France is pretty much closed on account of labor strikes. However, the captain said at table we will be allowed a berth. The stevedores are working.

Olga the Russian stewardess Hoovered Agatha of the Lake District out of her cabin this morning, and Agatha came in to chat with me. She sat on my bed and told me of her forty years married to Howard, a boat pilot out of Heysham on the Belfast run. "Before the Occupation, they commandeered all the vessels and Howard was sent to Dunkirk to evacuate three thousand women and children. Of course, the Channel was mined. My, what an adventure! After he retired, he went to creative writing, my Howard. He published one of his little stories in the *Reader's Digest*. The poor dear only lived one year after retirement. He got the lung cancer . . . Howard was too lazy to sail. You have to pull on the wellies and shove her off, you know. If I wanted to go for a sail he'd take the pilot boat out in the Channel."

Agatha said she had meant to bring a book, *The Precious Present*, but she must have forgotten. "My mother was always one for planning for the future and she died at sixty."

Lunch (noodle and mushroom soup, sardines on toast, gooseberries, cheese, and tea). Ernie of Tennessee: "I love to steer. When I was in the Navy there was no such thing as an iron mike [the automatic pilot]. You had to be ready at all times in the Navy. You had a man on the wheel. Reckon it's still that way."

May of Tennessee: "You don't know that."

Ernie: "I reckon it's still so in the Navy. We didn't know whether there might be a vessel in distress or a sub or whatever. But you had to be ready for action. That's the reason the Navy's out there. And they didn't leave the doors open like they do here. Them doors had to be dogged down so you could move."

On the bridge, easing into Dunkirk in swirling fog, the captain tells a half dozen of us on the wing: "If you'd mind the noise, and keep aft. It's a tense moment, and languages to be dealt with." My mates disappear. I stay.

French pilot: "Cut the engines. When you feel the steering stop, say. You understand?"

British first officer: "When you feel the steering stop, say. All right?"

Russian second officer: "When you feel the steering stop, say."

Russian helmsman: "Yes."

Second officer: "Yes."

First officer: "Yes."

French pilot: "Good."

In my view, it was like steering a floating Empire State Building in blinding fog up a treacherous ditch through concrete revetments, with instructions in three languages, a six-foot margin for error either side.

Walked into town in the fog from the quay. There was a traveling fair on the outskirts, roustabouts just setting up. Carousels in the main district. Little Peter bounced along beside me. All wrapped and bundled up against the cold, he looked like Sleepy. Or Dopey. Sometimes I think his innocence is bogus and kick myself for being so uncharitable as to think like that. He comes across as a naïf, though, and yet he got himself back to the ship by public bus in Antwerp yesterday. That was adventurous. He has been places. I understand he once worked in Brazil. He makes his own wine.

We followed the railroad tracks to *centre ville*, fog so thick you could only see your feet. Well, *I* followed the tracks. Little Peter followed me. He fretted we were going the wrong way. He fretted we might lose our way back. I lost my patience and said, "Choo-choo track go one way, Peter; choo-choo track come same way back." He fretted he had no French francs and I introduced him to a late-twentieth-century banking convenience called the automatic teller machine (or ATM, to the *bankerati*). Peter does not have a bank card. A cautious man, he explained that if someone stole it and used it, he would be liable for the charges. He also said he isn't the sort who needs a quick infusion of cash on a Saturday night. Then he told me he got an American Express card after his last trip abroad because he got tired of having to take off his shirt and trousers to get to his money belt. I said that must have been some money belt. He said he was kidding. He said, "Surely you must have a sense of humor."

Then Peter said, "But I have thought of a situation where a man was having a tryst, or however you pronounce it [Peter pronounced it "traiist"], and he totally disrobed but got up to put his money belt back on. I find that such an amusing image."

June drew me aside for a whisper after supper. The lack of service, the tasteless or oily food, the curries she missed so (Leicester was right; Bangladeshis cooked, served, and crewed on June's last voyage)—but she would stay on, show her grit, and sail with us. She would jump ship for a better berth in the South Pacific.

I have a difficult time understanding June after she has been drinking. I feign it is the noise of the engines, or the clatter of dishes, the acoustics in the dining room, but the fact is, it is the accent the boozy June slips into in the evenings. It comes out of the nasal passages, picks up thin vibraphonic assistance from the palate, and jackknifes sloppily off the flat of the tongue. "Dear boy," June said, "if I'm going to give you these pearls *en passant*, the least you can do is strain to hear me."

December 11, 1995
Dunkirk

In town this morning, Leicester of Devon and Dick of the Lake District were looking at model cars in a toy-shop window (I was looking at a French board game called the Puzzle of Love). Corvettes. Dodge trucks. Thunderbirds. "Remember the little ones?" Dick asked Leicester.

"Dinky's, you mean? Oh, my boys loved them when they were small. Worth a bloody fortune now." It triggered a memory in Leicester.

"My wife gave up smoking," he said. Leicester's wife died eleven years ago. He left her watching television, wasn't out very long at all, and when he got back she was gone. Her family tended to go that way; fit in appearance, no complaints, one day you look away and a heart attack claims them. "She began buying these china dolls." With the money she saved not buying ciga-rettes, I gathered. "I think she paid five pounds apiece for them. Lovely crinolines. Beautiful things, these china dolls. I think I have twelve or fourteen of them. Worth one hundred pounds apiece now. I think I have twelve or fourteen of them."

It was freezing out. In the patisserie to our left, they were selling little pink sugar Baby Jesuses, but we just kept staring at the playthings, three men at Christmastime, the oldest of us born in 1912, our noses pressed to the window of a shop full of toys.

Supper. Toxic June on one side, Tennesseans on the other. If we had had them, the seating cards would have read: Rock. Jaynes. Hard Place.

June: "I was with the accountant today. In my cabin. A Mr. Moss. He said, 'Have we misled you?' Yes. The food is inedible. The heat is claustrophobic. The pool is a disgrace. It is the bot-tom of the rung for your shipping line. And I told him—my dear, he is just an accountant, but I told him, 'This mattress doesn't even fit the steel girder it rests upon!' As if we were all deserving of custom-fitted steel girders, you see."

To go or to stay? June said she told the accountant, "I'll make your life miserable either way." She cackled. I snorted. I thought it was quite funny.

The Tennesseans were in an indecipherable frame of mind, antagonistic and insulting. And silly with alcohol.

December 13, 1995
Le Havre, France

Dinner.

Tennessee Ernie: "It seemed like to me a nice little old French town. I wouldn't want to live there, but a nice one."

June: "You know a lot about Europe, don't you, Ernie?"

Ernie: "No, ma'am. It might seem like it, but I don't know very much about Europe at all."

June: "Well, every time we talk we're in Europe."

Ernie: "But I know a lot about the South Pacific, wouldn't you say so, May?"

Tennessee May: "Um, hmm. Okinawa."

Ernie: "I couldn't ever forgive the Japs. I wouldn't drive a Jap car if I had to walk. I got a Jap camera just 'cause it's the only kind you can buy. In the Philippines—"

May: "Now, Ernie—"

"—in the Philippines, they'd th'ow a little baby up in the air and shoot it to pieces while the mother was watching. How're you going to forgive that? Seems like to me the Germans are trying to get along with people, but the Japs . . ."

June: "Heinz mayonnaise. Agatha, do you know Heinz mayonnaise?"

Agatha of the Lake District: "It's for people too lazy to make their own."

June: "Do you know Heinz mayonnaise, Leicester?"

Leicester: "Yes, I use it, with pleasure."

June: "See there, old Englishmen like it, but I find it ghastly."

Tennessee Ernie: "Some people in my country are saying we shouldn'ta dropped that bomb. I didn't start that war. The Japs did. I was sixteen when they hit Pearl Harbor. I saw a lot of terrible things. It messed up a lot of fellers. I know one my age still can't drive a car. Shell-shocked."

Agatha of the Lakes: "Look, Dick, the meat is already cut up for you in this curry. This is a dish you can eat American-style, just using your fork. It makes no sense to me to spend all that effort cutting your meat as they do and then cross your fork from your knife hand . . ."

Ernie: "Just like you people didn't start that war with Germany. But that'd been the end of Europe if it hadn't been for the U.S.A. savin' you."

Agatha of the Lakes: "Helping us, dear, not saving . . ."

Ernie: "But then we got people in the U.S. today don't believe they wouldn't be walkin' around on two legs and speakin' English if it wasn't for them bombs of ours . . ."

June: "Don't you find Heinz mayonnaise appalling?"

Ernie: "I bet you like that English mustard. What they call mustard over here ain't mustard to me."

Leicester of Devon: "Don't you find the meat a bit tough, lately?"

Ernie: "Seems like to me everything's cooked plenty. Don't you BLIEVE! it is?"

Tennessee May: "BLIEVE! it is."

June: "What's that, Leicester? I think Leicester let go of his tongue for a moment."

Leicester: "Silence is golden."

~~~~~~~

December 14, 1995
Le Havre

We are supposed to be away, but there is a problem with a brake lining on a crane, and hardware coming from Rotterdam. We were delayed a night in Hamburg, I think it was—I failed to note it—when errant water flooded the steering gear. I don't know what any of this means, just that there were seamen down below drying manly machinery made of steel with ladies' hair driers, at midnight. The passengers aren't supposed to be aware of this, but Priscilla, the wife of Ettore, the Italian chief engineer, told me behind her hand yesterday.

I eased over to the breakfast table with Priscilla and Ettore this morning, after answering Ernie the Tennessean's greeting, "Still cold as whizz out there?" with a theatrical little shudder. Ettore said this ship "is like a used car that has been papered over. You don't know what you're getting." He said he has been dealing with "small problems" with the two big diesel engines and that he won't really know what shape we are in until we start the long run for the Panama Canal—when we leave this berth.

Ettore flew to Bombay last year to assist in taking possession of this ship and to see it back to Liverpool. He found it had been "barely maintained—they had no money. For example, the propeller blades should have been changed at eight years. We are on twelve years with these." He nearly starved to death on the voyage, he said, because they ran out of most of the food on board and the Russian crew had nothing left but bread. But, what was worse, the compressor on the air conditioner failed. "The tables in this room were melting," Ettore said. The engineer jumped ship at Suez and flew back to England, leaving it to the Russians to nurse her to Liverpool.

I asked him about the tense, foggy approach we had into Dunkirk and he said that was nothing; the last time he entered this port, Le Havre, he was engineer on the *City of Durban*, a 65,000-ton freighter, three times our size, and the harbor pilot wanted to show off and arrive by helicopter. After some macho aerobatics, the chopper let the pilot down a rope to a stacking on the bow five containers high. There wasn't a ladder long enough on board to retrieve the pilot from his ignominious perch atop the containers. The Frenchman had to remain out there forty-five minutes until the helicopter returned, plucked him from the bow, and set him down again astern. Then the wind shifted abruptly and the ship caught the corner of a lock. It tore a gash in the hull large enough for a man to walk through. The ship was two weeks in the Channel ferry yard being mended.

We talked about the bulbous bow for a bit. Bulbous bows aren't new. They are modeled after the noses on dolphins (bottle-nosed dolphins), in my view a truly elegant and efficient piece of marinery. But a bulbous bow like this one, not an organic part of the ship but just stuck on the hull of an icebreaker whose own natural nose caved in like a fighter's—that's new, and untested. Ettore says it is supposed to work only when it is just below the waterline, so there is some tonnage arithmetic to be minded if you are looking for fuel efficiency. "It's supposed to give us one point seven knots and reduce our fuel consumption 38 percent," Ettore said. He shrugged, saying, "You never get something for nothing."

Caught a ride into Le Havre with our French shipping agent. The moist gray sky hung so low it mussed your hair. Had a piece of fish in a café. Not much beauty to the town, but then I may not have been in a mood to appreciate the sights. I may just be desperate for diversionary thought, but I was beginning to see something cinematic in my situation there for a moment: a man—me!—feels himself beginning to creak only to rediscover his youth while in sequestration among the old. The man (me!) finds meaning (*The Precious Present*) in lessons from the sweet elderly. In the bargain, the young man—me! relatively—puts a spring in their aged step, adds allegro to the triple beat of a pair of feet and a cane coming down the hall, as it were.

But more like it: gradually, one discovers old people aren't necessarily nice. If they could be bothered to pass you advice, they would say life can turn out pig-ugly. Live sorry old life long enough and you, too, will leave your family at holidays for their good and yours. And when presented the opportunity you will inflict your hatefulness on strangers (me! the young'un!).

Barry the Purser was moaning to me about Toxic June late this afternoon. He recalled a time on another voyage when he had lunch with her ashore, at her invitation, and she said, in the presence of others, "Fuck you, Barry." Barry was shocked. "Ladies in my circle do not speak that way." I said I had been observing June closely lately because I was helpless not to. It was my theory that she is struggling with physical ruin, lost appeal, and while she is still saucy and full of attractive fire (at least in her own eyes—and mine, in a certain light), she is a menace, really. For all that, it was my impression that June commenced every day resolved to be a nice person, but as her Sisyphean labors pushed her ever backward—Barry finished my sentence: "She finds at sundown she's back to being a nasty old cow."

Precisely.

I caught Harry, a retired civil engineer from Wyoming, a quiet man who is married to Gerda, a woman open to conversational adventure, looking at me funny in the lounge. When Harry reads, he reads *The Milagro Beanfield War*. I, on the other hand, read all over the block to keep from reading *War and Peace*, which I began reading in Liverpool. Among the books I employ in my procrastination is one I have had in my possession since 1979. It was recommended to me by my friend Carey Winfrey, a correspondent who was my predecessor in Nairobi. I had not thought much about its title until now. *Endless Love*. Nor had I been overly conscious of its pink jacket.

I have been a successful card and a cutup in my day, but this is a tough crowd. At table tonight talking of pets, I volunteered I had a wife once who had a dog who wouldn't let me come to bed. The dog blocked me, growling, a great show of teeth, night after night. This is one of my better entertainments. Done with the right sound effects and an expressive face, it is a sketch I have relied on in the past to start the ball rolling at many a dull party. So I contorted my face into a mad dog's and then that of a thwarted young thruster (actually, one and the same, you think about it), and showed them the battle I had on my hands to gain my own pillow. At the end there was embarrassed silence where, in other venues, there had been tears of helpless mirth. Finally, Little Peter asked, "Was that your dog or your wife's?"

~~~~~~~

We are away from Europe now. Our heading is two hundred thirty. We are circumnavigating on a slant, a diagonal, on the bias, to stay south of the thirty-fifth parallel and out of the winter storms. There is about a ten-degree roll to the ship. She rolled all night. It feels at last as though we're headed somewhere. Linens were changed this morning. Fresh towels were put out. Pancakes, flatter in taste than in configuration, and peculiarly spongy, appeared at breakfast. Soggy pucks. The cook is Russian; root crops are his specialty. He is being tutored by Barry the Purser, whom no one has ever accused of cooking well, if at all. The iron mike has the wheel. The sea and the sky meet in their gunmetal colors. I doubt you'd find their hue on any decorator's palette. Fancy something in a North Atlantic gray for the sitting room? See how it picks up the depression?

There is a sense of settling in. We will be nearly thirty days before setting foot ashore again. In the middle of this period comes the Panama Canal, a dramatic slip from one side of things to the other, at least in my mind. I'm trusting the anticipation alone will keep me from going barmy.

There are forty-one of us in this strange village. Our components are: seven Americans, eight English, one Irishman, one Italian, twenty-three Russians, and one Scot. We live in a white six-story building called the accommodation block, or stack. It rises off the main deck, roughly four fifths of the way back from the bow, and it is about the size of an Iowa grain silo. But for one architectural difference, the place we live in resembles public housing in the Bronx, or council flats in Dublin. The difference is that the structure sports a wide-brimmed hat (the hat being the bridge, or wheelhouse, the sixth story). Twenty-eight of us each have our own room, of about one hundred square feet. The rest—high-ranking officers and couples, and an old woman from

Boston named Mary, who appears, at first blush, tipsy and skit-tish—live in larger quarters, but not as large as, say, a modest one-bedroom apartment in the suburbs of Cleveland, Ohio. On the fifth deck are the captain's cabin, as well as mine and those of Agatha and Dick of the Lake District, Leicester of Devon, Little Peter, Mary of Boston (whom I glimpse occasionally drop-ping an empty whiskey bottle in the trash, muttering, "Another dead soldier . . ."), and Harry and Gerda of Wyoming. The pas-sengers' lounge stretches across the rear of this deck. There are weighted chairs in there, a couple of coffee tables, a half fridge, a television connected to nothing, a card/chess table, and a writ-ing desk. There is no view because the windows give off on the exhaust stack on the stern. An Italian-made one-stroke washer and drier are also in a room on this deck.

On the deck below us, number four, are Ernie and May, the Tennesseans, and Toxic June. On that deck, too, you begin pick-ing up the higher-ranking officers and then it runs on down by rank, deck by deck.

None of us has a kitchen to ourselves. There is one kitchen, situated between the two dining rooms, on the main deck, or the ground floor of the accommodation block. The Russian crewmen use one dining room; when the door swings back, a yellow cloud of nicotine pours forth, nearly solid as a wall. People who kid themselves they are eating higher on the hog than the Russians use the other dining room, the officers' dining saloon, where no one smokes. In the officers' dining saloon there are two long tables and one square one that seats four (and is reserved for the captain, though he eats with us when he is not pressed for time and decisions). The food is unremarkable to terrible, but once in a while it tastes ambitious; well-intentioned but hardly paci-fying curries are appearing in direct relation to Toxic June's vo-ciferous distress. The mood in the dining room stays mostly on the boil when June is in our midst. Last night, for instance, as the rest of us were given failed crepes (they fought mastication impressively, however) for dessert, June demanded, and received, strawberry ice cream. Seeing this, I managed to catch Galena's elbow and I said, "Madame will be unhappy unless I receive strawberry ice cream as well." I got it, and June said to me, sotto

voce: "Dear boy, I like your style."

Unless you count Monkey Island, on the roof of the bridge, our village has no common green. No walks. No trees. If we had a general store, it would be what is called the "slop chest." This is managed by the purser (who also manages the mail, so he is the postmaster as well) and consists mainly of alcoholic beverages, spirits, and non-alcoholic beverages that mix well with alcohol, and cigarettes. The store, née slop chest, isn't an actual place. You never shop. You tell Barry the Purser what you desire, and directly a mammoth Russian stewardess bangs on your door and grunts, and you open the door and she slings in a case of beer and a case of gin, or whatever. You receive a bill at the end of each month, typed neatly on Barry's word processor, and you are expected to pay up on the spot, cash or traveler's checks.

We are a segregated community. We are not exactly separate but equal, since theoretically the passengers and officers get better accommodations and food, but we are indeed separate. In the main, the Russians speak only among themselves. The bosun is a Russian, and he deals with the Russian crew. The first officer is a Brit, and he deals with the bosun. Neither speaks the other's language, but they communicate. The second officer, third officer, radioman, and electrician are Russians. They are the only Russians—other than the three stewardesses—the captain routinely speaks to, or deals with. The captain does not hold full-tilt assemblies, does not address the troops, does not hold staff meetings, if you will, as the manager of a Buick dealership would. The captain cannot put all the names together with the faces. The first mate probably could. Because the bridge is somewhat like a country club with a members-only policy, it is likely that there are members of the crew who have never seen the captain.

I have always found exclusivity a grand disappointment. Take conversation in the officers' dining saloon, for instance. I am beginning to fear that conversation among the elite may prove unimprovable. Little Peter turned to me today and said, "I haven't followed American literature, or any other, since Faulkner and Henry Miller. I don't have the patience. What's been happening?"

I said, "Peter, that's nearly forty years of contemporary lit you're asking me to cover over canned pears in cheap claret. Do I look like a *Reader's Digest*?" A feeble bon mot, to be sure, but all I had in the chamber, and I fired it only in the interest of play. I wanted Little Peter to come out and play with me. Instead, he dropped interest in me, turned to the table mate to his other side, and fell to discussing the Brussels sprouts before them. I went on silently pondering an answer for him, should he return to the subject, even though whole semesters, whole academic years tackle questions with less breadth than the one Little Peter blithely put to me.

Down at the other end, Tennessee Ernie was saying, "I BLIEVE! music's supposed to soothe you or make you want to get up and dance. Seems like to me now music's got kind of primitive. They're just beatin' on things, seems like."

Below the main deck is the entrance to the engine room and also on that deck are the ship's laundry, a sauna that does not work at the moment, a drained swimming pool (June calls it "the cess-pot") that, when filled, will be capacious enough for two swimmers to dog-paddle without bruising each other, and a gymnasium. In the gym is a primitive Russian treadmill that works on steel rollers with a stone wheel you could use for a whet and bring up the edge of a knife. The skipper had a trot on it barefooted a couple of days ago, and the rollers blistered his feet through the thin rubber tread. "It was worse than stepping on a bloody eel," he told me.

Other gym equipment: a parallel bar set permanently so high you have to shinny up a pole to reach it; a rowing machine missing oars; a one-hundred-pound single-piece barbell; a table for table tennis; a climbing rope; two netless hoops on the bulkheads at opposite ends of the chamber. We are looking for balls—

basket or Ping-Pong, it doesn't matter; we aren't likely to pass a sporting-goods emporium any time soon.

The captain is a boyish-looking forty-three years old. He has brown curly hair and he is fit, and, according to Agatha of the Lakes, who seems to have an eye for such things, he is "dishy." The captain's wife is a scratch golfer. He has two children who are mad for sports. He has been going to sea twenty-five years—"man and boy; man and boy." He is always pleasant and always seems to make time for a question. This morning, in his office (actually, his suite: office/conference room/cabin, it sweeps around the starboard corner, forward, of this deck, my deck), the captain told me the Russian crew is, for the most part, working out, though one sailor or another occasionally gives the skipper the impression he is unaccustomed to work. Alexander, the radioman from St. Petersburg, told me this ship, when she was with the Soviet Union's merchant navy, had two alternating crews, numbering ninety altogether, so they had many more hands than tasks. Those few who survived the change of ownership quadrupled and even quintupled their salaries. The A.B.s (able seamen, the lowest rank) and the stewardesses went from two hundred dollars a month to one thousand. The rest had to hit the road.

"This ship had a full-time doctor," the captain told me. "All the Russian ships did. They had nothing to do. Maybe one patient a day. And they gave them nothing else to do. They volunteered to stay on with us for two hundred and fifty dollars a month. Can you imagine two hundred and fifty dollars a month for a doctor? But we don't need a full-time doctor. We'd have to give him cabin space, for one thing."

I asked the captain how long it had been since he sailed with a British crew, and he said he never had. "It's always been Asians, until now, with the Russians. It's been Asians for much of this century. We couldn't do it with a British crew. The cost of the crew is the difference between profit and loss. It's true."

Sitting with the captain, I could see through his open door that I had been drawing dirty stares from the direction of the laundry room. It suddenly occurred to me my socks and drawers must have finished the wash cycle and I had, by leaving them unattended, thrown a wrench into someone's morning. I excused myself, saying forthrightly my hosiery must be done, and went to put the matter right. Ettore the chief engineer had told me that on one ship he had sailed a few years ago two American men, both over eighty, feuded over laundry until they were rising earlier and earlier to use the laundry room—"literally only washing one handkerchief," Ettore said, "just to block the other one"—and finally the crew had to separate the old men's fingers from each other's throats.

I went into the passengers' lounge and made an effusive public apology. There were polite nods. I think now it was rude of me to make a big show of contrition, even ruder than not paying attention to my wash. These people are better at the rhythms of living communally than I am.

Andrey, the third officer, has the eight-to-noon, eight-to-midnight watch on the bridge, and I've been paying calls. Andrey is twenty-nine years old. His wife and five-year-old son live four hundred miles east of Moscow. He wears his hair in a Prince Valiant, a style and length that annoy my older, conservative mates. Andrey learned English because he liked music, all music, but he learned the language through pop. I asked him whether he pulled this quartermaster duty every day, and he said, echoing a Beatles' tune, "Eight days a week." He has a guitar on board. He asked me this morning if I played. I said I did, a long time ago. He asked what kind of music. "Folk," I said. "Rock. What we used to call shit-kicking country." He looked puzzled. I should have kept that last one to myself. To retrieve him, I said, "Bob Dylan." He brightened. " 'Mr. Tambourine Man,' " he said. " 'Blowin' in the Wind.' " He said I should come to his cabin to talk and play music. "The third deck on the accommodation ladder," he said. The accommodation ladder, in Andrey's nomenclature, is the stairs.

Spain is out my porthole somewhere in this dark. We set our clock back an hour tonight. I devoted my hour to *War and Peace*. Andrey the third officer said he read it when he was fifteen. "It was how you say obligatory," Andrey said, "but it was a good book."

Nescafé and aft to pipe up the sun. Leicester of Devon emerged from the dark behind me. "Morning, Leicester," I said.

"Who's that?" Leicester croaked (he hadn't got his voice yet), looking up toward the bridge, then out beyond the stern.

"Over here," I said, standing straight before him, not ten feet away.

"Oh, you will-o'-the-wisp. My eyes are just adjusting." He smiled at me and looked east, which is to say off our port stern. There was little wind to speak of. The sea was scarcely ruffled. A bar of buttery light appeared above Portugal. "My God, we're lucky sods," said Leicester of Devon. We watched daybreak with no words more.

The sea began showing some muscle again at midmorning, and I went up for a word with Andrey the third officer. Benjamin, a Russian ordinary seaman who sprained his ankle on deck the other day and has been given light duty until he mends, had finished cleaning all the dials and faces of gauges on the bridge and had turned to tidying up all the national flags we carry. He was unfurling and flicking away specks of dust and fussily furling again. "All the flags of the world," said Benjamin, pulling Old Glory out of a cupboard to let me know he knew my game.

"How many flags are there in the world?" I asked.

"All of these," said Benjamin. "I tsink two hundred."

Andrey was looking at the sea and the sky, then at a meteorological publication spread out before him, then back out beyond the bow. The photographs showed the sea at various wind-whipped stages, Force Seven, Force Eight, and the like (Force Ten, a gale at forty-six to fifty-two knots, is when a larky day goes as dark on you as you'd not soon forget). I'm not keen on grasping every recondite piece of information on navigation at my disposal here (if a man wishes to work, there's always *War and Peace*), but my every visit to the bridge yields something anachronistic in the middle of technology. There is no dial, no gauge, no computer up here that tells you what the wind is up to, for example. Mariners can tell you by the look of the sea. That is all there is to it. If you desire a second opinion, consult a picture in a book. That's what Force Seven looks like out yonder beyond the fo'c'sle, and that's what it looks like here in this publication, so enter it in the log. Or you can step out and lick your forefinger and . . .

"When do you use your sextant?" I asked Andrey.

"Sextants are good for breaking nuts," he said.

Actually, sextants are used by trainees, cadets (we have one on board, Nick), and bored duty officers indulging their romantic streak, but much of the time they stay shiny in their teak boxes unless every scrap of wiring on board crashes and burns. Satellites tell us where we are. The SatNav readout is in the chart room. Radar tells you where you are, too, in its way. Radar was also telling us just then we had company: a squall line was about to rake us. Andrey turned on the Russian windscreen wipers. There's a bank of twenty windows across the bridge, each one about a meter square. The wiper blades cleaned them about as well as my bare elbow would, in a couple of groaning, desultory swipes.

My eyes fell on a sheet nailed to the bulkhead that gave the *Tiksi*'s maneuvering capabilities. There were things on it I couldn't fathom, but I did work out that if we ripped back the throttle from full ahead (where it stood at this moment, giving us a speed of nearly eighteen knots) to full astern, this floating fat lady could be brought to a complete stop by our twin diesel engines (ten and a half thousand horsepower apiece) in three minutes and ten seconds. A dime. The fillings in your teeth, however, probably would not survive the vibration.

Andrey asked me if I knew the words to three Bob Dylan songs other than "Mr. Tambourine Man." He said he knew the words to "Mr. Tambourine Man." I said I probably did, I could probably find them in that hamper where you store useless memories you really should dispose of but you're too stubborn to do so. Same thing you do with unmatched socks—and hope, eternal, and the rest of it. He said he tried to "make rhymes with words" for a time and it was working pretty well because he was depressed during that period, but when he grew happier the words stopped coming. I said there were other states of mind besides depression you could draw inspiration from. Andrey said, "Yes, being in love with a beautiful woman."

Along about then, both of us felt about a Force Ten blow through the heart.

The captain had the Tennesseans on either side of him at supper tonight. "Man like you," Ernie said to the skipper, "I 'spect you've probably read all there is to read about Captain Joshua Slocum."

"No, I don't believe I have," said the captain.

"Well, you know who he is, don't you?"

"No, I do not," said the captain.

"Why, he was the first man to sail around the world single-handedly. He was an old square-rigger, and when steam come along he didn't want to mess with it. He'd been a captain a long time and he give it up. He was on a train going from Baltimore to Boston and a old seaman said, 'I tell you what. Here's what I'll do. I'll give you a boat. Here's where it is.' So it was s'posed to be in Connecticut somewheres, and when Joshua Slocum went to the place he found out it was a apple orchard or some kind of orchard. Fruit trees anyways. He said, 'Why, this is a orchard of some kind,' but when he got to lookin' a little closer he saw there was a boat in there. A ketch. You know what a ketch is? Had that what you call it mizzenmast way back aft."

Ernie's wife, May, said, "Get to it, Ernie."

Ernie said, "I'm a-buildin' the suspense, May."

Then Ernie said, "It was in pore shape, so he took to pullin' off planks and replacin' 'em with his own planks and after while he sailed that thang all around the world. Cape Horn. Strait of Magellan. Oooh, he had some adventures. Indians come aboard while he was sleepin', but he had spread tacks out on deck. Smart old boy. Eighteen and fifty I BLIEVE! it was. [It was 1895–98, actually, but it's Ernie's story, so the hell with it.] That's when steam was comin' on."

May said, "When was it, Ernie?"

"I BLIEVE! it was eighteen and fifty," Ernie said.

The captain said, "It took courage then." The captain was thinking (he told me later), "When men were men and sheep were scarce."

"I like history," Ernie said. "I was born in 1925."

"You baby," said Mary of Boston.

Ernie said, "What would you give to be my age?"

Mary said, "I really would rather not have to do it again."

We set the clocks back another hour tonight. Another hour of *War and Peace*. Ernie hefted my copy in the lounge this morning and said, "That's a lengthy book. You enjoyin' it?"

I said, "It needs a real long runway for takeoff." Not that Ernie and I are consanguineous, but I happen to speak Tennessee.

December 19, 1995
At sea

We are thirty-two degrees north of the equator, and thirty west of the Greenwich meridian. We are below the Azores. The Cape Verde Islands are behind us, and Morocco. We are directly opposite the Atlantic Ocean from Savannah, Georgia. The sea is a blue-black and we churn it into a froth and color that looks like we added Tide, or 20 Mule Team borax, the detergent Ronald Reagan touted for a living in the years between his failed acting career in California and his thespian comeback in Washington.

The sun: the sun! The mood of the ship is sunny. Hatches are open. Doors are open. Portholes. Clean wind whooshes through the passages, pastes our shirts and our blouses against our breast-plates. The captain appeared at the breakfast table in white shirt, white shorts, white socks, and sandals, raising the sartorial flag (just a tad prematurely, I'd say) on the tropics. Leicester of Devon is taking the sun on his face out of the wind back of the port wing of the bridge. Agatha and Dick of the Lake District have been listening to cricket on the wireless in their cabin, Dick in shorts, Agatha in a sleeveless dress, their portholes letting in oceanic bouquets.

A chatty day for me. Been picking up a load of "gen," as the war-generation English still call intelligence, information, gossip. In fact, in Britspeak, you don't pick up gen, you "suss it out." I've always found little old England's slang seductive. From Ettore the chief engineer: Seven Russians work for him. Each man does one job and one job only and does not know how to do anything but that job. They do not share; they protect their jobs by not telling anyone else how to do their jobs. Then another discovery: The engine room is fully automated but no one ever activated it—gave it its head, if you will. It was, however, designed and constructed to run itself. When Ettore figures it out, the engines will at least be allowed to look after themselves overnight.

Lastly, from Ettore of the Dolomites, who ventured to Liverpool from Italy in the early sixties to learn English and sounds today like an old, gray Ringo Starr: The Russians are cunning. The Russians told the British buyers you could run this ship on thirty-five tons of fuel a day. Maybe forty, tops. When told this, Ettore thought: That is fantastic fuel efficiency for a twenty-thousand-ton ship. What the Russians did not say was you can get that kind of mileage only if you go slow, and if you run on one engine. If you need top speed, as we do, and two engines, as we do, then you will burn sixty tons of fuel a day, as we are doing. Ettore disappeared down a hole to his place of business.

To the bridge, then, to see how the captain was faring. The captain was wrapped up in the weather. There is a low in the mid-Atlantic and we are feeling the edge of its churn. On the black-and-white satellite photo it looks like a circular saw blade, whirling counterclockwise, or a tumbleweed drawn symmetrically perfect by a computer—anything but freehanded wind from a whimsical god, screwing down the atmospheric pressure. Trying to stay out of it, we first veered twenty degrees off course, then thirty, to keep heading south, but one of these days we must put out a hand and turn right, else the Panama Canal (which serves as the last-stop-at-realistic-prices gas station between us and Singapore) will be lost to us as a viable course. What I mean is, if we don't steal a march on this depression soon, and shoot straight across the Atlantic, we'll be way down yonder, and it's a long, fuel-guzzling trip to Tahiti if you go around South America first.

I probed a little for the captain's history. The third officer, Andrey, was standing this watch, so there was a window in the old man's responsibilities here. "Old man" is seadog talk; Barry the Purser, who is fifty-seven, calls the skipper, who is forty-three, the "old man" all the time. The old man said as a lad of five or six on holiday with his family in Dartmouth, he admired the smart Royal Navy men and aspired to be one himself in time. As a young man he went up for a scholarship but was turned down. Then merchant sailing was proposed to him. He sought out several shipping lines, had his choice of three, and chose the one he serves to this day, twenty-five years later. He apprenticed himself to the line (it's such a Pip world, this England, still), and the firm paid for his schooling, and, outside the classroom, gave him his practical education on its ships. He remembers that, in 1970, his earnings amounted to room and board and twenty-nine pounds fifty pence a month. He remembers each licensing examination he had to pass before shipping out as a third officer, a second, and then master: "You cram so you think your head will explode."

The bow rose and crashed. There is a microphone on the fo'c'sle, and a speaker on the bridge. The sound was heavy and shocking. The captain must have seen something in my face. "The vast power of the sea is always unbelievable," he said. "Here we are riding all this steel, and she still sends a shudder through you."

We went through the captain's career, his ships, and a few of his tales. He has a ten-year-old son, an eight-year-old daughter (he was drinking from a coffee mug that said "Dad"), and a wife who teaches physical education. Seeing to bringing these four Russian ships into the company these last two years, he has been able to stay pretty close to home, which is just north of Liverpool. This is the first time he has pulled a four-month (or longer) assignment in a fifth of his son's life, a fourth of his daughter's (this is the captain's arithmetic). "The last week around the house I was like a bear with a sore head. I should have handled myself better," he said.

We talked about the voyage so far. The captain said he was just now beginning to relax (a wave threw the bow up; the amplified sound of the crash filled the wheelhouse; my eyes sprang open bigger than quarters). There were some tense parts early on, he said, in Antwerp, in Dunkirk. Fog. We went through a concrete cut thirty meters wide in that fog. We are twenty-five meters wide. Eight feet of margin for error either side. That's tight when you weigh what we weigh. The captain didn't have a feel for how she maneuvered yet (the engines shifted astern of their own once, coming into Dunkirk; just did it, no explanation). A little wrong wind in a squeeze like that and we could have been introducing the hull to a wall.

But she's his ship today. He looked out over her familiarly, and I felt a pang of nostalgia for a nineteen-footer I used to run in the creeks and marshes and off the coast of Georgia. I knew that boat; felt it an appendage when I had the wheel. My boat, the *Miles Getz* (Miles Davis and Stan Getz died the year I got around to naming her) weighed six thousand pounds. Approaching an immovable object, a dock, with a fourteen-foot tide sweeping me into it, I was afraid the first time, but by the third I had achieved something like an apotheosis. The *Tiksi* weighs six thousand tons more than the captain is accustomed to. "She feels heavy." The tide rushing us at the berth in Dunkirk was forty feet. She has no bow thrusters. It is no wonder the captain is relaxed now. He didn't mention an apotheosis, though.

Seven p.m. We are still bouncing smartly. I couldn't sleep last night and probably won't again tonight. It's the pitch, not the roll. The roll soothes like a lullaby (so far). But the pitch feels like a hard landing in a big commercial jet, and each time our great bow and the ocean collide I hear in my mind those metronomic instructions to stay seated until we reach the gate, then make sure I've collected all my belongings, and have a nice day.

In all this rough contact, our deck has taken on the air of a romper room for the aged. I have begun to see that if you are ambulatory, and modestly fixed for cash, a ship is a fine place to be old. Just because of the ever-present possibility of foul weather, a ship is tooled out in as accommodating a fashion for the physically unstable as any nursing institution I've ever visited. Handrails are everywhere. The furniture, the cabinetry are friendly; all the sharp edges are rounded off (in the living quarters, that is; the working areas are a dangerous business). The toilet seats are high. And even the worst of the food must be inoffensive if your taste buds are shot.

Speaking of age and offense, Toxic June has confined herself to her cabin all day. I have never prided myself on being literal-minded, but, just in this instance, I can say I know someone who is, verily, under the weather. Barry the Purser says she has taken some fruit, some cheese, and some ice cream. The turbulence in here has put Dick of the Lake District on the bench, too. He remarked a while ago that a boisterous sea didn't bother him at all when he went to Singapore on a troop ship during the war.

"It must be your age now that makes you more susceptible, Dick," Dick's wife, Agatha, said. "I don't like getting old myself, you know."

"You don't?" asked Ernie of Tennessee. "You don't like getting old? Well, there's one thing for sure: if you live long enough, you'll get old. But hardly nobody likes it. I think just about ever'body thinks they'da liked to stay young."

"Oh, I think I would," said Agatha of the Lakes.

"Have you ever heard of Ponce de León?" asked Ernie. He pronounced it the way you would imagine. Then Ernie's wife, May, pronounced it better, by a Tennessee mile, but not quite correctly all the same.

Agatha of the Lakes was about to say she was aware of Ponce, but Ernie (I am convinced this is a special, unstoppable lingual gift of his) was already out of the gate so fast if he'd been a horse he would have thrown a shoe:

"Ponce de León was from Spain. Come over to America looking for the Fountain of Youth. You just drank the water and you stayed young. He reckoned he found it on the east coast of Florida, down about ninety miles south of Jacksonville. Place called St. Augustine. You come over to America and I'll show you. Ponce de Leon Lighthouse. And Ponce de Leon inlet. You know an inlet? Well they got a Ponce de Leon inlet there."

"Like Shangri-La," said Dick of the Lakes.

"Say what?" said Ernie.

"Ooh, Shangri-La," said Agatha of the Lakes. "Ronald Colman. What a splendid film that was."

"I don't know Shangri-whatever," said Ernie.

"The film was *Lost Horizon*," said Dick of the Lakes. "A Tibetan village where you stay forever young. But if you left it you got old."

"Was that what happened with the fountain?" asked Agatha of the Lakes. "If you stopped drinking the water you got old?"

"Well, Ponce de León died," said May of Tennessee.

"Oh, I don't know," said Ernie. "I don't know whatever happened to that feller."

"Indian got him with an arrow," I said, but nobody listens to me in moments like these, when I am regarded as too young to know what I am talking about.

~~~~~~

Occasional Force Ten winds continue to dog us out of that depression in the Middle Atlantic. The weather has cut our speed to ten knots and a fraction, and put back our ETA at the Panama Canal from December 27 to December 31, unless the ocean calms and we get the lead out. Until then, we stick to the captain's strategy, a familiar military tactic to a cracker American like me: we keep trying to outflank the low, as Grant did Lee, all that spring of 1864, from the Wilderness to Cold Harbor, from Cold Harbor to Petersburg—we keep moving southwest around the storm's right.

We hit a rogue swell at five-thirty this morning that gave us a thirty-five-degree roll that woke up the ship and set off false alarms. The captain's quarters are strewn with charts and manuals and the contents of various drawers. Everyone came peeking into the passages like earthquake survivors. Leicester of Devon in his pajamas, his day clothes soaked by a flying teakettle. Everyone had furniture and lamps rearranged, glass breakage. Toxic June lost a bottle of whiskey and a bottle of gin, shattered against a bulkhead. Barry the Purser had June's booze replaced immediately; no fool, Barry.

Everyone I've seen (it is nine o'clock) is coolly collected or wearing a cool disguise. As we continue to roll and roll, and one missile or another whistles past me (a shaving cream canister a moment ago), I gain more appreciation for the sand in these ancients with whom I sail. If something—something of nature's the strength of that rogue swell—had hurled me from my bed at home, I'd be knocking back a third double rye and dialing real estate agents by now. All that my fellow passengers are doing, however, is complaining about the shoddy carpentry, as wardrobe doors and drawers bang open and shut in every cabin. The latches are cheap. "I'm ashamed to say it's British workmanship," said Agatha of the Lakes. "It's rubbishy."

I'm impressed by these people this morning. I think I have been selling them short. I was beginning to think it was ten limbic systems and me on a long ride. But this kind of buoyancy isn't wired in and involuntary. Way to rodeo, you old farts.

I hear Little Peter next door playing with his radio. Sometimes I think Peter is playing with *me;* sometimes I think he is just weird. He has been reading *The Decline and Fall of the Roman Empire.* Peter says the Romans would have had a longer run if they hadn't taken all those hot baths, heated up their testicles, and, well, everybody knows how the big picture blurs when you've got hot balls.

Every day, Peter counts the number of spots he is able to monitor on his shortwave. Sixty-five was a record. Abu Dhabi was a first for him yesterday. Before that, Djibouti.

Old men seem to like to count. Dick of the Lake District told me as we passed through a lock in France he had counted one hundred and ten cars on the deck of a passing freighter. Leicester of Devon counts less than the other old men, but he counts— I've heard him. Ernie of Tennessee is nothing but numbers (BLIEVE! it was . . .). Peter has gotten nineteen days, so far, on one eight-hour charge of the battery of his Norelco shaver. Peter informs us it is fifty-eight steps on the accommodation ladder between us on the fifth deck and the officers' dining saloon on the main. To count constantly means you have to take into your count the most irrelevant things. What I don't know, nor have the cheek to ask, is whether all this counting helps the old men pass the time, or helps them slow it down. I remember one Sunday I was tucking into a fried chicken dinner in Georgia when I overheard an elderly woman in the next booth remark to her companion, "I'm so old my days fly by like a picket fence."

For two or three hours before dawn, I saw Sirius through my feet, out my porthole, our brightest star, like a diamond stoplight, blinking between my big toes. We are still rolling in the residue of that big low up north. My bunk is situated athwart, which is to say I run no risk of sliding out of bed as we roll, but the placement does come with its own set of aggravations. Because I like to gaze out the porthole while I repose, and because my reading lamp is affixed to the bulkhead opposite, my head, when in bed, is to starboard, my feet to port. This means that when the ship is rolling and I am trying to sleep, I sometimes wake because I am feeling incredible pressure on my neck (because, due to the roll, I am actually standing on my head) or, when we have slid over to port, there I am in bed awake and standing on my feet.

Sea life without stabilizers: none but the heaviest drowser could take refreshment from these nights. Stabilizers are what you pay for on passenger liners; on a cargo ship, it's a matter of pride to take a mauling from the sea. On a cruise ship, your champagne glass runneth over only when you overpoureth. On this ship, when you ask for a glass of water, which is as close as you'll get to champagne, the stewardess first half empties her water pitcher onto your tablecloth, for traction, then she fills your water glass and bangs it down before you. That's the kind of class we are.

Some of the stiff upper lips in my crowd have lost their starch as the shoddy drawers and doors continue to bang about and even the items you thought were properly stowed are emitted back at you like bullets and end up raising a bruise. Agatha of the Lakes has a mean blue splotch on her upper left arm, for one.

———

After lunch today I made my way to the bow for the first time and gained respect for, and complete understanding of, the word "awesome." Thirty-ton containers, the size of railroad cars, stacked on the one side of the slender walk along the rim of the ship, the gunwale on the other, and a moist deck underfoot moving to the primordial rhythm of the deep. The sea came over in great cold sprays. There is a foremast with a lookout post the Russians manned when they were breaking ice (the man forward, espying a fracture, would guide the bridge to aim the bow at the crack and force it), but the Brits had never had need to staff this station, and now it was forlorn. It looks like a little air traffic control tower, or an enclosed crow's nest on top of a short shaft. The captain has never been in it, nor did he know whether it was locked, but he made me welcome to explore. There was some rust, and the hatch did not want to cooperate, but I managed to dog it open with my shoulder. Seawater sloshed inside. I found a light switch. Iron rungs ran up the bulkhead through what felt like a one-man vertical tunnel. Very close in there. Wet, thick air. I emerged into a kind of cockpit. There was a lifejacket, and a bench with a busted slat. The windows were crusted in salt. There was a black phone, to the bridge I assumed, with some instructions in Russian. I appeared to be the only one at large on the ship outside the accommodation block. The Atlantic Ocean parted before me, for me, majestic and frightening. So this was the vista afforded barebreasted wooden maidens on the bows of ancient galleons. It sounds far more unpleasant than it was, but the truth is, for the half hour I spent in that outpost, I felt utterly alone on the world.

An invitation under the door from the Tennesseans: drinks before dinner Christmas Eve in the passengers' lounge. It is the
only holiday evidence around.

Long talk with Andrey on the bridge and much of it derailed
by language failures. We talked about Russia. St. Petersburg is
the soul; Moscow is the heart. I did not tell Andrey when he told
me that I had heard this a hundred times. The two times I visited
Russia, I may have heard it more. The people are more interesting in St. Petersburg, says Andrey, who took his maritime
training there. Yes, I say, I gathered that when I was there. Moscow has "two millions" coming in on the trains each workday,
he says; "two millions" departing each night—too busy for soul.
But old slow Petersburg, there you have patience and time for
art and conversation. I am thinking I get enough of this in *War
and Peace*. But we are trying to become friends and the language
makes it slow work. Of course, said Andrey, it is best to be in
St. Petersburg with a woman.

Andrey, said I, after a long balloon of silence, gray sea sprays
bursting over the bow, just about everything goes better with a
woman.

I wear eyeglasses, but my vision is fine within about four feet, so
I need no help in reading. Also, because I can see my food just
fine, I don't bother with spectacles at meals. This evening in the
dining saloon, Toxic June sat at the other table, directly in my
line but separated from me by twelve or fourteen feet. At that
distance, through the softness of poor sight, my eye picked up
her face as it must have looked before it went under the harrow.
My God, I thought, what strength and bravery it must take to
watch your beauty fade until it's gone.

"What's new with you?" I say to Andrey on the bridge.

"What do you expect?"

Silence.

"Do you play cards?" Andrey asks me.

"No."

"It is a passer of time."

Silence.

"Well," I say to Andrey, "tell me about your life."

"My life is a dark place."

I asked him if he had translated the words of a song he mentioned a few days ago. He said he thought I would like the song. It was written and recorded by a Siberian rock group, Nautilus Pompilius, from Ekaterinburg, the former Sverdlovsk. He said he had written it for me from memory. He gave me a folded paper from his pocket. These are the lyrics:

When all the songs I don't know become silent
My latest paper Steamship will scream in the astringent air
Good-bye America where I've never been to
Farewell for good
Take a banjo and play for me at parting
Your frayed jeans became too small for me now
We have been taught for so long time to love your forbidden fruits
Good-bye America where I'll never be
Will I hear the song that'll be stuck in my
                        Memory for ever

"When was this song written?"

"In the Cold War. Before Brezhnev died."

"I would guess it was written after Reagan called the Soviet Union the 'Evil Empire.' "

"Yes, I know."

"Well, of course you know. It's me that's doing the guessing here."

"It was written after the South Korean airliner."

"Now, that's putting some meat on the story, Andrey."

"Yes."

"Is the group still together?"

"Yes. In St. Petersburg. In Russia, if you are artist—"

"I know, I know—like Nashville."

"Yes, I know Nashville."

"Only better with a woman."

"Only better with a woman."

Drinks with Toxic June in her cabin one deck below mine. Her cramped quarters—same size as mine—are wallpapered with cards. She has Christmas greetings Scotch-taped to every surface, sent to her by friends around the world before she boarded. She has me choose one from three cards and starts to write but stops. "It's Gregg with two G's on the end, is it?"

"No."

"To Greg, then, with love. Happy Christmas."

I learn June lives on the Channel Isle of Alderney. It is, she says, "Two thousand alcoholics clinging to a rock. We have sixteen pubs." June is having gin. I am having club soda. She is reading a book called *The Rise and Fall of the British Empire*. We get on immediately, probably because June confesses first thing that she is not a snob, then says, "I know you are an intelligent, interesting man. So tell me, are you picking up something I cannot find, or am I losing my mind, or are these people truly terribly boring?"

I told her I felt there was a ship full of comedy at our disposal if you looked for it, or a fair amount of blues-inducing sadness if you looked at things that way. I told her I kept to myself a lot. Other than at meals, the only time I regularly see our fellow passengers is when I am thrown out of my cabin by Olga, the stewardess, who Hoovers the carpet at nine-thirty and makes my bed into the same bewildering twist of linens I encountered in hotels and inns all the way across Russia four years ago. When Olga knocks, I go into the passenger lounge, usually to find Harry and Gerda, who use it pretty much as their sitting room. I haven't gotten to know Harry and Gerda yet. They are amply nourished waddlers from Out West in America. They are plain folk, a little stingy with a smile. Given the environment, that's not enough in my book to begin awarding demerits. When he speaks at all, you hear Harry say things like "I think after November all professional football games should be played in enclosed stadiums." One day I was lamenting the sorry state of some primitive pulley weights in our so-called gymnasium, and Harry said, "You'd do better with a bucket of sand." I've been waiting for another one as good as that.

Oh, and Little Peter is usually there, and he has counted something already—radio stations or something—and he would be sharing that. But other than being put out until I hear the silence of the vacuum cleaner, and can then retire to the diabolical jigsaw Olga has made of my sheets, I'm not with our mates much.

June said she was getting on with this May of Tennessee, whose double cabin is next to hers, but said May's husband "is thick as a stick." I thought the expression was "thick as a plank," but I didn't feel it was my place to oppose June on Ernie's density. I personally think Ernie is a natural man. I don't think there is any guile there. He certainly has a gift, though, for turning any conversation into a recitation of his personal war in the South Pacific. I let this annoy me for a while, but I watched one of Barry the Purser's videos the other night and it brushed me up on what happened at Okinawa, where Ernie was (there were 182,999 other men in that assault, too). A force of 60,000 hit the beach the first day. The Japanese launched two days of the most devastating suicide attacks in the history of modern warfare; there were 350 kamikaze attacks in one day (Ernie counted 50). In three months, the Japanese sank 30 ships, damaged 368, killed

5,000 sailors, wounded 5,000 others, killed 7,400 GIs, wounded 30,000 others, and lost 107,000 of their own. Forty-five thousand Okinawans perished. In my view, Ernie has earned his obsession, and he can talk about his piece of that place all he wants.

May of Tennessee, however, seems to enjoy insulting me. She has somehow placed me in her ledger under arrogance, mistaking what I see as merely a lack of common ground. I'm polite to a fault.

But I don't tell June any of this. Mostly I just listen. She tells me again she is not a snob. We get on the food. "All I would like to see is a simple roasted chicken and a nice salad. Is that too much to manage?"

Yes, I say, and I tell her it's more than we can hope for from Tuber, my name for the chef, the Russian root crop specialist. But we must be generous and extend him kindness in our thoughts. In the recent bad weather, the Force Ten gales, Tuber endured whole lost meals flying around the galley, and boiled more potatoes and cabbage, an occasional involuntary whimper the only evidence of his stress. June, as I think I have mentioned, lost a bottle of scotch and a bottle of gin to the weather; they smashed against her bulkhead (today her cabin still held the bouquet of delirium gone to waste). When the captain looked in on her, he found June and her stewardess, Nadezhda, wrapping her surviving jugs in towels and placing them under the mattress for safe passage.

By suppertime we had given everyone a thorough running down—or, rather, June did, but I encouraged it. She called my neighbor Agatha of the Lakes "Miss Marple. Snooping into everything. Smelling like a rose herself." I couldn't let Agatha go undefended, but June cautioned me that "getting matey" this early in the voyage showed poor judgment. I said I'd try not to form any friendships hastily and we left it at that. June said she had decided now to leave the ship in Singapore. "I've done the Suez countless times," she said. "And the Med will be cold anyway."

Flying fish everywhere off the bow. Water royal blue. Northwest of us is Necker Island, owned by the Virgin Atlantic wonder Brit, Richard Branson, where Princess Di and her sons occasionally holiday. I spent some time there writing a story about the place for *Life* magazine a few years ago, and it comes back to me as I see it on the charts this morning, but I decide against mentioning it on the bridge. Name-dropping. Almost always diminishes you in the eyes of others.

The skipper comes up before breakfast, mug in hand, bag under eye. I tell him I was writing about him in my journal the other day, about how I sensed he had the feel of this twenty-thousand-ton ship the way I felt at one with my three-ton boat. He said not quite yet. It's a matter of how heavy she is (a few thousand tons more than he's ever mastered), and the propeller that is really too small for the weight. And it isn't the weight she's carrying; it's the weight of her herself, including the extra thirty centimeters of ice-breaking steel that sheathes her hull like a condom. Her scantlings. Now, a new ship, the captain said, is a pitifully thin affair. He saw one off Durban not long ago, built by the South Koreans, and his first mate remarked, "She looks hungry already." The captain looked and found "she did. You could see her ribs." We, on the other hand, are so dense the skipper worries about stopping us. You don't go full astern to stop, he said. You reverse her gradually, giving the propeller a chance to bite. But this ship surprised him, concerned him, how long she took to slow. He still shivers thinking how it could have gone wrong back in Europe.

Leicester of Devon came alongside and we all got talking where we were a year ago on Christmas Eve. The captain said he was coming home to England from Le Havre and he reached home at eight o'clock that night, "which is exactly how you're supposed to do it on Christmas Eve. And there was ice on the trees that looked like a storybook."

"Oh, I know," said Leicester of Devon. "I have a former wasteland behind my bungalow [I think he means a municipal dump] where they've put about six football pitches and a slope going down to it. Never been good for a thing to me, but last winter my five-year-old grandson got a sled ride out of it."

I was in piney old Georgia last Christmas, and all day I've been lonesome, wishing I were back there still. By tomorrow I expect to be covered in sentimentality, and pretty unresistant about it.

May of Tennessee managed to insult me again after lunch. She and Ernie are giving a little cocktail party in the passenger lounge at five—in just a few minutes, in fact. I went up to her as lunch was ending. "I have two boxes of cookies," I began saying.

"Well, good for you."

"And two big bars of Belgian chocolate."

"Well, are you going to give a party?"

"No, but I wondered if I might contribute them to your party."

"I didn't know you could be nice."

"I beg your pardon."

"I didn't. I didn't know you could be nice."

I said nothing, just left the dining room, whereupon I said to myself, "Why didn't you tell that woman to go piss up a rope?"

～～～

December 25, 1995
The Caribbean

My tongue was a very ungrateful color this morning. I'd call it a New World blackberry. I drank last night, not like a man with a thirst, but steady on. It wasn't one of those once-in-a-lifetime rationalizations. I did not raise a glass and think: Only on Christmas Eve when I'm on a Russian icebreaker . . . I simply decided it was time to allow myself to drink, and I told myself I would deal with the consequences later. I had a glass of scotch, Famous Grouse, and then I had another. I felt the third one spread out in a spidery way inside my skull, just beneath the crown of my head, like the flip side of the beginning of male-pattern baldness. I became chatty and then, as my late grandmother used to say, I "sulled up like an old bull." Later on, my moods stopped swinging. Predictably, remorse is with me now. I will put off the analysis for another day.

Came into the Caribbean through the Sombrero Passage in the middle of the night. St. Croix off the port just now. Leicester of Devon is up taking the sun. He got a call through on the satellite phone to England at six-thirty. "Reception was very good. I rang my friend who was taking her crowd to the Christmas meal at the Gipsy Hill Hotel in Exeter. Actually, in Pinhoe, on the outskirts. Save the cooking, you see. Spoke with my son. He said it was a hard frost and cold. Very lovely, he said. My friend could have been with me here now, if she'd wanted." I let it go, selfishly, for the temporary protection of my own heart. I do not wish to know of Leicester's bruised affections today. I gather her name is Silla, which is probably short for Priscilla. She has sailed with him before.

Awoke to presents at my door. A little stuffed bear and a card from Mary of Boston. A whiskey glass and a tube of Chinese ginseng toothpaste from Barry the Purser. A card addressed to "young Gregory" and another stuffed bear, this one wearing a Santa hat, from Agatha of the Lakes, who kissed me with passion last night. I had never had such a gesture from an old lady. I would like to think that my displeasure with it had nothing to do with her age; that it was just something I did not want. As I say, I'd like to think that. She told me she was "very naughty" when she was a young woman. It was the gin, I suppose. She's nine years older than my mother.

May of Tennessee told the captain, "If I had your figure, I'd wear short pants all the time." I got this from Toxic June, who Englished up the quote, I'd bet. May probably said "legs" and "shorts." June says she abstains from booze every Lent. During this dryness, she said, "I find everyone at cocktail parties talking very stupidly."

June said to Ettore the Italian chief engineer, "Do they have stockings in your country?"

"Yes," he said.

I said, "What about telephones, televisions—the wheel?"

"Yes," said Ettore. "And ice-a-box."

Cocktail party talk.

"Peter, you're gettin' low," said Tennessee Ernie.

"What?"

"You're gettin' low. Can I top you up?"

Ernie is a beer drinker, has no idea how to mix a drink. You ask for scotch and he asks you whether you want some tonic with it. Or 7UP. Or mulligatawny soup, if there happens to be a tureen nearby.

The radio was blaring on the bridge this morning. Sounded like a traffic report. I said to Andrey, "What's that?"

"I don't care."

"All right, so you don't care. But what is it?"

"Some Americans talking."

Andrey and I haven't gotten into religion, but I know he goes by the Russian Orthodox calendar, an old calendar. His Christmas is the sixth of January.

Another cocktail party this noon in a room opposite the dining saloon on the main deck. There's a Russian stand-up piano in there. And an ice maker Ettore installed yesterday. Everyone very convivial. Many photos taken, especially of me, who am made to stand alone while they flash away like paparazzi. I can't think why and it makes me very self-conscious. I hear Agatha of the Lakes exclaim sorrowfully of her camera, "But it's giving up at twenty-four when I paid for thirty-six."

Then in to dine. There are wine bottles on the tables, a first. I am staying with water. I am a little frightened by the ease with which I returned to alcohol last night. I really thought it would be more of a struggle; evidently a Slinky toy has a stronger spine than mine. Today I must return myself to the successful teetotaler I have come to respect. Barry the Purser seats me at the head of one table, the captain at the other. I'm at a loss thinking why I deserve the honor until I realize Toxic June is seated at my left. I think Barry has learned she enjoys me. On her other side is Alexander the electrician, to whom June says, "Darling, have you beeeeeeen in the tropics before?" She advises him to take salt tablets, says she has brought hers along.

I should have bit my tongue, but instead I volunteer that the value of salt tablets in our circumstances is dubious. They used to give us salt tablets in gym, thinking it was good for us to restore salts lost in perspiration. But now it is known that perspiration has a far lower concentration of salt than blood, and so when sweat is pouring off you, you're mostly losing water. Throw more salt in yourself and it only accelerates dehydration, and that's bad for you. Thing to do is drink plenty of water.

This infuriates June.

"Darling, I think I can safely say I am the only person in this room who has crossed the Sahara twice."

"I'd say you're right," said Little Peter enthusiastically.

"Peter saw dolphins this morning," said Agatha of the Lakes.

"I counted five," Peter said. "Maybe it would be more believable if I said four."

I was thinking: Have I crossed the Sahara twice? Then I got my wits back, and I told myself that even if I have crossed the Sahara fifty times, it's best not to mention it.

So June set sail on a story of how she restored the health of some bloody stupid dehydrated non-foresighted Frenchmen. In the Sahara. With salt. Among other ministrations (I shudder to speculate).

I said, "I could drop my trousers right now and let you flail away at me for my impudence. Or I could say that salt supplementation may be necessary in extreme conditions, I will admit, but on an air-conditioned, heavily insulated ship, venturing on deck thirty minutes a day to sun oneself, extra salt is not what I'd call a good idea. But it would be more fun if I took down my pants, wouldn't it?"

"Oh, I do love you," said Toxic June. And the hateful fire went out of her eyes and the Lord decreed it was good for all.

It was the best meal Tuber has presented us. Barry the Purser was in the kitchen at his side with a *Better Homes and Gardens Cookbook*. We had goose, duck, and ham. Melon balls. Roasted potatoes. Gravy, after a fashion. Rum cake and strawberry ice cream. The captain toasted the Queen. "Long may she reign," said Agatha of the Lakes. (There is a portrait of the young, horsey-faced Elizabeth on one bulkhead of the dining area.)

Then the captain toasted absent friends. "Absent friends," said everyone, including me, with feeling. Whatever it was I was running from, I was thinking, I could stand being back in the bosom of it, if only for this day.

Yes, a bounteous table, but I spent much of the meal distracted and remorseful, until at one point I found I had been staring at a blown-up color photograph opposite me on the bulkhead until my food had gone stone cold. I had been looking at this landscape for twenty-five days with the distinct feeling I had been there. Birch trees in autumn. Paper birches. And a two-track lane down to a blue lake. Alexander the radioman, who was at my table, settled my mind. It's a Russian scene, about one hundred kilometers west of Moscow. I stopped to relieve myself by the side of the road there in 1991. A little Christmas present: true déjà vu.

My good deed for the day was to be kind to Peter, who has seemed sadder than most for the last few hours. I had heard him say he had a place with one hundred and ten acres in upstate

New York, close to the Canadian border. I had heard him say he bought it a few years ago on a day when a brook on the property sparkled, and deer appeared up on a hillside so that he saw the sky above them and between their legs. I asked why he wanted a farm and he said the answer would take a long time, but that there was a farmer in Indiana who blocked an interstate highway from dividing his property by saying he would put an ax through the head of the first construction worker who stepped onto his land. "That's freedom," said Little Peter. "That's independence." It was a surprising revelation from what I've come to view as so timid a fellow, but timid in a weird way, I must say. Timid and cheap and anal: Peter has a piece of string tied to the earpieces on his glasses; Peter has the keys to his luggage on a piece of string around his neck. But I detour. What happened to the good deed I set myself?

Peter went on to say he keeps two geese on his land because he finds the winters too silent. Canadian geese leave his area in August, and after that there is nothing but blue jays until March. Then come red-winged blackbirds, cardinals, and robins and, after them, one warm night, Peter opens the door and hears thousands and thousands of peepers down in the pond, and he knows spring has come to him again.

I thought, well, Peter, you dog—a lyrical side to you. Then he changed back into old boring Little Peter again. Peter signposts his conversation, overguides: "And now, this is the really interesting part . . ." And of course it turns out a yawner. I don't know whether it still does, but *Playboy* magazine used to have a page of awful jokes with a heading at the top that said in big bold type: HUMOR. This offended me in some way. It was as though I had turned a page and been instructed: LAUGH NOW!

Peter's divorce cost him three hundred thousand dollars. I haven't a clue why he told me this. I had a divorce once. I can't remember what it cost. Toxic June, Agatha—they're mad to know the personal details of my life, but I hoard them. Yes, married twice. Yes, children—grown. Yes, married now.

Where's the little woman? The little woman is in New York. Why isn't the little woman here? The little woman missed the boat.

Ha-ha! I take your point. One mustn't pry.

They would prefer that I give them a drama. I don't have a drama. I don't feel like being married. I haven't for some time. My wife? She thinks being married is okay, could be better, loves me all the same. Me, I don't want to hurt anybody but I don't feel like sticking around. Think I might sail away. All right then, go. See you sometime. See you sometime.

I am going to bed sober now. But first, once more, the clock has to go back one hour. Briefly now it will be the same time on the ship that it is in Georgia and New York. The little woman is in New York. In Georgia I have a daughter who is married and six months pregnant. She lives a clean, modern, upwardly mobile life. I have a son just up the road from her in a cabin on the side of a mountain. His life is a little earthier and more static than his sister's. They are so different. A few years ago I used to say my daughter never wore anything that did not have to be dry-cleaned, and my son never wore anything that had not been owned by three or four people before him. This is no longer literally true, but they are still as unlike as that. Merry Christmas to all, and to all a good night.

I miss you.

December 26, 1995
The Caribbean

There, now—there's the proper face in the shaving mirror. No question of experience and an accumulation of years, but no puffy assistance from the Famous Grouse and friends. Still, there is Boxing Day to be got through, the British excuse for a second acquiescence to compulsory drinking before the run-up to New Year's.

This daybreak reminds me of a Dreamsicle, an ice cream bar from my youth that was tangerine outside, vanilla within. It's a Dreamsicle sunrise this morning, in a cumulus pastry. Haiti is off our starboard beyond sight. I was there on assignment in March of this year. I decide not to mention it. Can't risk the social demerits.

Agatha of the Lakes told me this noon she would like to smoke a marijuana cigarette. She asked me if I had ever. I could not tell a lie. She asked if I might purchase marijuana on one or the other of these islands up ahead. I think I demurred, if that means respectfully declined, or maybe I was just vague. I'm too old to be busted in Papeete out trying to score some dope.

We will be in the Panama Canal tomorrow night.

〜〜〜〜〜

December 27, 1995
The Caribbean

Toilets all stoppered, showers scalding—Barry the Purser's life a nightmare. He begged them—"I did; I did, I begged back in the shipyard"—to replace the Russian sewerage with pipes a size or two bigger. A cigarette butt stops up what we have. The engineer blows out the system and we are all in a terrible mess (I won't describe it, but I shall never forget it). The stewardesses are coming around with disinfectant.

"I never smoked," Leicester of Devon told me on Monkey Island as we waited out the toilet brigade below. All the Russians smoke. We have assigned the toilet blame to the Russians, all of us non-smokers have. "One of my sons smokes, but he doesn't smoke in my house; he goes into the garden. None of my grandsons smoke. I never could see it. Taking that smoke into your mouth, then . . ." Leicester made a disgusting blowing noise. "In

West Africa during the war I had some long nights sitting on about five hundred German prisoners. I made some inquiries about a pipe. I was guided to Four Square tobacco, quite a well-known product. I managed to acquire all the paraphernalia and up I lit. I only barely made the toilet.

"Now, the quartermaster had some Egyptian cigarettes. I never touched them. He had thousands and thousands of them. Couldn't give them away. They said they were made from camel dung. Even the wogs wouldn't smoke them."

I allowed that I used to smoke and dearly loved it. I said I could never be a hypocrite about smoking, condemning the poor nicotine fiends as many of my reformed friends do, because, in my heart of hearts, I am still a smoker. That said, I do harbor one objection. In New York, which has pretty much banned smoking indoors, you can't enjoy the out-of-doors these days without walking in a cloud of smoke. Since all the smokers have been banished to the elements, the sidewalks have become as smoky as the expectant fathers' waiting rooms of old. I have thought of proposing a law, modeled on New York City's alternate-side-of-the-street parking law. You have to move your car from one side of the street to the other every morning in New York, so the street sweepers can do their job. I would humbly propose alternate-side-of-the-street smoking. That way, the smokers could walk on their side, and the rest of us could walk on the other. I don't hold out much hope for alternate-side-of-the-street smoking, but merely pondering it made me, in Leicester's view, a typical American. Dreaming up a law to satisfy my selfishness.

Passed through the Panama Canal last night, and a full night's work it was. The toll, according to a slim brochure one of the two Panamanian pilots dropped off on the bridge, works out to about two dollars and a quarter a ton for cargo, one seventy-five a ton for ballast, and a buck and a quarter for every ton we displace. We're twenty thousand tons. I don't know how much ballast we carry. We displace thirty-four thousand tons. Call it a hundred grand. It seems a needlessly complicated formula. The captain said it cost $135,000 the last time he transited the Suez, not counting the baksheesh, which is still an onerous business, highway bribery (smokes and whiskey, mostly). Here, for at least another four years and three days (the canal becomes entirely Panama's on December 31, 1999, thanks to Jimmy Carter, an unpopular move politically for Goober, as were so many, but a right one, as were so many), going in one side and out the other is still an aboveboard business, and no strong-arming for presents.

The pilots, and a trainee, came on in fog and rain in Limon Bay, at the Cristóbal breakwater. You are required to take on, and pay for (the captain is not sure about the cost), a second pilot if you are wider than eighty feet. We are eighty feet and five inches. A ship one hundred and eight feet abeam is called Panamax. The locks are one hundred ten feet wide. The canal is fifty miles long, from deep water Atlantic to deep water Pacific. For yellow fever victories and the rest of the saga, see David Mc-Cullough (*The Path Between the Seas*). As for my captain, I gave him John McPhee (*Looking for a Ship*). The captain, who has been around the world by sea twenty-five times, told me this morning that he did not know, until he read McPhee, that in the Panama Canal the pilots really are in charge. Elsewhere in the world, they are, technically, nominally, paid-for advisers (in Dunkirk, we were ill advised and we almost ran aground, the captain concedes—he winces when he tells me this), though in many places, particularly when the pilots and the tug skippers are communicating in a language the captain does not understand, the pilot has the helm. Even knowing the law, courtesy of McPhee, the captain said he had to make allowances for the sluggishness of this ship when the pilots called out their commands. If they wanted him to advance at four knots, for example, he would have to shove her up to eight to achieve it, and if they wanted deceleration, the equivalent of four knots, say, he'd have to force her full astern. So it went. No sleep for officers and crew and everyone still keyed up this morning as we lay off Balboa, the bone-white skyscrapers (why am I surprised?) of Panama City glinting in the sun. We took on eight hundred tons of fuel while at anchor and sailed for Papeete this afternoon at one.

Longest conversation yet, with the captain, as we bunkered. I think he had some nervous energy to work off he didn't know what to do with. He began by telling me he declined the pilots' offer to see him to our anchorage last night, thinking he was saving a penny, only to find our main gyroscope was on the fritz, knackered. This is down by the engine room. We have a second gyro in a great green globe on the roof of the bridge (Monkey Island), but it was not plugged up, so to speak. The captain was cross with the Russians for not having the backup gyro up and running, as it should have been, and uttered, as far as I've heard, his first biased words. "Typical Russian," he said. What it all meant was that we had to find a parking spot in this crowded bay without a reliable compass. "I just had to find a hole and anchor," he said.

Off he went, then, in an explanation of why we couldn't trust God's own magnetic poles to tell us where we were. Variations and deviations. First, no matter where you are, your true-north reading on the compass in your pocket, no matter how much you paid for it, is going to be six degrees off.

"So how was that factored in on the first charts?" called out sly Little Peter, who had been eavesdropping on my primer from his perch on a deck chair off the bridge.

"I'm a user, Peter," said the captain, sounding mildly annoyed, "not an explorer."

Second, we are at the equator (I thought the air felt clingy), meaning we are spang in the middle of two rather significant force fields. And third, "it comes down literally to the direction in which the steel in this ship was milled." I played dummy—it wasn't a stretch—and said, "So you're saying that between the pull of the poles and the pull of the milled steel in this ship, an ordinary compass would be too confused to tell me diddly?" With just the faintest sigh of exasperation, the captain said again he simply had to find a hole on his own, and anchor.

Well, while I had him sailing by the seat of his pants, I got a fill on SatNav and GPS (Global Positioning System). Satellite navigation, which we do not rely on, despite its prominent oc-cupancy in the chart room, comes from twelve satellites on a polar orbit. You get a reading once an hour, and for the other fifty-nine minutes you are on dead reckoning (speed and direc-tion) until the next reading comes down. GPS, which has been available since the seventies, is twenty-four satellites parked out there. We go round; they don't. You are always within sight of six of them, and the system will tell you where you are within forty meters ("I'd accept a hundred," said the captain. A little later, Ernie of Tennessee told me GPS was accurate within six feet, could read the license plate on your car. Whatever). Before GPS, it took an extra day to reach Papeete because the best you could do was make a landfall in the archipelago to the north of it and then swing wide and west to avoid some dicey atolls and volcano tops. Now, with the pinpointing satellites, you pick a narrow passage and slip your big clipper on in.

After this, we talked about what men at sea talk about. The

captain remembered "getting a skinful in Singapore, in old days—I'm really talking old days now."

Up on Monkey Island, Leicester of Devon, in his graceful fashion, was talking the same language to Toxic June. "So why isn't your friend Silla along on this voyage?" asked June.

"She's experiencing a land slip at the end of her garden and her stupid son thinks she should attend to it."

Leicester left June in the sun, sipping a Heineken from the can. She didn't quite understand his explanation, and it fell to me to try to flesh it out. I told her Leicester had told me this, exactly this:

"My friend Silla would have come along if it weren't for her stupid son. She is in number twenty-nine and I am in fifty-five. It's a row of bungalows. She looks out on the river. I told her there was another single cabin available on this ship and she was in a great conga hoop over it. But her son—remember I told you we had that slope to that waste ground behind us?—he said she had to do something about it and he talked her into waiting a year. He's a bank officer. Fifty years old. They just declared him redundant. Yes, a conga hoop, Silla was—even had Lloyd's to manage her bills while she was away."

June said to me, "Is it your journalism training makes you act this way?"

I asked June if I could have one of her beers, and she dispatched me to her cabin to fetch two.

It truly is insidious, this drink thing, just as all the drunkards say. Just like that (I just snapped my fingers): I said, June, may I have one of your beers? Emboldened by my ability to drink Christmas Eve and to cut it out Christmas Day, here I go again. I remember in Tehran in 1979, when they took away all the alcohol. The first couple of months, while Khomeini was getting the feel of things, you could still drink. There were mini-bars in all the rooms in the Inter-Continental Hotel, and fine wines in the cellar. Then one day a gang of mullah thugs came in and seized it all. There were grown men literally dragged down the corridors clutching the shank of a bottle, the Ayatollah's boys pulling on the neck. That day they smashed two million dollars' worth of wine in the alley out back of the hotel.

I thought I would never get out of Tehran, and when I did, when I was sitting in first class on a jumbo waiting to take off, a flight attendant asked me if I wanted champagne. I said yes and drank down a glass. I looked out my window at the mucus-colored pollution of the city that ran right up to the Elburz Mountains, up there where the Shah had lived in the clean air, and I asked for more champagne every time the cart made a round. Finally those big jet engines began to roar, and one of the attendants came to collect my flute. More champagne, please, I said. Turning to the galley, the young woman shouted, "Hey, Adrian, fetch a magnum for Champagne Charlie up here in seat one-A!"

That was drinking without restraint. I was pacing myself now.

Saw Little Peter in the lounge tonight, having a glass of wine. He had been reading *The Peloponnesian Wars*. He counted something today; cormorant or something. Fifteen.

~~~~~~

December 29, 1995
6 N / 8 4 W

Watched *Zulu* last night on video, the young, toothy Michael Caine, and woke up this morning thinking/dreaming about physical courage. In those small instances when my life demanded it, I have not been let down, but a lack of courage of the other kind, it discourages me to report, may be what turns a man into a writer. Only way to have the last word, isn't it? Is it the heat in these parts makes me cut myself so little slack? Should I see Toxic June for a salt tablet?

Seem to be striking up a friendship with the captain. Could be a generational thing. He is a company man (although the company had them all bugger off one afternoon in 1991, declared them redundant, had them go offshore, incorporate with a personnel firm, pony up the quid for their own benefits, pitch in for their own retirement, etc., and come back the next morning, hat in hand, to be rehired en masse, sans fringes) and as such thinks twice about fraternizing with the help. That leaves the passengers, all of whom are a little old for him, except me, four years his senior. He came in to see me to retrieve some navigational books for the cadet, Nick, who was allowed to make a course change last night (don't hit the Galápagos, son; turn right!). I told him I was unable to turn up the word "scantlings" in the meager English dictionary I had scrounged from the Russians. He said it was a nautical term, or, perhaps, at its broadest, industrial. In turn, I gave him the word "kerf." My friend Patrick Lynch gave "kerf" to me about twenty years ago. Such a good-for-you word. I try to use it, like garlic, in everything, and I remember I found need for it, or manufactured need for it, in this journal back in England, as I watched a server in a Liverpool hotel carve into a roast that was done to the national liking: dry as a two-by-four. Said the skipper, "Just to make sure: you are saying 'kerf' is the space the saw leaves?"

"Correct."

The captain and I had a small "company" talk. He has just reached that age where a few of his peers are starting to pull ahead. It is dismaying at first, I told him. It feels like an unnatural hierarchy, being governed by your chums. Even more troubling is to see people you trusted turning duplicitous. Of course, it is only human to enjoy being on the first team, and to do what one must to protect one's position. But it is painful all the same to witness the degree of change in public face, hypocrisy, denial. So rarely are they frank enough, once they have outclimbed you, to admit that they must lie to hold on.

I tell all this to the captain, but I have to issue a caveat and he tells me to continue. I'm not terribly well schooled in the elements of self-deception, I say. Denial is not an issue with me, I say, for I cannot think of anything I have ever denied myself. I have been known to go right down to the gutter on a good debauch . . .

—But your point? said the captain.

The ugly-baby syndrome might apply here, I said. What I mean is, there are people who think there is no such thing as an ugly baby, particularly the parents of an ugly baby. I honestly don't think parents of ugly babies have the ability to see ugliness in their baby, even though *I* can tell an ugly baby when *I* spot an ugly baby. I don't think this is ego-distorting vision; I think this is love. It's a form of self-deception, yes, but it's benign, even beneficent—it makes parents genuinely believe their ugly baby should replace the Gerber tot on the baby-food jar. Now, who is to say the ugly-baby syndrome doesn't apply as well to an ugly business that a man has managed to claw his way to the top of and cannot for the life of him, from the top, see reason to alter its nasty course toward the good of man? To the successful striver, a mean little firm in the black is a thing of beauty, and you would no more radically modify the way it runs than you would haul your infant off to a plastic surgeon to change its Scarsdale hooter to a fine, thin nose from Beacon Hill.

You may say, I said, that there is ego involved if it's a business. You may be right. But it may be true that a thing that is yours alone blinds you in a way. He may be an S.O.B. but he's our S.O.B. That sort of thing. My mamma, drunk or sober.

The radio officer came down the companionway looking for the skipper and the skipper drained off his beer and excused himself, saying, graciously, he did not want to interrupt this discussion, but if I would excuse him for just a moment—and hold on to my train of thought, he'd be right back. When he got back, I offered this coda:

In my own experience as a company man here and there, I achieved a few precocious successes simply by earning the high regard of my superiors. Without having to ingratiate or perform in any unseemly way (which is only to say there was no fellatio, or proctology, involved), I had exploited this gift since the earliest grades of school, until it seemed to me so natural to possess special dispensation from the boss that I suspect my bearing reflected my golden-boy status. This is not a wise way to behave, I told the captain. If the play runs long enough, they change the cast. Before you know it, the ex–teacher's pet is selling pencils on the street, or bound for Samoa bellyaching with the skipper of a woebegone Anglo-Russo tub that last saw service *north* of Siberia.

The captain thanked me for my views and left. He looked stunned. I would, too, if I had just heard such a speech. It's what comes of being deprived of conversation for a month. Seems to make me rant.

Got an unflattering glimpse of Harry last night. Retired civil engineer. Long time on Guam. After five years of free naval housing, they kicked him out and he had to buy himself and his wife a condominium. They were so reasonably priced, he bought two. Nine two-year contracts later, Harry was able to sell out, and with his profit he and Gerda retired to their native state, Wyoming, the dull, flat side (not the Grand Tetons, where the President of the United States has been known to holiday). He was a sour man last night, Harry. He talked about Panama putting twenty hands aboard to pay out a line as though all of them were millionaires, rather than the fathers of shoeless children they probably are. The last time I looked, there was only one Manuel Noriega, and he wasn't out there pulling on a sodden heavy rope all night. A selfish pensioner who imagines ghosts stealing the dole, Harry.

So I went up top to look at the stars. You can make out about two hundred and fifty in a city, I read somewhere. In a wilderness, away from light pollution, you are supposed to be able to see about twenty-five hundred. Out here it has to be clearer than wilderness; the star count has to be twenty-five thousand if it's one. The night sky is ablaze. It is brilliant. You could drink from the Little Dipper.

I went into the wheelhouse for a word with Andrey, who was on watch in the dark. I asked him what he thought about, looking down at the dark sea.

"Vodka," he said.

Russian tragedians.

~~~~~

Toxic June was mixing bloody Marys in her cabin ("Last year when I came on board [another ship in this line] they didn't even know what bloody Marys were; by the time I left they were living off them") and talking about 1949 in Canton, when they still had chit coolies. That's what she said, "chit coolies." A line from Hemingway kept running through my head: Old days good, now heap shit. She said a woman named Jorgenson, who was married to the American consul, sent a chit coolie round to her asking for her immediate presence. June rushed to the woman's side and found her black and blue, a walking bruise. She suspected wife beating, but was wrong. The woman was a filthy rich alcoholic. A self-batterer, if you will. I was having a hard time following the story. The captain had put a paper on my desk earlier, entitled "Doldrums, Intertropical Convergence Zone." I may have been leaning on it for an excuse, but I really did feel dulled.

"He's simple," June said.

"Who's simple?"

"Darling, I'll have just one little baby drink more, but then I must rest for tomorrow. I want to feel miles better for drink on New Year's Eve."

So she saw this woman again in Los Angeles. And they went out to the airport and got in her plane—"Darling, she had two planes, and two pilots, all her own"—and flew to La Jolla. "You flew to La Jolla from L.A.?" I said. "That must not have taken but a few minutes."

"Darling, she had to give her pilots some work."

The great North Carolinian Joseph Mitchell once wrote a story about being hit on the head with a cow (they had a heifer hoisted in a belly sling and she slipped, or something) and how he couldn't parse much of anything once he regained consciousness. June can make a man feel like that.

Barry the Purser came in. June had ordered him to. She had ordered him to send up her tomato juice and then, as a second thought, invited him for a drink. Barry said Agatha of the Lakes complained so much about the special treatment she thought June was getting, at one point she asked wouldn't the shipping line pay to fly her home. He said if the company ever got started on a policy like that, "I'd be flying passengers home right and left."

June said in her letters to friends she was calling our vessel a "prison ship."

I've not been writing letters. I sent a few holiday cards from Europe, but nothing much else. I have the excuse of having no place to post mail. There is also the excuse of having no place to receive mail until we make land. Keeps you from feeling sorry for yourself. Receiving mail is an unreliable affair on a freighter anyway—another reason to tell yourself it's not you that's unpopular, it's the damn system that's keeping your hungry admirers off your tail. You are always off schedule, and it is up to the shipping agent at each port to forward things and try to catch your correspondence up with you. Between some of these tiny islands, we will be expected to pick up and deliver mail, as will the ships behind us. You can't expect a ship following us to overtake us to bring us our mail. It is best to forget about mail, or try.

Curiously, in lieu of mail, diary writing seems to relieve loneliness; I had thought it might abet it. Keeping a diary does not feel as much of an interior act as it is. In my head there is always an audience (just as there is in all writing). Sometimes the audience is singular. Sometimes there are friends around a table. It is satisfying to write in a diary. It is also bad for letter writing, in that once I've settled the day's score in my journal, it feels like work to do it again in a letter. In any event, in one form or another, I feel I will publish a good deal of this someday. In a way, it is that anticipation, of circulating the thing, maybe even hamming it up and reading bits aloud, that's keeping me company. This story I'm living, though—I wouldn't complain if the plot picked up a little.

December 31, 1995
1 N / 9 6 W

Agatha read *War and Peace* in 1965, when she was in a car accident and broke her femur. A teenager in a Jaguar rammed her head-on. It was the day Winston Churchill died, January 24. She was laid up nine months, and it took her that long to finish Tolstoy. "Well, people tend to visit you, don't they?"

January 1, 1996
The South Pacific

I blew the whistle at midnight on the bridge. It is actually a horn of some deep authority, but it is called the whistle on the instrument panel, and I saw it, and I blew it. More than once. In another environment, a sound that fulsome could stop a church service, or independent thought—a sound of that power could override a call to order of the National Security Council.

Quite a day for me, New Year's Eve. Two hundred dolphin in a feeding frenzy, churning the water. And three whales, blowing their own year out. I had seen, oh, perhaps twenty-five dolphin at once before. But this was stunning. Here I go sounding like Little Peter: counting.

The latest is laps around the deck. They reckon five laps make a mile. So Peter walks six. Dick of the Lakes, not to be beaten, walks ten. "I've done me ten," says Dick, who has a funny walk. I remember reading once about a prospector in the Klondike who, upon hearing gold had been struck in Nome, bought a bicycle and pedaled down the frozen Yukon to get in on the action. An Indian who was witness to this spectacle exclaimed, "White man, he sit down, walk like hell!" That's Dick, without wheels.

To stay trim, the captain skips lunch, and to be pretty, he tans himself for an hour on Monkey Island. I also hear him grunting in his quarters, and I suspect push-ups and sit-ups, though—no, I would: I started to say I wouldn't rule out sex. The captain is smarter than that. And the stewardesses aren't that desirable. Except maybe last night, when somebody must have moved the bar on the standards of desire down a notch or two.

As far as I know, the skipper stayed above it, but others seemed to be sloping off for a snog every which way you looked. Lust was in the air. You could smell it. It smelled good. But for my abstemious part, all I did was watch the traffic in and out of the passengers' lounge. I drank right smart whiskey while I watched, though.

Agatha of the Lakes said her new husband, Dick, had to wear those long Bermuda shorts of his to keep the eponymous Dick modest. Dick blushed. In her cups, Agatha spoke wistfully now and again of "my Howard," who was her husband for forty years until he died. "Isn't it daft of me to keep speaking of my Howard with *him* sitting right here," said Agatha, smiling at Dick. She met Dick, whose first wife had died of cancer, as Agatha's Howard had died of cancer, doing cancer counseling. "It was more the cricket than anything," said Agatha. They shared a passion for the game, and one game led to the other. "I wasn't fussy about getting married," Agatha said. She had told me this before, but it wasn't New Year's Eve the first time she told me. "My daughter acquiesced to our living arrangement, but she did tell me I was setting a bad example for the grandboys. 'How does it look?' she'd say."

Lots of huggy-kissy at midnight. I clung to the horn, for dear life.

Six hours before the new year began for all of us, the captain was here in my cabin having a chat. The first officer, Ben, poked his head in and said, "Happy New Year, Captain. She's only just now gone." It was midnight in London, in Greenwich, to be precise.

The Englishness of it. I was touched.

The captain had come to return my copy of *Looking for a Ship*. I had to press him to get him to say he admired McPhee's skill in reporting and writing the book, because what he was most taken with was the salary in the United States Merchant Marine. No wonder they went under (the Lykes Brothers, American shippers who let McPhee hitch a ride, have gone belly up, according to the captain), he kept saying. There's a second officer in there McPhee ships out with who makes twelve thousand dollars in six weeks. The captain, my captain, is paid one hundred twenty-six pounds a day, and he is paid only for those days he is sailing this ship. It works out to about forty-five thousand dollars a year, we figured. I did a quick piece of math in my head that I kept to myself: If what he makes to be responsible for our lives works out to what our lives are worth . . . I was offended that my own personal value toted up to such a knock-down sum.

Is there anything going on in the world? Barry the Purser told me Dean Martin died on Christmas Day. I have a shortwave radio in here, but the last time I tried it, it was all Christmas carols, and they depressed me. Though come to think of it, in a downtown mall in Liverpool, where I went bookshopping, there was Dean Martin on the sound system singing "Rudolph the Red-Nosed Reindeer," which was originally Gene Autry's song.

Am I even approaching conveying just how boring one can become as one bobs around the world?

In my head I hear a squad of hecklers, interspersed among a crowd clapping affirmatively, the hecklers hollering, "Shut up and go to bed!"

January 2, 1996
2,400 miles from nowhere

I think we are all having a very bad time. I know I am. I don't see how people can live this closely for four months. Toxic June told me to make myself scarce until Tahiti, otherwise I would find out just how easy it is to start a little drama at sea. I saw Ettore the chief engineer have it out with Barry the Purser yesterday. Barry likes to have his dining saloon cleared after one hour, and Ettore made the mistake of tarrying. The matter of Barry's insubordination was taken to the captain. I haven't seen any of the principals today.

Except Toxic June, the most delightfully insubordinate person I know, who quite agrees one cannot allow standards to slide or we will all be lost. This is one of her favorite topics, high standards. Nevertheless, June said, one can only harvest the best chums one can on a ship. Adhering to this pick-of-the-litter philosophy, she said she was given "quite the ticking off" on her sail last winter for doing so much socializing with the Bangladeshis in the crew. June said to me, "Darling, you haven't a clue about protocol, do you?"

"No."

"How have you got by all these years?"

"Charm."

But speaking of drama, Toxic June organized it for us New Year's Eve. The Brits against the Americans in a couple of home-grown skits. I think I was thought to have quite some cheek for declining to contribute. It is just that I am trying to give up cutting the fool in public. But others carry on, with shining success. The Americans pantomimed what it is like to be old and to bring a what's-the-hurry frame of mind to the table here, where three large Ukrainian women think the proper dining rhythm involves quick pronging, fast swallows, and a withdrawal from the arena so swift there's food still in line on the tongue waiting to enter the dark maw, like traffic backed up at the Lincoln Tunnel. The Americans pulled off their sketch with dash. The big surprise was that Little Peter wrote most of it, and performed his own work beautifully, portraying himself in a dither (easy labor that it was). He intended it as comedy, and it worked, and I don't find him naturally humorous. In fact, most days, Little Peter makes me want to weep and beg God Almighty to release me from the ship.

And then the English. I couldn't tell whether it was the New Year they were bringing in with a dummy baby in their silent bit, or what. The one thing I found funny was the way they had gotten up our first officer, Ben. He is a very proper man, and bright. He is slight and quick and crisp. And here they had him in Toxic June's nightie, a white cotton affair for the tropics (which I found very fetching) and a lacy, old lady's nightcap the likes of which I have only seen on the wolf in "Little Red Riding-Hood." And the women who used to portray W. C. Fields's wives in the movies. Brits and farce. It didn't matter that the skit was a muddle; visually, June's troops were superb, and I kept hearing her cackle from the wings, "Absolutely brilliant!"

June tripped on her long gown before the night was over, and Gerda, being a practical woman, tried to help her, once she was on her feet again, by tucking the waistless garment into her panties—free up her feet a little more, you see, a tailor's solution. But June wasn't wearing any knickers, or any undergarments at all. Saucy old wench; makes me like her even more.

All that frivolity, and since New Year's Eve everyone has been utterly foul. It is too hot. The air-conditioning does not work. Little Peter, who has a device, makes it eighty-six in his cabin, which is next to mine, wherein I sit, naked and aglow with perspiration. The toilets are backed up. We've been sailing too long from Europe here (we were very slow in heavy seas). And the showers are scalding. I washed my hair this morning one filament at a time to escape raising blisters on my scalp. Everything on this icebreaker was made for cold weather. I've never seen so many heaters. Ettore, with whom I've just supped, says there is a heating element affixed to every workable part of the vessel. It is stifling in here, and Ettore is sensitive about it.

If you want comfort, he told me curtly, take a passenger ship. We were in the dining saloon and all you heard was talk of the heat. I had sweated through my shirt trying to make it through my dumpling and mushroom soup, which was the hottest it has ever been served. As Ettore put it: this ship was purchased because the price was attractive. It was refitted and put into service before anything, really, could be tested. We are testing it now. As Ettore barked: that's what we bargained for! We passengers will hear no complaining from the crew. The crew works in heat. In the engine room, where Ettore toils, it is 140 degrees Fahrenheit, or nearly pork-roasting temperature back where I come from.

I thought it best to leave Ettore alone, and let his jugular stop popping out like that. What had got his goat, I learned later from Ben on the bridge, was the loudest moaner at the other table, Agatha of the Lakes. Normally, you start cooling down a ship the moment you leave Europe bound for this clime, Ben said. It takes a while, but by the time you strike the equator, it's pretty temperate indoors. But Agatha said she was cold and made an issue of it. To shut her up, the engine room kept the heat firing far too long, and now it's so oppressively hot inside, the brain-frying equatorial air outside feels like the crisper in your Frigidaire.

Up on Monkey Island to get some after-dinner relief, I ran into Gerda and Harry. "We ain't seen nothing yet," said Harry, talking about the heat. Gerda said she would not sign up for a voyage like this again: too long between ports. People are cross all right. Harry groused about how much it was costing to be this uncomfortable. Gerda said you got to watch out for people's nerves on a ship. Gerda said, on Guam, she and Harry saw a Japanese captain put a whole Filipino crew ashore and order them not to bother returning to the ship. Gerda said the captain had been driven furious by the Filipino habit of using their fingers in the sugar bowl.

To bed, stickily.

Ten p.m. We have cool air. It came on in a rush. I am on a chair with my bare chest pressed against the blower above my cabin door.

January 3, 1995
The South Pacific

My guess is that when you're feeling the bite of age you don't much enjoy the gummy old chomp, and so creature comforts become paramount the closer you approach the great mystery. I've seen the indignities. Toxic June excepted, I've seen their broad-bottomed, heavily paneled panties in the wash. I've seen a tough beef Wellington make a wienie out of a high-tech dental appliance. Obviously, you get older, beat-up, and resigned. You don't ask for a hand in this game, but you have to play it out.

I myself, who was hearing the creak, feel like the colt in the crowd, and I recommend this kind of mixing as a tonic in the early stages of anyone's decline. But be careful to self-medicate with moderation. You can despair of looking at how you're going to end up. Or you can be a chameleon about it, and take on some of the churlish characteristics of slack-jawed, wet-lipped, barbaric maturity a little ahead of your time. Until the return of air-conditioning last night, and the opportunity to bathe this morning without boiling my hide, I believe I was closing in on an anger I hadn't felt since that time I backed over an Arab.

The captain and I had a moment of bonding the other day when we discovered a mutual link. Neither of us has thought highly of the Saudis we have encountered. I cannot be contemptuous of a whole people; it would diminish me severely in my own bleeding heart. But, my word, these were supercilious fellows, and it doesn't take much arrogance to wear thin with me. It's arrogance you can't back up with talent of some kind I'm speaking of; I say a man's hauteur has got to be defensible.

I was in a left-turning lane of a busy thoroughfare in Dhahran in February 1991. I had been in and out of that part of the world since Iraq invaded Kuwait the preceding August 2. I was driving a rented Toyota Land Cruiser, a big black one. The sun was fierce, it was four o'clock in the afternoon of another difficult day, and I couldn't find enough space in the oncoming traffic to make my turn. For all that, a Saudi in a white Chevrolet Caprice behind me was honking impatiently. And suddenly I felt a bump and realized he had hit me with his car. I looked in the wing mirror and saw him shaking a fist at me. When he bumped me again, I started to get out, but then the thought occurred to me that I was considerably bigger than he was. I shifted into reverse, and began backing my four-wheel-drive vehicle, slowly. Never, not even in the movies, have I seen such terror as entered the face in my rearview mirror. He could not reverse, for the line of cars behind him was flush against his rear. I did not stop until I came up over his hood. Then I went forward, and in the doing pulled off some of his grillwork. Then I got out and made for him, with the intention of ripping his damn silly dress off and throwing him in the Persian Gulf, which was on my side of the highway and would not require a left turn. But a cop was Johnny-on-the-spot and had seen the whole thing. He let me go without a fine (Americans were in high, fickle demand in that neighborhood in those days), but he said, "I think you have been too long in my country."

A week later, I was on a plane to Paris.

———

Lunch: Agatha of the Lakes got a pea from the soup down her windpipe and gave us all a scare, but she managed to dislodge it after a noisy struggle.

"Wasn't it lovely how cool the cabins were this morning?" Agatha chirruped when she was herself again. "Was yours over-heating as well?"

"Oh my, yes," said Gerda.

"Dear Dick had to go on deck."

"Harry has trouble with the heat, too."

"I can't sleep when I sweat."

"Oh, even at home, I try to keep the temperature at sixty-four in the winter and no higher than seventy in summer. I like it cool."

"It was lovely out in the moonlight."

"Are you unhappy with the steak-and-kidney pie, Peter?"

"I put my hand over it on the menu, but I guess she didn't understand. I have about thirty-five pounds of kidneys at home in the freezer. When the ground thaws, I'm going to dig a hole and bury it."

"In America, do you have a nice cup of tea in times of crisis?"

"Whiskey."

"Whiskey? Oh, we might have whiskey around, or a gin, but we always seem to require a nice cup of tea."

"Harry's right. It would be whiskey or scotch."

"Why do you have thirty-five pounds of kidneys in your freezer, Peter?"

"I try to buy in bulk on the theory that it saves money. There is a place near Rochester where I buy meat. I have three cats and I feed them meat—not exclusively, but they like a little meat snack every afternoon. Steak, liver, kidneys. I put it in Baggies, serving size, and I freeze it. But they've decided they don't like kidneys, and the only thing I can think of is to bury it. One of them is a very big cat."

"Her Majesty isn't coming to lunch?"

"Leicester, be nice."

"She's having an apple in her cabin."

"Couldn't we have the girls take these bread baskets away and just put out a cheese board after our pudding? Mind you, I don't want to trouble them to bring the whole thing, but I like a little cheese after a sweet."

"You know, methanol can blind you. But if you pour it through a slice of bread it purifies it. There can't be any holes in the bread, though."

"That's nice, Peter."

I don't think *War and Peace* would be so thick if it weren't so full of people talking twaddle. Despite the war, like life, *War and Peace* drags. But I'm off on a wrong foot; all I really meant to say here was that Tolstoy throws in tea in times of crisis, too. For example, early on (which is as far as I've got and may ever), when Count Bezuhov is having his fourth stroke and third unction, and there is all this snookering going on over slanting the will in whopping favor of the bastard boy, Pierre, and people are moving their mouths without sound as if they have ague, the family breaks out the service, the delicate china cups without handles, and the French doctor, Lorrain, says, "There is nothing so reviving as a cup of this excellent Russian tea, after a sleepless night."

Leicester of Devon has taken to calling June a "la-di-da toff."

Just two thoughts more before setting the clock back an hour, and to bed for another long night of Magic Fingers. That is what they used to call those beds in cheap motels that had mattresses that jiggled for thirty minutes if you inserted a quarter into a slot on the nightstand. Every low-rent connoisseur of the lunchtime liaison knew about *Magic Fingers*. With the vibration of this boat, my bed never stops trembling. It gets into your thoughts and your dreams and most visibly into your libido. I don't believe it can be good for you to have yourself shaken all over incredibly fast for four months; either that or it's unimaginably wonderful for you. Isn't priapism something one should see a professional about? That is not a joke.

But I don't know how to approach my shipmates about sex. I mean, I'm embarrassed to. I mean, if Toxic June thinks I'm ignorant of protocol, wait till she finds I was considering asking an English sea captain: Do you wank?

That's pre-slumber thought number one. Number two:

I have consumed more than one hundred meals on this ship, and from the experience, I must uncharitably report that I believe these people in the galley got their culinary training helping wolves gnaw themselves out of traps. How else to explain the gamy, mostly sinew-and-bone, cuts of meat that appear with such frequency? And the rest of the abysmal cuisine I shall leave as the subject for another day.

~~~~~~

<div align="right">

January 5, 1996
The South Pacific

</div>

Rats! Rats! Rats! Rats! Rats! No, I don't mean vermin—although the Brit shipping-line reps don't mind divulging they paid ten thousand dollars to exterminate the cockroaches on this vessel after they bought her from the Soviets (it's either some kind of bigot boast or a gloating victor deal, or both). I mean "rats!" in the sense of: bloody hell! Somewhere in *The Diary of a Nobody*, that fine old piece of Brit parody by and for Brits, Charles Pooter, one of my mentors in this diary business, turns up with a missing page. Pooter suspects theft. I have suffered the same loss, but I regret to say the blame probably lies with the wassail of the holidays (had anyone asked me, I would have suggested rechristening *Tiksi* the *Anti–Betty Ford*, since all it is is a world-class hole in the water for what used to be called "a harrowing descent into alcoholism"). In my real life, I am no longer a drinker, largely because, as Tolstoy describes me in my nineteenth-century Russian incarnation: "We all have our weaknesses. *He* had a predilection for Bacchus."

This may just be the delusory assessment of a drunk, but I believe the paper I have lost was a wry ramble on the state of affairs around me. While even I might doubt the cogency of the dissertation (only because it was written late one night between Christmas and New Year's), I know me and I know it must have seemed like a terrific idea at the time. I also know myself well enough to know I may have disposed of the thing on purpose. It's a rare opinion written by an inebriate that deserves a stay of execution.

Nevertheless, with nothing better to do today out here on the bonnie blue, I wish to try to reconstruct my thesis. I remember, using as an example the stewardess Nadezhda, who is Ukrainian, I made several sweeping generalizations about the Russians. Not only did I misstep with geography (these days a Ukrainian of lesser refinement than Nadezhda would bop me for roping her into a fulmination against a Russian), I generalized, which I am loath to do. I do, I loathe it when anyone tries to group me (you Americans; you Southerners) and generalize (are all paranoid about your health; like to take filthy pictures of your sisters). But in the case of Russia, I made an exception and popped off in the most general terms. I said that, just as in India, where the rich tend to run to fat and silk and the poor to skin and bones and rags, in Russia the stereotypes apply. Gloomy, moody, stolid, yet can be made—at least in my experience—easily to laugh. Drunk. Sentimental. I am made up of these parts as well, and thus have them in common with the Russians. But where the bough breaks between us, leaving me aloft and clinging to a branch, is tragedy.

I borrowed Nadezhda for an illustration, even if she did hail from another country, because she alone among the crew has voluntarily given me fragments of her past. Nadezhda. Born August 23, 1961, Ukraine. As she learns English, these are the four stories she has managed to get across to me: (1) Her bank failed and took all she had, twelve years of savings. (2) She bought an old American car, floated it home on the deck of a Russian freighter, and took it to a mechanic, who stole it. (3) She was married to a sea captain, who died. (4) She was a discus thrower, but something happened (injury or nerve) and her prospects diminished. I believe my point was not whether the stories were made up to gain my sympathy and, by extension, my purse. My point was that in the month I have known this woman she has not revealed to me anything in her life that wasn't sad. Surely, since 1961, the clouds broke for the sun one, just one day.

The Russians brood. They aren't open. They aren't forthcoming. It's all true. There's a hangdog look about them, too—but they're proud.

The Brits will tell you how much better off the Russians are now that the *Tiksi* flies the Union Jack. The Brits will cite the rise in pay. The Russians were practically starving before, but now they've fattened up, the Brits will tell you. The Russians are well looked after now, the Brits say, but for all the better conditions, the Brits cannot coax much needed information about this vessel out of the Russians. The high command is in the dark about the *Tiksi*'s crotchets and eccentricities, feeling out the ship's nature as we sail. And the Russians are indisposed to labor, according to the Brits.

It is correct that you have to search hard to find a Russian who was ever made to work, really work. One of the sureties of the grim life under Communism was that everyone got a job. Since there weren't that many jobs, this meant that you could wind up sharing one job with ten or fifteen other people in the ever-bloating system, but it also meant that you had to perform only one-fifteenth of the labor. And if they couldn't find a job for you, they'd let you stay in school forever, collecting degrees like charms for a bracelet, there in the most overeducated nation on earth. The stewardess Nadezhda, who is on my mind for many reasons, not the least of which is a haircut she has promised to give me here in my cabin at three this afternoon, holds a degree in electrical engineering.

A diploma and a job allow a man in dire circumstances—like totalitarianism—to hang on to a piece of his dignity, his sense of self-worth. You can't eat these things. They won't keep the rain out. But pride and self-respect can help pull you through a mean existence.

So why, if the existence is less mean now, aren't the Russians on board this ship happy all the time, especially since the yoke of Communism itself has been removed?

Because they were deceived. They thought they were a world power. They were broke but strong in their minds and in their shared miseries. Then they were thrown overboard like jetsam from the distressed mother ship, Russia, and then, shame, shame, the Brits plucked them out of the waters of unemployment and put them to work. The Russians lost mates and familiarity and, obviously, lifetime job security. Wages improved but rinky-dink British regs arrived (protocol). In a way, the Russians simply went under another boot, perhaps with a softer heel, but for all the new rewards, what they heard was an unctuous voice from a dominator saying, "Now, doesn't that feel better? Let's be friends. You take the bottom."

Speaking of heels, I badly worded some question about the present arrangement versus the previous, and the Russian third officer Andrey growled at me, *"C'est la vie."* And turned and walked away.

They feel emasculated. Soul-wise, they've been downsized.

And the Brits? Same difference. Their company threw them over. The shipping line, in declaring them all redundant, and having them link arms with a Britannia-waves-the-rules offshore manpower agency, so that they were able to return to their same jobs next day stripped of all benefits, all employer contributions to health and pensions, all job security—*that's* not emasculating? Trouble is, it's hard for me to tell an emasculated Brit from a masculine one, they do such a good job of never hollering uncle.

Among this ship's group of British officers, only the Italian-born Ettore, who moved to England in 1960, when he was twenty, is incapable of disguising his discontent. There was a time in this company when you worked four months at sea and got four months off, with pay. Then it was four months out and two months home, with pay. Now it is pay only when you are on the ship. In 1995, because he had to stay at sea in order to support his family, Ettore was home three weeks. That is why his wife, Priscilla, is along on this voyage, as a paying spouse— so that they might see each other. Ettore wouldn't give you spit for loyalty to this company.

Ettore has also had it with the potluck rotation of the crews. One time out he draws a Bangladeshi crew, unfamiliar with the ship and some unfamiliar even with seamanship, and the next time around he has Poles. Next, Russians. And because the number of hands hired seems with every voyage fewer and fewer, he's running the length of the ship, and down through its bowels, stanching hemorrhages. "Horrific things happen," he told me, declining to tell me more.

In any event, the Brits have just cause to pull the same long faces as the Russians, only not the tradition of doing it.

That leaves the passengers, who occupy the cabins that once housed a corpulent and extraneous tier of Russian senior officers. We all know it is Father Time that is calling in the markers on the passengers. *They're* risking money if they buy a green banana. From Northern Europe to the South Pacific, on a Cold War surplus vessel, crewed by the vanquished, captained by the victors (ha-ha), they sail to scenes of heroism and conquest in their great hot war (and watch videos at night in which Richard Burton and Clint Eastwood and Telly Savalas remind us, in *Where Eagles Dare* and *Kelly's Heroes,* of what blue steel bucked up the Allies' mettle). They sail a Russian icebreaker that came on the free market when the Cold War thawed, and now, in her first service unto British capitalism, rebuilt by British hands, the used Marxist tub overheats like a 1953 MG TD. That's a load of cheap irony, that is.

The passengers on the *Anti–Betty Ford*, née *Tiksi*, drive me to drink with their drivel, but there is not an intentionally mean bone among them, not even in Irritable June (I think). June's not mean, just angry. June's is the spirit Dylan Thomas had in mind when he wrote his signature line ("Rage, rage . . ."). June will do anything to shake up the complacency, God love her.

And me? What did I say of me in my lost analysis? I think I said it was my aim to use this voyage to shim up my life, as you would a draggy door you want to rehinge and set swinging smoothly again. I think I said, all thoughts of circulation to my friends or general publication to the contrary, I'm keeping this journal as an exercise, as Little Peter counts things—anything— out of fear that if he doesn't do something with his mind his brain waves will flat-line. As far as what's bothering me goes, I can report that all I seem to have gained in the way of remedy may be nothing more than a geographical poultice: for a while, distance, like chemotherapy, seems to put troubles in remission. At the moment, making it to the end of this journey sober appears to be the biggest hurdle before me. That and *War and Peace*.

Today is Friday. On Sunday, we are due to see land, two tiny islands, Tepoto and Napuka, five miles off the starboard bow. They are called the Iles du Désappointement, so I'm not expecting much. We have not seen land since Panama, and we transited the canal in the night, so we didn't see anything to speak of. The last time I stepped on land was France, a long time ago. I miss land.

I have seen two terns this morning. But first came the flies. We have had flies since last night. I told the first officer, Ben, so much for Noah, the dove, and the olive branch—it's the common housefly will let you know there's high ground in the vicinity. Flies, though good news to those of us despairing of ever seeing land, do take a little of the shine off the tale of the ark, I said to Ben. Ben speculated that the progeny of the long-gone flies which came aboard in Panama may have just hatched, that's why we have flies. Then we decided not to mention Panama flies so that I might go on debunking the Bible. In any event, besides the forty other souls on this ship, the two terns and the flies are the only living things I've seen—above the waterline—for days (Little Peter would know how many days).

Nadezhda came to cut my hair. Because I have carpet here in my cabin, and because I have many hairs, we repaired to an unused office with a smooth floor on the deck below—the easier to Hoover the cuttings. A Russian army officer's jacket, green with red epaulets, hung on a wire hanger hooked over a shelf of a bookcase jammed with arcane Russian manuals, their covers powdered lightly with sea salt. On the bulkhead was a manufacturer's schematic drawing of one of our two diesel engines. There was a heavy black phone in there, an Iron Curtain kind of a phone, sinister even in disconnection. You could stick up a 7-Eleven with that phone.

Nadezhda told me her mother worked forty years for the good of Ukraine in the Union of Soviet Socialist Republics, and now her mother is retired on a pension of twenty dollars a month. She said her mother has always told her, "Those who feel, see tragedy. Those who think, see comedy."

Nadezhda's barbering, which cost me a bottle of wine (eight dollars), is much like the other two Russian haircuts I've gotten in my lifetime: a valid reason, for once, to kill yourself.

January 6, 1996
The South Pacific

A fire drill at half-past ten this morning. All we are required to do is put on life jackets and muster at the station that has been assigned Little Peter, Toxic June, Gerda and Harry, Agatha and Dick of the Lakes, May and Tennessee Ernie, and me. Two decks below, aft. A covered lifeboat hangs on davits there. It looks like a big orange lozenge. We are always dismissed moments after we show up. "But what would we do if we actually needed to do something?" Agatha of the Lakes asked Barry the Purser.

"You'd be well looked after, dear," said Barry.

A meeting later in the passengers' lounge to discuss Tahiti tours. The purser needs to know how many are interested in a guided day of Mooréa, Tahiti's heart-shaped sister island, just across the Sea of the Moon. I'm aware Melville was there, working on a farm, writing *Omoo*, and I am vaguely interested. Also, there's a Club Med on Mooréa, for what it's worth (good lunches at those things, if I remember correctly, and an eyeful of cinnamon skin). There's some discussion of fees.

"You don't take a round-the-world cruise and haggle over the price of a pineapple," the purser says naïvely.

Little Peter sneaks out of the room, or squeaks, as tight things do.

Everybody seems to be mad about something at supper, and holding it in. Toxic June does her best at the next table to be provocative, but she's slurring a little, and nobody wants to fight. Agatha of the Lakes trills that the British lottery is forty million quid tomorrow, and wonders what she would do with the money.

"The first thing I'd do is buy this boat," says Gerda at my right, clenching her teeth. "And then I'd get in that kitchen . . ."

Gerda, more than the rest of us, seems to be letting the poor quality of the food attack her sweet disposition.

Ascending the accommodation ladder after dinner, Leicester of Devon said of Toxic June, "That's the laugh of a hag." He sighed. "Well, we're a third of the way there." If he were happier, Leicester, an inveterate sailor, would have said a third of the way "round," not "there."

Ten p.m. "Well, that went over like a lead balloon," Toxic June said, sipping a Famous Grouse as I took down all the Christmas cards in her cabin. Her cake, like an American fruitcake, but containing six liqueurs ("darling, it's the only cake I make"), had been the centerpiece of her Twelfth Night party, with port, in the passengers' lounge, after supper. The cake was solid and heavy as a cinder block, but it was moist, I can attest, since I had the largest slice, and a second, while watching the holiday-besotted crowd down a fair slug of port and Bailey's Irish Cream.

"Let me see all the kinds of nuts on your cake," said May of Tennessee, sitting next to June and helping to serve. "Walnuts, pecans—oh, niggertoes!"

June cast a curled lash down at her creation.

"That's what we grew up calling Brazil nuts," May said.

"How fascinating," June said, and her eyes rolled up until I thought her pupils were gone, gone for good. June has exquisitely derisory gestures.

The party was indeed a bust. Leicester of Devon crept across the passage between the passengers' lounge and the exhaust stack, trying to see through the drawn curtains whether I was in there. At the last window, at my back, June spotted him through the glass just as he poked his nose around and she barked "Leicester!" and he flattened his eighty-three-year-old self against the hot bulkhead holding back the diesel fumes, but was caught as surely as June had shined a light on him. There was nothing for it but to come in. Like a sheep. He declined the cake, though. "My wife used to make one every year," Leicester said. "I wouldn't eat hers either. Vile things." Leicester had port.

The tanned captain came in and stayed the distance. They must send ships' masters to small-talk school (How to enjoy tedium! How to be tedious!). Not so the chief engineer. Agatha of the Lakes, who never rises for breakfast but is served in bed by her husband, Dick, was talking about how much more civilized it would be to serve an hour later, at eight-thirty, while saying she understood the need to serve the crew earlier, for they had work to do. "Oh no," said Ettore, his face darkening. "We just serve the crew by accident."

The party went on too long, but the worst of it was June had insisted the captain, Ettore, and Priscilla and I come to her cabin afterward for drinks and to take down her Christmas cards. I got there first, removed her cards, and tried to run.

"You could have just a baby drink with me."

"No, I can't."

"Darling, even alchs manage—"

"I can't."

Fine, then, she would ply me with gossip. June said she thinks Little Peter doesn't want to take one tour or another because he wants to get on a motorcycle and find a tart. June has regarded Peter as a sex fiend ever since Christmas Eve, when he told her that the reason men wear neckties is that they serve as great big arrows pointing down to their most significant piece of anatomy.

I said he's cheap, he's heard he can rent a motor scooter, not cycle, and I just couldn't imagine Peter in the fleshpots (although I could possibly see myself there).

"He's cheap? I thought he was strapped."

"Not strapped, cheap." I told her about the eyeglasses on a string, the dollar wristwatch, the constant tabulation of shaves he's gotten on a single battery . . . "Don't you think that's cheap and weird?"

Evidently, June had had enough of talk about Peter. "There's more to the captain than I thought," she said abruptly.

"Like what?"

"I asked him, I said, 'When you were a child, did you ever play Happy Family?' He looked at me and he said, 'Yes.' "

Happy Family, I gathered, is one of those fantasy games in which you place yourself in a unit that is a lot more pro-you than the one you are growing up in. The way June swelled and puffed as she passed me this information, I could swear I saw canary feathers on her lips.

Suddenly, her mood swung to self-pity. Where were the others? Surely a misunderstanding, I said. Why did no one thank her for furnishing the wine at Christmas dinner? I don't think anyone knew, I said. I think everyone thought the ship footed the bill.

"You go along," said June. "I am going to sit here and get quietly smashed."

One of the things one just can't do in my circumstances is say just how much one would enjoy getting quietly smashed, too. I made two tidy stacks of all her Christmas cards, and crept away.

Just two or three cabin sweepings as we approach Papeete:

1. Barry the Purser stopped me after breakfast and said, "I'm sure I don't have to tell you today is the King's birthday."

Elvis would have been sixty-one today, fourteen years older than me and too young a man even at that age to be a passenger on this ship.

Down through the years since the Big E died, people who know me have passed along practically every awful piece of Presleyana there is to be found. Because I was reared in Memphis, sending me some Elvis keepsake (teddy bear key chains, hound dog charms—they are available everywhere still, like his spirit) is an easy way wandering friends have of letting me know I have crossed their minds ("Isn't this precious? Found it in Yamoussoukro . . ."). Usually I let the tacky booty pile up until it gets in the way, and once or twice a year I chuck the lot.

It feels to me as if it has been a long road of mockery and dismissal for poor old Elvis. No one under forty, after all, could be expected to know much of him beyond the grotesque figure he cut in his final years; Elvis himself in his last performances became the first Elvis impersonator. And no one under thirty could be expected to grasp how the world could have been so musically Milquetoasty, such a short while ago, that a thing like Elvis, the marvel of him, could shock it silly. He was a phenomenal deal.

When I think of Elvis I remember moving to Memphis from

the Alabama sticks back when Memphis seemed the biggest place on earth, when the country rolled right up to the city with no girth-defining beltway to penetrate, no long, suburban, catfish-chicken-rib approach—just one minute, cotton field; next minute, bam! metropolis (high cotton). How ridiculous we 1950s sophisticates were to our rural kin, warning them not to sunburn their throats gawking up at our giant constructions (we had but one slender contender, and I have since come to find that it wasn't so tall, I was just small, but in those days we thought the Sterrick Building scraped the sky). In our bragging we made the Mississippi River wider than the Nile, and faster than the Thames, which we pronounced the way it's spelled. And though none of us imps lied, we implied we hung out with Elvis, when we had a mind to.

In truth, not one of our mothers would have allowed us even to wear the sort of raiment the King favored, so loud in pink and black, tailored, tapered, and pegged so they made him look like a hip, truck-driving carhop, or a supercool matador of the night. In truth, while we sat in class, our mothers swore one another to secrecy, and cruised the Big E's house, the one he bought before Graceland, on Audubon Drive (I know this only because mine—with my Aunt Sue riding shotgun—drove rubbernecking by and had a flat).

Aw, well—as if it mattered. Go on, Elvis.

2. Vibrating through the lounge, I came across Little Peter telling Gerda and Harry about a clever piece of workmanship a neighbor pulled off back home in upstate New York. The man's water system was a gravitational affair from a nearby hillside. Some repairs were required near the entrance to the pipe that came out of the brow of the hill spouting water. "Now, how do you think they shut off the water?" Peter said. I was just whistling through, but I thought: Peter's giving Harry, a retired civil engineer, an engineer's riddle. I took a seat.

This was a god's deal, I gathered, not counting the pipe. I mean, it wasn't like you could go and shut off a valve to replace a worn washer on a leaky faucet. You had to stop nature. Harry shrugged. Gerda shrugged. Peter looked at me. I said, "Your deal, cowboy."

"Now, now—this is the clever part." Peter doesn't like to surprise you. If it were a dumb part coming up, Peter would be sure and warn you about that, too. "They followed the line back up a little higher on the hill, dug out around it, and packed it in dry ice."

We all thought don't that beat all. Froze the sucker.

"Peter," I said, "one time I had a wife who had an electric blanket. I hate electric blankets. And I had a pump on my well and the pump froze. We had no water. I wrapped the electric blanket around the pump, and thawed it. I restored water. But there was so much packing grease and other filth in the well house, I ruined the electric blanket and it could never be used again. I thought that was pretty clever."

Peter looked at me, and Gerda looked at me, and Harry looked at me. After a while I got up and left.

3. Toxic June's outdoor salon is the talk of the lounge. Most of us are on deck five. June and the Tennesseans are on deck four. June is pretty lame. Arthritis. Walks with a cane, which the Brits always call a stick, and I admire them for it (calling it a stick). Stairs give June a hard time. There's an elevator in this accommodation stack, but it goes only from the main deck to level five. The bridge is six. Monkey Island is seven. To get out of doors and sun yourself, you have to climb. The Brits, who are born and grow up and grow old and die in a kind of half-light, don't seem to have a care about melanoma; wherever there is full sun, there are exposed pink Brits with thighs like blue cheese.

There are plastic lounging chairs with cushions out on the wings of the bridge, and on Monkey Island they have three or four slatted, wooden torture chaises longues you can lie on like a wurst on a grill. I don't use them. Little Peter isn't much for sun, either. And Gerda is allergic. Gerda goes out for the air, but wraps herself like a Muslim. Well, not *exactly* like a Muslim. A Muslim woman in her natural habit looks like a Darth Vader pepper grinder. Gerda gets herself up like something that would jump on your back in a pumpkin patch at Halloween and choke you graveyard dead. Come to think of it, I've never seen May of Tennessee in the sun, either. Like Gerda, May has thighs the size of the bells on tubas. She may just be self-conscious.

But this was June's piece. The outside stairs, or accommodation ladder, take a little dogleg at June's level, leaving about a fifty-square-foot corner of deck exposed to the sun, port side, aft. A couple of days ago, a lounge chair with cushions suddenly appeared in this ultraviolet patch. Then another chaise longue. Then a straight-backed chair. *Voilà!* June's salon. For stargazing. After-dinner drinks. And she suns herself there in the middle of the day rather than go in for lunch. In describing the reaction, I can't decide whether I want to connect the anatomical "tongues" with the fowl-like "clucking" or the fowl-like "fluttering." It seems to me fluttering is faster than clucking, which would be the case.

June's new arrangement led her to discover a secret of mine, which in turn led us to words. I have joined her in privately snickering about the old men walking round and round the deck, and calling out their number of laps publicly as though they had scaled Everest. What I kept to myself was that I did the same thing, only I did it when no one was looking. I have exercised all the sober days of my adult life, and some that weren't, and when I came on board here I began with the primitive torture devices the Russians left in the gym-cum-boiler-room below-decks. Hot when we were in Europe, that room would set you on fire now. I had to move outside. The main deck is an obstacle course of vents and turnbuckles, wildcats, cleats, exposed fittings, sharp edges, leaking fluids, uncoiled ropes as thick as anacondas, and ladders up and down. You can't run. If the deckhands are out, it's mostly take a few steps, get out of the way, clear sailing for forty feet—whoa! Here comes Little Peter, let him down the ladder, now hold up for the bosun coming through with a spool of spun steel.

I settled on noon for my own exercise. Everyone is eating. The deck is clear. I can't run, but I'm surefooted enough now to speed-walk it. But it won't get your heart up. So, for every lap, I began taking the outside ladder to Monkey Island, across, and back down. Seven flights up; seven down. Do it for an hour. Wear a hat. And keep what you're doing under it.

Then one day: Full stop! There's June on Level Four: lotions; creams; elevenses. June doesn't hold with physical exertion that doesn't return pleasure. She ridiculed me. After making a great show of turning her back each time I hurled myself by, she began applauding sarcastically (June can do that). Finally I spoke sharply to her. It would be ungentlemanly to say what I said, but I hurt her intentionally. She stopped picking on me. Now each day I climb past her and if I look her way she is always there blowing me the tiniest little kisses. I just won't abide a bullying granny.

4. Supper tonight was exceedingly bad. A can of corn in a bowl with a quarter of a stick of butter on it for an appetizer. Turkey bones and Brussels sprouts and Tater Tots. A ring of canned pineapple in a pancake (June bellowed for brandy and a match and wanted to light hers, but was ignored).

I had had a word with the purser earlier about the food. I have recently learned that after thirty years of taking in passengers' complaints Barry has ground his teeth down to the gum line. I have also learned (a man does not ascend the heights of journalism that I once ascended without a certain dash of resourcefulness) that Barry feeds the crew on five dollars a man a day; he feeds us on between eight and nine dollars. "It's not the food," he said. "I do my best with food. I'll be in the market in Papeete tomorrow. If a passenger wants escargots, I'll do me best to provide escargots. It's not the food. The man just can't cook."

Our chef: Tuber. The root crop tsar.

Back at the table—Lord love the midget devil in her heart—Toxic June was trying. She was working, trying to get a conversation going with Dick of the Lakes, who sat opposite her. She asked his interests, besides cricket, which she had heard about.

"I like natural history."

"Do you collect plants and bring them home?"

"No, I like plants, identifying some, but I'm not that keen on plants."

"Birds, then?"

"I like birds."

"Do you follow birds?"

"I'm not a twitcher, if that's what you mean."

~~~~~~

January 9, 1996
Papeete, Tahiti

I've been on this ship forty days and forty nights now, and I think I see that being old is kind of like being drunk all the time. I don't see how Toxic June manages being old and drinking, too. This morning, May of Tennessee said to me, "Have you ever been here before?" In the last forty days, I have told May or her husband, Ernie, forty times I have never been to the South Pacific. I said to May this morning, "One last time: from here to the Suez Canal, I have never been anywhere we are going."

Ernie said, "I thought you said you went to Africa one time."

I said, "We aren't going to Africa. In the Suez, we're going by it."

Ernie said, "But I thought you said you went to Africa one time. I just heard you tell May you never been anywhere."

Up on Monkey Island, as the sun rose behind Tahiti and we waited for a pilot boat to take us in, I drew a sketch of what this fabled rock looks like in silhouette. Tahiti is two old volcanoes, connected by an isthmus. (If I knew it was going to be isthmus trouble, I'd have stayed home.) Backlit, it rises as though it had shoulders, then droops in the middle to form a jagged saddle. The more I looked at it, the more birdlike it looked. Dramatic, though. Headless eagle. Then I thought: The bat signal! I said to Little Peter, who was there with his binoculars and his camera, "You'd know who I was talking about if I said Batman, wouldn't you, Peter?"

"No," Peter said, "your point would be lost on me."

When the sun was full up, everybody was up on Monkey Island. They were pointing their Instamatics and their video cameras straight at the sun. Miles of film and videotape that will come back blown flat white with overexposure. No images. No telling them.

I kind of pictured myself in Tahiti amid the crusty-footed French layabouts and the melon-breasted, dark-nippled Gauguin ladies who used to fancy Brando when he was one-third the physical man he is today, and twice the cerebral one. I saw myself in a white linen suit and almost packed it. I did not see myself trying to rack more points with the Lord for continuing my gerontological mission, but there you are.

Walked into Papeete this morning with Leicester of Devon, out of the port through packs of mangy dogs and down a hot, two-lane road lined with Australian pines and sea grapes. The smell of coconut oil was at first delightful and then sickening as it began to overpower. The oil was in storage tanks there by the water, at a processing plant, just down from the Coca-Cola bottling plant, its big logo red against the sky. There was everywhere more traffic, noise, and smarting carbon monoxide than a little island should bear, but I didn't have experience enough and time to make any judgments or to criticize. Sort of a honky-tonk town, though. Captain Cook and, two and a half centuries before Cook, Magellan, had only the natural beauty to furnish their journals. The Citroëns, Peugeots, and Renaults fall to me, to say nothing of the French nuclear testing offshore. But I cavil.

Leicester enjoys stretching his legs, and after all we had been a month at sea. But I had to step along because I was due back at the ship to collect Toxic June before noon because I had promised to accompany her to the island of Mooréa for lunch. Since Leicester loathes June, this was rather two-timing of me, but I concealed nothing from one to the other, saying I had taken a vow of polygamy from here to Singapore, at least. So we changed some money, had a quick tour of the central market, I bought Leicester a fresh-squeezed orange juice, then left him to fend for himself. I checked the hydrofoil schedules for Mooréa and learned if we didn't make a noon ferry it wouldn't leave enough time on the other island for lunch before the last boat back. To shorten this: I dashed to the *Tiksi*, and while I was hustling June out of her cabin they had to move the ship a few meters down the quay, so they removed the gangway for an hour and a half and there was no way off our vessel. And no way to reach Mooréa.

We passed the time speculating on Little Peter's day. The last we heard, the old skinflint was going to rent himself a motor scooter. I haven't observed much physical coordination in Peter, so I imagined a menace on two wheels.

Early afternoon: Got the police at the port gate to call a taxi, talked the police into allowing the taxi beyond the gate by telling them June was my stove-in grandmother, collected June, Priscilla, and Ettore and, two taxis later, was deposited six kilometers straight up a pig trail at a restaurant called Le Belvédère that also has a heliport. We were too late for lunch. "For people who eat all the time," Ettore said of the French, "I never seem to be able to get any food." But what a vista. Papeete and the harbor below, Mooréa beyond. A movie set. My companions drank beer and I stayed high and dry with a hot-fudge ice-cream sundae. The Polynesian music playing in the open-air restaurant sounded like the Sons of the Pioneers, accompanied by ukuleles, doing birdcalls.

Then it was an hour in a taxi down the mountain, through ferns and eucalyptus and flame trees, oleander and bamboo. Priscilla screamed and caterwauled as we descended, just as she had done when we made our way up, saying to her husband she was going to be sick, saying the terror of the switchbacks and steep fall-offs was more than she could bear, saying she was going to be ill, twisting Ettore's shirtsleeve into a corkscrew and making the rest of us exceedingly uncomfortable with her histrionics.

On flat ground we repaired to a quayside bistro, and no acknowledgment was ever made of the woman among us who had lost her mind twice, in two taxis, this afternoon. We ordered sandwiches. All of a sudden our view and ocean breeze were spoiled—completely blocked out—by a rusted panel truck delivering onions to the establishment. As the van's sound system blared a brain-cracking din, two sweaty Polynesian teamsters wrestled onion crates around our sidewalk table. One, catching our eye, stopped to shake our hands and I noticed he had been surgically stitched up one side and down another and had what looked to be a gangrenous foot. Obviously a casualty of Little Peter's motor scooter.

At this table, my opinion of Ettore rose yet another notch when I learned he had encountered a managing director of Ford at a business affair in London; and, upon learning that Ettore, a chief engineer, drove a new Ford of a certain model, the motor car executive inquired how Ettore liked it. Ettore said it was "rubbish." To convince him otherwise, this man sent a chauffeur around next day to pick up Ettore and a couple of his chums, to take him to the plant to observe the manufacturing process. They laid on a bus that seats seventy, for the three of them. At the end of a seven-hour hearts-and-roses tour, the managing director asked Ettore what he thought of Ford now. And Ettore said, "You've just shown me how you make the rubbish."

My three companions made their way back to the ship by taxi and I had a moment alone in Papeete at sundown. A Russian ship, *Korvov*, sat the tide rusting at a berth right there at the foot of the town. Our pilot this morning had said she had been there three weeks, for she could not pay her bills, and she had been impounded. Sunburned Russian seamen were barbecuing on *Korvov*'s poop deck. Laundry hung from the accommodation stack. On the quay, food vendors were setting up colorfully lighted trailers, firing up the gas grills, and laying on the sausages and flounders. Either the subtleties of cosmetics have never been learned in these parts, or I joined for a short while a parade of demimonde. I sort of enjoyed it, but I could have done without the goosing from a demonstrative little pudge who seemed to have greased herself in seal fat. Slightly unnerving, too, was my growing awareness that a number of these tarts were men.

We were to sail at eleven. On the ship there were prawns on ice and champagne for potential clients the shipping agent had brought aboard. The captain, tan in his dress whites, looked every inch a courageous, handsome mariner. The captain has composure and assurance; he would never be mistaken for a scholar, but it would be a mistake to put a scholar in his job. On the deck the first, second, and third officers had sweated through their white coveralls working the livelong day to meet a deadline established merely to impress. We're a bigger ship than came calling last time, a newer ship, a refitted Russian ship, and we're more efficient, and faster, so they say. To show off our new capabilities, the crew worked straight on off-loading and onloading and everyone went without sleep for about a day, and the captain cut a fine figure among the champagne and prawns, and we were loaded at twenty-five till eleven and we were sailing at eleven. The representatives from head office could fly back to the U.K. now (the way of the world: the crew is fed slop on five bucks a day; accountants fly business class from London to Tahiti to toast the good work with champagne). On the ship, everyone was exhausted. There would be no need to meet such a ridiculously unnecessary turnaround for nonessential goods (coconut oil; a trimaran bound for Vanuatu) again on this voyage. It was all for show. Just as the captain, the driver of a smelly old lorry of the briny deep, is shined for image and representing a kind of marine theater, or tradition, that no longer exists. In reality, we're just a truck, a twenty-thousand-ton truck of the sea hauling and making deliveries around little islands with Third World economies. We're small, which is how we get in here. There are four-hundred-thousand-ton tankers out there; there is no port big enough to accommodate them; lighters tend them at sea. But we're class-minded, I guess, otherwise how would I explain the kind of skewed culture on board here, where it seems to make some sort of difference who sits closest to the truck driver, in his dress whites?

This morning, Ernie of Tennessee asked me if I had ever been to Suva. "I have never been to any place we are stopping between here and the Suez Canal," I said. Ernie had a tooth attended to in Papeete yesterday. It is way in the back (" 'Tis the aftermost grinder aloft, on the starboard quarter," goes the old sailor's direction to the dentist), and it has been giving him trouble for years. Someone—Priscilla—asked him why he doesn't just have it out, and he said he didn't want to get AIDS.

Tonight at supper the appetizer was billed as "chili fingers." It was a half slice of white bread with melted Cheddar cheese out of a tube, squirt cheese, and a dollop of Tabasco. You could eat it. One night Tuber tried to serve us bananas and garlic in maple syrup for dessert. You couldn't eat it.

I have made a major decision. I have been living outside my own generation, and letting another generation live in my diary. If it is at all illustrative, let me point out we have twenty-eight inoffensive videocassettes on board. You could call it the Jessica Tandy Film Festival (*Driving Miss Daisy; Fried Green Tomatoes*) or, for the gents, Big Men, Big War, Back Then (*The Battle of Britain, Where Eagles Dare*), or, for both, Let's All Have a Good Cry (*The Glenn Miller Story*). I walk faster, think quicker, laugh a lot, sleep less, eat more, don't sun, can't talk to a pile of rocks, don't need my day narrated (". . . and now the sun is going down"), don't drink, keep fit, possess a memory, curiosity, to say nothing of my own teeth (and taste buds to go with them!), ain't grieving, get horny (I am no libertine but it wouldn't take much encouragement to put me over the line), require stimulation. I have got to get some new friends.

You know, the thing about Tolstoy that gets my goat is he's not only high-handed, he's sure-handed, which makes him lethal. I was just reading where Princess Liza and Mademoiselle Bourienne are froofing up the plain Princess Marya to go down and see Anatole Vassily, who has come for Marya's hand (but in truth desires her purse). According to Tolstoy, as Moms Mabley would put it, Marya was so ugly it hurt your feelings to look at her. Yet the two women dressed her "in the naïve and unhesitating conviction women have that dress can make a face handsome." Her dressers just knew "with *perfect sincerity*" that the right raiment could make the woman.

Now, there isn't a good-looking woman on this boat, not one. But the other night, one of them—I shan't say who—leaned to me and whispered, doesn't so-and-so look beautiful in that color? I must have looked mystified, for my tablemate then added a qualification: "For a heavy person, I mean."

And here in Tolstoy is the Ugly Duckling's Dad, old Prince Bolkonsky, displeased at his daughter Marya's hand going anywhere. "Whether he was out of humour because Prince Vassily was coming, or whether he was particularly displeased at Prince Vassily's coming because he was out of humour, no one can say. But he was out of humour."

Tolstoy is funny. He has the old prince, upon learning that his people have cleared the snow on the road to his house for his daughter's suitor's arrival, command his people to put back the snow. Prince Bolkonsky's son, Andrey, is off fighting Napoleon. My Andrey, the Russian third officer, is reading Philip Roth. *Portnoy's Complaint. The Professor of Desire. Goodbye Columbus.* The piece of American writing Andrey really likes is Henry Miller's *Tropic of Cancer.* If I remember correctly, that's the one with the apple and the cold cream. Me and Tolstoy, we're shoveling snow back on the road.

My mother will tell you that I set off afoot and roved widely, or struggled against parental restraint and tried to roam, from the time I was three, maybe earlier. I have been compulsively adventurous all my life, but sailing was never a passion. I cannot say I ever once dreamed of sailing around the world. But since water covers a little more than seven tenths of the world, it was inevitable I would come to this. What did not cross my mind, however, was how restraining a ship can be. Well, you could leave. You could say: Big mistake. And pick a port and split. But if you choose to stay the course, you really have no choice in anything. Direction. Victuals. Companions. No choice.

A tour of Hades—the engine room—with Ettore this morning. It is so hot you need gloves for the rails on the ladders, though the he-men who work down there don't wear gloves, don't touch the rails. Down there are welding shops and fitters and the tools and raw materials to make whatever we need to keep us running. John the Scot, the second engineer, was in the cool control room with a Russian–English dictionary in his lap. You can't hear, with or without your ear blockers. Ettore would point and mouth to me that such-and-such monstrous vat broke down our bodily wastes chemically and discharged them liquidly into the ocean, this bubbling black nightmare chamber cleaned our eighty-dollars-a-ton crude oil, the dregs of the fossil fuel that our vessel devours. And there, side by side, were the two fourteen-cylinder diesel engines that keep us running, the pistons in them the size of barstools (I picked up a spare to learn its heft). The work of the two motors then goes into a single gearbox that steps down their revolutions per minute to the one hundred and ten our shaft turns. The shaft leads into the thrust box, a square of iron and steel the size of a fast-food restaurant that absorbs the entire push and pull of the prop: the power isn't spread out over our hull; all the force of twenty-one thousand horses, ahead, astern, is taken in the thrust box. This engine room arrangement, these twin diesels, would be fine and efficient for a ferry on the English Channel, says Ettore. But global voyaging? The company was penny-wise and pound-foolish with this purchase. The maintenance costs are going to eat the line alive.

This particular vessel might be ill suited to the assignment, but it struck me no advancement in cyberspace can make what we're doing and how we're doing it obsolete. A single gearbox stands between Tahiti and aged cheeses, aromatic brandies. The people where we are going will not get what we are bringing them on their keyboard, on the Web. It's crude oil alone that's responsible for delivery of the household furnishings, the clock radios and televisions we bring in forty-foot containers. We've got a railroad car full of walnut breakfronts, ash coffee tables, yellow pine sideboards, and china down below. That's right. Teacups.

At supper, Tennessee Ernie told his war again, this time to Toxic June. How he was eighteen in '43 and joined the Navy. How this admiral and that was from his part of the country. He takes you to Okinawa, to April 1, 1945, when he was steering one of those landing craft fetching dead and wounded from the beach. He describes the morning, how it was neither pleasant nor unpleasant, and how at noon the big guns opened up and for two miles back from the beach it looked "just like the ground does when you turn it to make a garden." Then the fighting. Ernie thinks he brought out the first casualty, an American shot through the hand by his own people. "Oooooh, he was mad." Then he takes you up to Day Six, still in his landing craft, being lowered sandwiches in a bucket, three hundred and fourteen kamikaze attacks, Ernie counting fifty before being too busy loading dead to keep counting suicides in the sky. Hauling bodies back—"I couldn't tell you whether they were dead or not"—and at night, eleven hundred vessels firing from offshore, every third round a tracer. "It looked just like—you know when you're burning leaves and you stir the fire with a stick, how the flames jump up?" Three men he served with had a failure of nerve. One he still sees back home. "He can't drive. He don't talk. He follows me around. Lots of times he just stands by me quiet, like a dog."

"So you come here with tears in your eyes," said June.

"Naw, it don't bother me. You're different when you're eighteen, nineteen, twenty. You're not even growed up yet. It don't bother me nothing like it would now. I couldn't stand it now."

January 13, 1996

Apia, Western Samoa

Dawn and there lies Western Samoa, long and low, aswirl in mist. I can see curls of smoke in the hills from cooking fires. The exhaust stack is our only sound and it is a muscular bass, not a "boom! boom!" with exclamation marks, but a mean, two-stroke "boom, boom" all the same. And when I see these islands in these circumstances, from a cargo ship, being such a child of the movies, I imagine in the jungle beyond the shore a great timber gate, and before it a slew of pagans dancing wildly, chanting, "Kong! Kong!"

Well, I do.

We lay off Apia all day while a New Zealand freighter that beat us to port by two hours discharged. There's one quay, one wharf—it's a one-boat town. The captain was anxious. He seemed cross. He finally explained to me that at dawn in these parts, the hour he had intended to come alongside, it is becalmed. But the offshore wind picks up through the day. If we come alongside at dusk it means we have a wind astern. Also, there's no breakwater to speak of in this harbor. The swell breaks at the pier, so we'll have wind behind us, and we'll be riding a surge.

Two Samoan pilots, one very small, one very large, board us off a tug at six-thirty. Epaulets. Sandals.

"She's very heavy," the captain advises. "If you ask for slow, if you want her to stop, she's likely to carry on. It's best to ask for dead slow, then stop."

"Is an anchor ready on the port?" the short pilot asks.

On his walkie-talkie, the first mate, Ben, says to Andrey, who is on the fo'c'sle, "Andrey, put the anchor in the pipe for emergency." The hawsepipe.

We start in. A tug positions itself off our port to give us a bump in case the wind and the swell conspire to carry us aground. She—the tug—wouldn't have the strength, but it's a nice gesture.

As we approach, First Officer Ben orders Third Officer Andrey to call out the distances between the bow and the wharf.

"Fifty meters."

A few seconds.

"Thirty meters."

The captain: "You've got to watch the steering at slow speeds. She's very heavy. Just give her an occasional kick."

Big pilot: "Full astern."

The captain moves the telegraph back to full astern.

"Ten meters.

"Seven meters."

Little pilot: "Is she full astern?"

The captain: "She's been full astern."

"Five meters.

"Two meters.

"Zero."

We kiss the quay. Don't even nick it.

A torrential rain. Customs and immigration do not board. I wait until nine o'clock, see a little break in the downpour, tear off for town. It's Saturday night, by God. At the foot of the gangway, I'm turned back by a bare-chested Samoan big as a column on the Parthenon. I can't go ashore until I've been cleared, and there's no one to clear me. Why did he wait to tell me until I had descended the whole damn thing? Back to the Jessica Tandy Film Festival. At ten o'clock, the captain brings the mail around. Someone has sent me a story from *Harper's Magazine*. Some pud-pulling writer took a luxury cruise ship out of Miami and swans on for twenty thousand words about it. Shithead.

Under the wide and starry sky
Dig the grave and let me lie.
Glad did I live and gladly die,
And I laid me down with a will.

It's Sunday. Robert Louis Stevenson's home, up on a hill three and a half kilometers out of town, is closed. Samoa is closed on Sunday. Has been ever since an English Godperson named John Williams brought the Good News to the heathens in 1830. They had nine gods before missionary Williams landed and declared eight redundant (the god of fishing, etc.), but retained the big fella (the god of life and death).

In town on foot outside a bakery I say hello to a whore. Indecision strikes. Piece of cake? Piece of ass?

I count five churches, two hotels (Aggie Grey's I have heard of—James Michener, *South Pacific*, Bloody Mary, and all that), two pool halls, and a clapboard cinema where *Die Hard with a Vengeance* is playing tonight at ten. There's an appliance store with a wringer washing machine in the window. I didn't know they still made them. Nine hundred Samoan tala. A clock tower that seems to be reliable only twice a day. The tower is dedicated to thirty-nine Samoan-born men who died in World War I. Only two have Polynesian names, a Private M. Ah Mu and a Private Togimau (no first name). Two magnificent banyans form a parenthesis around the tower. There's a sign in the grass pleading don't shoot the national bird. The national bird is a manumea, or tooth-billed pigeon, found only in Samoa. The bird symbolizes beauty and independence, the sign says. The Western Samoan flag flies from a staff nearby. It is red with a blue rectangle in the upper left corner. On the blue rectangle, in white, is the Southern Cross.

It's muggy here, but gorgeous, with all the usual flowers, shrubs, and trees: bougainvillea, frangipani, oleander, poinciana, baobab, mimosa, and the wonderful banyan. The cops wear sky-blue skirts. There are dogs asleep in the street and all along the seawall. Ugly, lazy mongrels. It was the same in Tahiti. You won't find them on postcards. The dogs of the South Pacific. Down from the clock tower is a piece of construction: the first McDonald's in Western Samoa.

A Mass is letting out at the Roman Catholic church, the biggest in town. The women wear dresses in primary colors. The men wear white shirts, black ties, black skirts.

I go to Aggie Grey's for coffee and a copy of the Sunday *Samoan*, the first newspaper I've seen since Europe. I learn that a Greek freighter, the *Amphion*, developed leaks in two holds and sank four days ago off Nova Scotia. All twenty-four hands were rescued. I don't think I miss newspapers much. Still, it would have been nice if this one had one word from my home, the United States of America. What's happening with the Republicans? Is Bob Dole out front? And the Democrats? Whither the Great Sweet Potater? Is anybody there?

Supper at Aggie Grey's with Ettore, Priscilla, and John the Scot. Both men are disillusioned with the company, fatalistic, and concerned that corners are being cut at the expense of safety. For example, there's a manual trolley that's supposed to run the length of the keel (something like those pallets on roller skates that auto mechanics use to scoot under cars), but in the refitting the shipyard put a pipe across the track. If anything went wrong in there, say a valve ruptured and steam burst, an engineer couldn't crawl out in time to save his life. Priscilla doesn't like this discussion and tries to change it. But John won't give it up. The complement in the engine room is one quarter what it used to be, and the workload is quadruple. A good ship meant to go around the world carrying cargo would have a six-cylinder, seventeen-thousand-horsepower engine. This one we're sailing has two fourteen-cylinder engines. In each port, they pull two pistons for maintenance (mostly to replace worn piston rings), so there is never any downtime. A ring job costs about sixteen, seventeen hundred dollars. Each piston has five rings. The firing ring alone is three hundred twenty pounds sterling. The water out of the tap in my cabin smells like paint because they painted the holding tanks and you are supposed to let them dry for three weeks. But the owners wanted this ship on line swiftly, so they got only a week to dry. The Russian captain of this ship, who was out of a job when Ettore came on board in Bombay, invited the engineer in for a drink. He had some rotgut he had bought in India that was labeled "Officer's Whiskey." Ettore said the skipper was distraught. "He had thought he had a job for life."

January 15, 1996
Apia, Western Samoa

This be the verse you grave for me:
"Here he lies where he longed to be;
Home is the sailor, home from sea,
And the hunter home from the hill."

I was going to Robert Louis Stevenson's home today, but it is closed on Mondays for dusting. That's what they said. Closed for dusting.

At first light we discharged four tanks for brewing beer and a Toyota. Now shirtless, barefooted men in skirts with rags on their heads are unloading eleven hundred tons of copra from flatbed trucks into our number one hold. They climb down on the coconut husks and open the burlap bags one by one. Andrey has the watch today from six until noon, and then I am taking him to lunch. He says the copra, which goes into cattle feed in Europe, smells like India. "It is really, if you will forgive me, the bullshit of the coconut." He has made up a new English word for it, "gargo." "It is combining garbage and cargo."

On foot, then, to the central market, to kill some time. One guidebook or another advises to get a hot cocoa and a delicious doughnut. So I find a stall selling cocoa and it turns out to be Nestle's powder in water, not even milk. And the closest thing to a doughnut is a deep-fried doughball the Samoans call a pancake. It is baking powder, flour, and sugar, and it costs a dime. There's a pretty brisk trade going in great hairy taro roots, bananas, fish, seaweed, and pancakes. It rains at fantastic volume all morning and I occupy a bench under the corrugated tin roof of the market. I have brought nothing to read. I watch Samoan women sleep on their sides by their stalls. Little puddles of brown women, all over the floor of the market.

At midday I rap on Andrey's cabin door. He has showered. His long black hair is dripping. He wears a T-shirt with a likeness of John Lennon on it, and cutoff blue jeans and sandals. "Would you like some brandy?" he asks.

"It's a little early for me, sport," I say. So we set off. Just judging from the spark of his eyes and his sudden willingness to talk, I'd guess he has had a celebratory shooter or two. "So maybe you will have an adventure," he says as we walk along the seawall. "This morning we have put a wire in the hold to tell the temperature. At fifty degrees [Celsius] the copra will ignite and there will be a fire. I have just learned this. It is thirty degrees in the hold now."

"That's just super," I said. "What an ignominious thing to have on your gravestone. Killed by the bullshit of coconuts."

"Igno . . . ?"

"Well, just embarrassing."

I show him to Aggie Grey's because it is the most expensive in town and I want to show him a good time. He likes fish. So we have raw fish in coconut milk. We eat quietly for a moment.

"In Russia," Andrey says, "when there is silence at the table we say another policeman is born."

"What does that mean?"

"I don't know. We just say it."

He volunteers he likes Toxic June. "She knows special words."

"Tell me one."

"*Zakuska.*"

"What does that mean?"

"Food for after vodka. Salted fish. Salted tomatoes. Salted cabbage."

It's a June kind of word, all right.

"What do you think of our stewardesses?"

I don't know what to say. "They are very large women," I say.

"I am ashamed for my country. They are fat and simple." Andrey says, "In Birkenhead, in the shipyard [across the Mersey from Liverpool], after they saw our stewardesses, they called our ship the *Piggy Bank*."

"Do the stewardesses fuck the crew?"

"One does."

"Which one?"

He tells me. I imagine for a moment having sex with this woman, but I can't quite put it together. Science would be against this kind of cross-pollination.

We have an afternoon together. I take him back to the market. Then to a bookstore. He buys a used biography of Jim Morrison. "I like to be alone," he says. "Even with my family, I like to be alone. That is why I like the sea. I like bad weather. I like thinking. I am trying to improve myself. I am seriously studying music, with no schooling. And books. I am seriously studying books."

I have a son his age, and a lot like him. Twenty years ago I wrote a book about him and my daughter and their mother. When the book was published I was in the process of getting a divorce. Timing. And coincidence. On the walk back to the ship I am thinking how nice it would be to see the boy. On the ship

I have a letter from him. He has been in New York, visiting his stepmother—my wife. He loves New York. He lives on a mountain beside a trout stream in Georgia. He plays guitar. Builds guitars. For a living, he guides incorrigible juvenile delinquents on thirty-day wilderness trips. Thirty miles south of where my son lives my daughter lives beside a man-made lake with her husband. In about six weeks, she is going to have a baby. At a scandalously tender age, I am going to be a grandfather. Before I left on this voyage, I went to see my children. On the refrigerator in my daughter's kitchen, there was a sonogram of her child in utero. I saw my grandson's penis. It may have something to do with why I'm on this ship, my life is changing so.

I read somewhere Robert Louis Stevenson said when you marry you willfully introduce a witness into your life. Stevenson said that, once married, you "can no longer close the mind's eye upon uncomely passages, but must stand up straight and put a name upon your actions." O Robert Louis, sometimes conscience is witness enough to make a man come clean:

Last night, in my cabin, I had a Samoan whore. I paid twenty dollars for her. Today I saw her feeding chickens in her yard beyond the seawall. She waved at me and smiled and poofed her hair with her hand, though it lay lank and black and flat against her cheek. Andrey said, "Do you know that woman?" I said yes, waving back and smiling, but I said nothing more. Some grandfather I'll make.

January 16, 1996
Apia, Western Samoa

Teacher, tender, comrade, wife,
A fellow farer true through life
Heart whole and soul free
The August father gave to me
1914

I'm just guessing that's Robert Louis Stevenson's wife those words are meant for. I've seen it punctuated differently in books, but this is the way the stanza reads in stone. It's chiseled at one end of his crypt. Someone has left a single flower, a bird-of-paradise, on the tomb. It's a one-hour climb straight up a muddy track through a rain forest to reach the grave. Stevenson was a consumptive (when he was my age, he had been dead three years) and never got up here under his own power. But the Samoans carried the body up. That was in 1894. His wife, Fanny, was from California. It doesn't say "Fanny" on the tomb, though. It says "Aolele." (Back in town I asked a waitress what it meant and she said, "Cloud.") I went to the Stevenson house and paid seven dollars for the privilege, but they were just starting a tour, with my own fellow passengers, and I just forfeited and walked on. I get enough of my shipmates on the ship.

Besides, I looked a fright. I had slipped on the trail trying to get out of the way of a barefooted Samoan with a single-shot .22 rifle. He had two dead pigeons in a plastic bag. The national bird. Manumea.

"What do you do with those birds?" I asked.

"Eat," he said.

We sailed, at sundown, for New Caledonia.

This morning I said to Tennessee Ernie, "Want to go out on deck?"

"I like the deck," he said. So I let him through a hatch and followed him onto the port side. It is something I have been intending to do for a coon's age (have a thorough chat with Ernie, try to last him out), and I'm glad I accomplished it. He has a passion for the practicals, is a way I have put it before. Born in 1925, I've heard him say. That makes him three years older than my daddy. He's a fair-skinned man, with a bit of a gut, wears his thin white hair in a severe cut, wears khakis, plaid cotton shirts, and suspenders—looks like a man you'd see whittling outside a feed store on a town square in East Tennessee. No pretense. I've seen men of Ernie's build in New York cinch themselves up so that their belts bit into their bellies like barrel staves.

Ernie is more curious than I am, which pisses me off. Also, he's not as smart as I am, but knows more, which pisses me off.

Ernie told me, as we hung out over a port rail looking for dolphin, that the sun was ninety-three million miles away. He told me the speed of light was one hundred and eighty-six thousand miles per second. He told me it takes three minutes for the sun's rays to reach me. (It's eight minutes, according to my sources, but why spoil Ernie's riff?)

Those were just a few things Ernie told me along the way to telling me many other things. When he was eight years old, he won a newspaper contest, naming the parts of a ship. He always wanted to sail. But he had people back in Tennessee and he did not want to leave them. So he went to work for the American government, in the soil conservation service, and he likes to keep saying "for thirty-five or thirty-eight years." He went around telling farmers they ought to look after their land better. We went off on phosphorus and potash for a while, but got back to something I know more about: trees. Particularly, trees in the South of the United States of America. He got them, the farmers, to plant some good trees. He delivered the seedlings to the farmers five hundred at a time. He'd give them white pine for a northern slope (shade-tolerant), but loblolly and yellow and shortleaf for full sun. I knew all this. And tulip poplar. Ernie said, "I counted them all, and I finally talked enough old farmers into planting a million trees, but it was way back yonder. I wrote it down when I got to a million, though. I really believed in it; I had my heart in it."

When Ernie got through working for the government, he bought a worn-out farm—"Oh, it was a pore old place," he said. He had been advising farmers ("for thirty-five or thirty-eight years") and he wanted to show he could do it himself. "I improved that place," he told me.

"Well, what did you do?"

"I got grass growing. And I ran cattle on it. I did a lot of things."

He never could kill his cows, couldn't sell them. "Cows are more intelligent than people give them credit for. They may not feel as intensely as people, but they feel. Have you ever seen what they do to 'em in a slaughterhouse? Hit 'em with sticks and shock 'em and things. Oooh, it's got to be a nightmare for 'em."

I don't know why, but I asked Ernie whether he believed in God.

"I'm glad my mother isn't alive to hear me say this," Ernie said. He looked off up toward where they told us in Sunday school the hereafter lies. He sucked in enough air to ruffle his nose hairs and blew it out in a thin whistle through his front teeth. "If this earth stopped for a second, stopped spinning for a second, the moon would fall," Ernie said. "Science, any science if you study it, will tell you there is no heaven."

Had lunch, cheese and biscuits, née crackers, with Toxic June on her new fresh-air salon. Born in China, she said she has lived her life on cargo ships; "it was the only way to get anywhere, darling."

I asked her to tell me how she turned up lame. She told me a fantastic tale of having a five-ton truck roll on her in the Congo, in 1972. Developed a hematoma along her right thigh. Wouldn't let them attend to it in Uganda, wouldn't let them attend to it in Kenya—flew to England to retain a plastic surgeon. The surgeon predicted that in seven years June would be crippled by arthritis. And so it happened, almost to the day. Sitting there in the sun, I examined the long scar on her brown and freckled leg, and I thought, in her day (June was born in 1918, but you'd never guess it when she's on her game), this brassy-faced creature must have been a heartbreaker (the captain once told me he reckoned she had been "a prick teaser").

As I let her thigh alone, June stunned me. She said she had seen me having lunch in Apia with Andrey the third officer. She asked if we had become lovers.

I said, "No. What would make you think that?"

I thought she was joking.

June said I didn't have to be defensive. She said this sort of thing was common among British officers, from public school on and what all.

I got up and fetched us another Heineken from the fridge in June's cabin. Have I mentioned that, after giving it up New Year's Day, I began drinking again on Samoa and I'm still at it? If not, I've been withholding information from my own diary. What a lily-livered thing to do.

When I got back with the beer, I told June about the whore I had back at our last port. It was a stupid indiscretion, but I felt challenged by this old woman. She asked me what the whore looked like. I told her the whore looked just like the two naked women in the Gauguin print on the bulkhead in my quarters.

June said, "Well, I hope you wore a cap."

She said that the reason she thought I was homosexual is that in her life, no matter where she traveled, she consistently attracted amusing handsome gay men. Isn't that what I am?

It is true that I can be amusing.

I think what June does to amuse herself is bait, reel, and pick apart the catch for insecurities. I think somewhere she convinced herself the only parlor game worth playing was stirring the pot. It is an especially good game for a cripple. Doesn't matter how sedentary you are: just sling your provocative chum out and wait for small minds to lunge. What she caught from me was the tale of my midnight liaison with the Samoan prostitute. God knows what leverage the information will give her.

January 21, 1996
Nouméa, New Caledonia

Our lives are so pitifully barren, we manufacture ritual. When we receive word a harbor pilot is to join us, we all gather on Monkey Island with binoculars and wait, watching, watching for the pilot boat. Then someone spots it first (Leicester of Devon today; just a brown speck; you have to have a practiced eye for this) and we all feel a tickle of excitement. Eons pass before the boat is alongside and our lads lower a rope ladder and the pilot ascends. He is hand over fist up our great hull, clad in its steel, icebreaking condom in blue water aboil from a fierce sun, and then he is on our deck. We have done our jobs, watching, squinting, anticipating. We all but congratulate one another, and go below. It is three hours to the wharf.

Barry the Purser was watching Nadezhda make his bed this morning and he said, "You know, Nade, in Ireland, for foreplay, we say, 'Grit your teeth.'"

Into town on foot alone. Town closed. Sunday. Shuttered and locked. Find a Café de Paris in an Hôtel Le Paris and take a seat under a blue awning. There are six Frenchmen in the place knocking back beers and unfiltered cigarettes. I used to smoke. Now I tell considerate smokers, when they inquire whether I mind if they smoke around me, that I did all the damage I could do to myself, so fire away. You don't have to be accommodating for the French, though. The French never ask. The French smoke in oxygen tents.

I am feeling energized and wondering why and it occurs to me I am surrounded by youth. The tawny barmaids. The tobaccoists. Youth. People need youth. Need to be around it more. If I get any more rhapsodic here, I'll wind up a kindergarten teacher, or a jailed pedophile. Meantime, I seem to be in danger, for the first time in my life, of leering.

Waiting to dock today, I went in to another one of Tuber the Root Crop Tsar's inedible lunches. He had a starter he called a casserole that was four bones in yellow grease. The main course was an omelette with asparagus, which he did not fuck up. But then he served a side dish of white rice, in a bowl, with orange wedges and pineapple chunks.

Into town afoot again, in a driving rain, with John the Scot, who feels a thirst coming on. I take him back to the only Sunday action I've been able to suss, the Café de Paris. We get on the subject of my vibrating cabin. I say: If this is the key to producing the horniest man in two hemispheres—vibrate his whole body all night every night for fifty nights, so far—maybe we should just call Guinness and get me in the goddamned record books.

John changes the subject to marriage. I tell him my theory that marriage is an unnatural act. I tell him I think marriage was invented when people got married when they were about twelve years old and the maximum life expectancy was about twenty-four. No time to do anything but sire and die. No hanging around thirty years on to catch the deflating sight of jammy crumbs stuck to the morning chin.

John interrupts; he has been married exactly thirty years, and if you can stick it out that long, it gets pretty good again, after some lean deals. He asks me why, if I feel so bitter, I'm still married. In truth, it is difficult to be bitter about anything in the Café de Paris, in New Caledonia, on a rainy Sunday night, with a dozen young, golden, three-quarters-naked women draped around the bar like fruit bats.

So I tell John the truth: At 1:25 p.m., on New Year's Eve, 1977, in a Japanese restaurant in Times Square in New York City, I began choking to death on a piece of raw octopus. Madeline Greenleaf, who was to be my second wife, though I did not know it then, was sitting opposite me. After first determining, quietly, for about one minute, that I could not breathe and therefore would die, I began trying to gag away the obstruction. I was able to blow through a blocked windpipe some noises so appalling that by minute number two the restaurant was cleared with the exception of the cook and the server, who peered at me in stark terror from beneath a curtain over the door to the kitchen. Now I was running out of strength to keep fighting and coming up on dead and knew it clearly. My life did not pass before me. I thought instead about how my mother would greet this news: "Raw octopus? Really? He put that in his mouth voluntarily?" Madeline Greenleaf, meanwhile, had got around behind me, got her arms up under mine, and then with all her might (she's little) struck me just where you should and dislodged the octopus that was bound to murder me. I have been unable to repay the debt ever since, and so have tortured her by remaining her husband. That's my story, on my grandmother's Bible.

John the Scot said he had read somewhere that Howard Hughes had been disappointed with Jane Russell's nipples.

God, I love this sailor talk.

Back to the ship on foot, soaked through by a cloudburst.

January 22, 1996
Nouméa, New Caledonia

I have come to think the most dangerous places to traverse in the world are ports when the dockers are hard at it. Forklifts the size of Ferris wheels roar down at you from all points of the compass and not a traffic cop for miles. No wonder the old wait for transport. I'm the only broken-field runner on the ship, but it's a dumb sprint, as reckless as a last-minute dash through a railroad crossing. I do it because I'm desperate, or pathetic. I'm running from the thing I ran away *on*.

There is a tour, but I don't think I can abide a whole day cooped in a minivan with the gummers. I elect to walk. I'm joined in the beginning by Little "Born to Be Wild" Peter. He rents a car everyplace. It's the American in him, I guess. He's cheap, too, but he still gets defeated. Peter rents cars for four hours, the minimum, on islands where there aren't four hours' worth of roads. I leave him at the Tourist Bureau, and strike off.

I go along to the market and charge deep into the interior on the road that runs alongside the McDonald's and up and over hills of palmetto and bougainvillea and frangipani, brown, vertical terrain to which whitewashed houses cling like cockleburs. I spend three hours in steep ascents and descents and emerge on the far side of the island. I walk off the afternoon and find good old Club Med. For some reason, they have a net and all the rigging for a complete high-wire circus act. If we still had Fellini, Fellini could work with that. I eat a grilled salmon outdoors beneath a thatched roof on the beach. All the naked people around would stun a lesser man blind. It is a visual feast. On the sound system is a Japanese bluegrass band playing "Under the

Double Eagle," a song my father in Alabama has flat-picked all his life.

~~~~~~~

At breakfast on this, the morning I have decided to leave the ship and get a hotel room ashore for one night, just one bloody night with a regular bath and some other amenities I have dreamed of, you could hear Tuber the Root Crop Tsar in the galley, wildly beating on something with a hammer. Tennessee Ernie said, "If that's a chicken he's working on, at least we won't have no trouble with the bones."

I got out here on a bus. Here is the Lantana Beach Hotel. There's no point in running on about it, it's just a ninety-buck-a-night hotel room. But it's four times larger than my cabin and it has a bathtub. Out the sliding glass door is the beach, and sails against the sky, and bare, golden women from here to eternity—pretty much what I had in mind.

Among the nuts-and-bolts chores I thought I had to attend to today was the repair of some tonsorial damage done to me by Nadezhda. I was seen to by a firm, brown Caledonian who possessed two words of English—"long? short?"—and fewer items of clothing. I said, "Short, if you mean my hair." I have calculated that, including air fare and hotel, it will cost me about four thousand dollars a month to keep getting the same haircut from the same young woman. She had a bird of paradise tattoed on her dark, flat belly.

—Hold on, this could be fun! I have found "Dallas" on the TV! Here in my room at the Lantana Beach Hotel. In French. Now I know I'm in God's pocket. I'm taking stairs three, four, five at a time, they seem so less vertical than on the ship. I'm slamming doors because they offer no resistance because they are not made of steel. I seem to be holding on to my drinking glass or cup all the time, even though a glass or cup won't walk off on you if you're back on ground. I'm lying on a double bed and I'm not vibrating. And now "Dallas"! My French is not what it should be, but in my translation, what J.R. is telling Pam right now is "If you don't change that hairdo, Pam, I guarantee you you're courtin' a damned jaybird attack."

January 24, 1996
Nouméa, New Caledonia

The sun, coming up, found me going down in the Pacific Ocean. Unlike William Holden, though, I could tell you a tale of a femme fatale (Ms. Sweet Bird of Paradise), and still get out of the pool.

Rushed back to the ship thinking we were sailing this morning. Did most of it on foot, but leaped onto a bus for the last half mile. Was surprised I was pleased to see her mustard-colored cranes and the Union Jack, from the far side of town. Came up the steep, rocking gangway like a seaman (I can do that now; sissies grab the rails). Learned quickly from the captain we aren't going anywhere soon. The dockers are in a labor dispute. They are slowing down, showing up two hours late. Plus, we are trying to unload all that French grain we took on in Dunkirk and Le Havre (they need it for their French bread; I personally have only eaten about three hundred feet of it in the last three days), and there's a problem with a pipe fitting—anyway, we're delayed. Maybe tomorrow noonish.

I go in to breakfast. Everyone admires my haircut. I tell them about the flower tattooed on my haircutter's abdomen. Tennessee Ernie asks, "Are you shore you only got a haircut from that girl? You look pretty pleased with yoreself. Don't he look pleased?"

Someone asks the whereabouts of Little "Born to Be Wild"

Peter, as if I were his keeper. As it happens, I have spotted him. I saw him returning his rental car. He didn't see me, although I was six inches from him and I said, *"Bonjour,* Peter." He was sitting there at the steering wheel, his nose deep in a map. The place he was looking for, the place to return his car, was directly across the street. I said no more.

"I bet you he could tell you how many steps it is to town, though," said Ernie of Tennessee. "You ever notice Peter shore can count?"

I'm having lunch outdoors near the quay (I have decided to forgo dining with Tuber the Root Crop Tsar unless it is breakfast—bran from a box—or I'm at sea) and Little "Born to Be Wild" Peter passes by on the hoof. I'm having a fine salad and spaghetti bolognese, and French bread for which I am personally trying to deliver the wheat from France. Little Peter is cross. He has been all morning trying to change his leftover local currency back into dollars. Finally successful, but I assume he had to stamp his foot. Little Peter said, "I almost said the only French word I know." I didn't ask. *Merde,* I guess. But after Peter let me be, I got thinking about these phony nations, all of them made up by greedy jerks from elsewhere, and their goo-goo currencies. It used to cost me my sense of humor back when I made a living writing for the papers about the broke republics. Their money is no good anywhere else. When they change your money, they tell you there will be no problem changing back to some hard currency when you leave (not that U.S. dollars are worth a shit anymore). Then comes the day you step to the teller's cage with a bag stuffed with about a billion garish bills, worth about a dime all told, palm trees swaying all over the notes, and they say you are sorely out of luck. Now that I no longer represent anyone but me abroad, I have perfected a line and a way of saying it that first got me out of this money jam back at Aggie Grey's, in Samoa. You say, "That's not what you told me four hours ago when you took my hundred-dollar bill, you asshole." You have to give it quite a snarl, and then they pony up.

If I were writing a travel book, that's the kind of advice I would pass along.

If I were writing a travel book and if I wanted to be honest, I'd have to call it *The Hostile Traveler*.

Is there some kind of worldwide Beatles revival going on, and no one alerted me? Liverpool, I could understand, but their music pours from every bistro in these islands. It carries me back to places in my mind I thought were gone for good. Lambent memories.

And some not so. I remember being in Kampala one December night, pinned down in a tiny office in Impala House as guerrillas opened up with their machine guns in the courtyard outside. It was late and I was on the floor, under a metal desk, with two colleagues (no, three: Jack White, Sean Kelly, Bill Campbell; all trying to get under the cover of one desk) and an enormous jug of J&B scotch whiskey. All of a sudden the telex machine clattered, and I was terrified the noise would draw the gunfire.

It was my employers in New York City. I had been feeling neglected in those days, and I had asked, if anyone could spare a moment, it would be nice if they got in touch. The message was "How you?"

By the illumination of a Bic cigarette lighter, I was able to type "Can't chat. Real nasty here right now. You okay?"

"So-so. Weather shitty. John Lennon dead."

January 25, 1996
Leaving New Caledonia

I think. The captain says maybe by two this afternoon. I see a dozen lazing dockers on the quay in the shade of a shed. The pipe to the grain in our hold is still severed. The captain says it is a union leader named Gaston who is holding us up with the dockers. The captain clutched himself in the crotch, like Roseanne, Michael Jackson, Madonna, or an Italian, and said, "They've got us, right here." Says we should be away today, though, only one day behind.

So it's shanks' mare back through the forklift beasts and out on the town of a morning. It's a New Orleans kind of town, with New Orleans humidity. Nouméa makes you thirsty. In an establishment called the San Francisco Hotel and Bar, I meet the proprietor, a man named Emery who is from Walnut Creek, California. He came to the South Pacific to work for Shell Oil in 1980, when he was thirty years old. He had a wife and a child. They had another child in New Caledonia. After four years here, he was transferred to Tahiti. His wife, who never quite became enamored of the culture, decided one day to take the kids back to California to see her parents. Six months later, Emery said on the phone to his wife, "Don't you think it's about time to come home now?" And she said, "I'm getting a divorce."

"It's kind of dirty in Tahiti. Well, different cultures. She didn't like dirt. I don't mind dirt."

The company offered Emery a two-year contract in Papua New Guinea. Emery had been in his employer's service briefly in Papua New Guinea, and he detested it (I did not ask why; since I am going there, I'm assuming I'll learn). He remembered once when he was a child his father's company offered him a transfer to Michigan. His father, a lifelong Californian, rejected the move. "They didn't fire him, but they sort of put him in a closet. I remember it as a very unhappy time for my father. So I told Shell to fuck it."

Emery got a job as a personnel manager at a casino here in New Caledonia. Six months later, he bought a hotel and bar. He had never been in the hotel or the bar—except on the day when he decided the price was right and he would buy it, and there were no customers—and even back home he did not go to bars. But the notion touched his heart—a bar in the South Pacific!—

and he plunged in. Basically, it was a nightclub, and the hookers got the rooms. The music was disco and Polynesian, the only two kinds of music Emery cannot stand. The first night, the whole first week, everyone in the place was gay. "I was in the Army, you know, and I never saw anything happen. But the Europeans, the French military, the sailors—well, a hole is a hole. They were swapping spit with transvestites all over the place. And everybody who came to the bar kept asking me, 'Where's Lulu? Where's Lulu?' And it turned out Lulu was the queer who ran this place. Man, I had to make some changes."

He threw away the disco and the Polynesian music ("You lose your whores that way; they like to dance") and installed B. B. King and George Thorogood and The Destroyers. He got out of the nightclub business and made it a straight bar. He renamed the place the San Francisco Hotel and Bar. He bought a vintage Harley-Davidson. It was the bike, parked at the entrance, that seduced me into the place. I had a Harley when I was young. Not a great big one, just a Harley. But I loved it. I had never seen so many Harleys in one place as New Caledonia. So I decided to ask someone why.

"More here, for the size of the population, than anywhere else on earth," Emery said. I said, why? "Oh, we're small. And a fashion is a fashion. Somebody gets something, or looks cool, and everybody has to. Me? I had paid all this money for tickets, made all the reservations, took care of everything, for my wife and the kids to come see me. They were going to come for three months. The kids were out of school. I hadn't seen them in four years. I'm talking to her on the phone and I say this is going to be great and she says, oh, we're only going to come for two weeks, the kids have such a schedule this summer. I'm yelling. I'm yelling into the phone. I'm saying I've organized all this and paid all this money and two weeks? You mean that? Two weeks? So I cash in the tickets and I see the Harley guy and I say, fuck it, give me one."

Emery lives with a woman but has no interest in marrying

again and likes the French culture for not pressuring him to. He is a hale-looking fellow with dark hair and a beefy physique. He wears cowboy boots. This is the only American-hangs-it-up-and-buys-a-bar-in-the-South Pacific tale I am going to bother to tell. But I suspect it is not the last I will hear.

So the captain said by two, and it's ten till five in the afternoon, and we haven't sailed. I go up to Monkey Island to see what's going on. Little Peter, Harry, Leicester, and Mary of Boston are watching them load empty containers (we're taking them back to the firm; part of the service), and they all seem locked into it. Is there a culture even to this? Way to load! Dazzling crane work! Peter is happy if there is something to count. The rest of them, something to look at. We can't leave the ship. They're looking at the clock. They won't let themselves drink before five. That's not true. Leicester scarcely drinks. Little Peter has a little wine. Harry is pretty steady with his beer. The ghostly Mary is the one who watches the clock. She does not rise for breakfast. She lives for her "elevenses," which is to say screwdrivers, vodka and orange juice, beginning, precisely, at eleven. She's fairly well left us by lunch. In the afternoon she naps, or plays cards in a haze, and breaks out the scotch at five. She has always seemed a little self-conscious around me, skittish. Once at lunch when the subject of her broad Boston accent came up, I told the story about the Renault 5, the automobile the French marketed in America as "Le Car." Only in Boston the decal on the side of the vehicle said, "Le Cah." No one laughed. Mary seemed stung.

The hell with watching the stevedores *or* the clock. Now I'm back in my cabin, scribbling this. I pour about three ounces of Famous Grouse into a cup of freshly made (I brought this stuff all the way here with me, and husband it like gold) Celestial Seasonings Tension Tamer tea. Today is Robert Burns's birthday.

Motorcycle dreams.

"Taking a trip?"

"What's that?" Bronson, played by the actor Michael Parks, leans a rocky pec across the teardrop gas tank of his Harley Sportster. Nine hundred cc's. He is stopped at a traffic light in San Francisco.

"Taking a trip?" The inquisitor is behind the wheel of a stupid Detroit machine. Businessman with a cough. Going home to the full catastrophe. About 30 percent body fat. Cholesterol level, like some fantastic peak, too high to see with the naked eye. A shoat near Bakersfield is already doomed to furnish him a valve.

"Oh, yeah." Bronson giving it an enigmatic smile. Glances at the signal, abiding law. Lean and loose in his jeans and his boots and his watch cap. He knows he looks like James Dean. You don't have to tell him.

"Where to?" California sunlight catches the yearn in the salaryman's eyes.

Bronson hasn't really thought about it. "Oh, wherever I end up, I guess."

"Man, I wish I was you."

Bronson shoots the trapped American a look of sympathy (don't mistake it for condescension; Bronson is the road god; he is free and kind; he is you if you had any damn sense).

"Well, hang in there."

The light goes green. Clank of Wisconsin transmission metal. The Harley's low growl is seduction from a tailpipe: follow me to world enough and time, Jack. The station wagon clatters (a tappet problem) on over the hill of defeat. To the shackles beyond. I turn twenty-one in Memphis watching the credits for "Then Came Bronson" roll up a twelve-inch, black-and-white TV. Just a year before, I had nearly gone blind trying to squint through the opaque breast cups Jane Fonda wore in *Barbarella*. But now it is 1969, the year of *Easy Rider*, and freedom from convention is on all our minds.

I vow never to become the soft man stuck in the Oldsmobile.

Mary of Boston fell down the accommodation ladder last night and may have broken something. She drinks, as I mentioned just yesterday. And she wears flip-flops. Bad combination on a ship. She's in her cabin just around from me, still in her dress. Agatha of the Lakes and Gerda are attending to her. Painkillers were located. We'll be in Suva, the Fiji Islands, at noon tomorrow. Won't know till then if her hip is broken. She's mighty stove in. She's old, too. She's coming up on eighty this Bastille Day. Her husband died three years ago. Alzheimer's. I think her way of mourning is to keep sailing and stay anesthetized. She has a suite all to herself. It is my theory she has been using one room to drink in, the other to throw up. That's far too harsh. Many afternoons she's clearheaded enough to play cards with Priscilla, which, come to think of it, is a no-brain act. If her hip is broken, I guess she will be leaving us now. She always seemed to go out of her way to avoid me. It seems I was always storming around a corner and startling her in the companionway, quite unintentionally, and she would unsteadily shuffle into the nearest door. I either frightened her or offended her. It's a mystery to me why.

Leicester of Devon napping in the passengers' lounge. Oh, he's upright, but he's asleep. I've gone in to read. The vibration in my cabin is hell on my concentration. Each time Leicester wakes, he clears his eyes and gives me the broadest smile. Leicester is eighty-three. They aren't his teeth, but I like them.

Finally it is lunchtime and I cave and submit my stomach to Tuber the Root Crop Tsar. Fat, gristle, and bone. For dessert, a cold bowl of rice with five raisins and the subtlest sprinkling of sugar. "You know," I tell Gerda, "before it's over, I'm afraid I'm going to break down and cry."

"I've already done that," Gerda says. "It doesn't help a bit."

Leicester of Devon is at my side. I tease him, tell the table, "Ask my friend Leicester to tell you about that duck he pinched during the war in Sierra Leone."

Leicester takes the bait. "I didn't pinch it, I tell you. The African bloke came to me and said somebody had been pinching his ducks. I said I don't know anything about your bloody ducks, get out of here! And that night damn if we didn't have duck for supper. But I didn't have anything to do with pinching it."

This is going so well I think I'll play the tummler. I say now to the table at large, "Ask my friend Leicester how Freetown got its name."

"I haven't a clue how Freetown got its name," Leicester the retired solicitor resists.

"Your honor," I say, "may I submit to the court that Leicester of Devon was dispatched to Sierra Leone to enliven the appalling war effort there. Furthermore, Leicester of Devon was charged with taking under his wing five hundred African recruits. And may it please the court, I will show the relevancy here: when Leicester of Devon landed to take up his five hundred native recruits, he found that four hundred and ninety-eight had craftily slunk on back to the bush. Hence the name: Freetown. Capital of Sierra Leone."

"Actually," says Leicester, the old solicitor in him moving here into rebuttal, "we made quite a good war effort at the end of the day. I got five thousand chaps to come along. Packed them off to Asia. Had a housekeeper named Mrs. Benjamin. She had a daughter named Sophie. She used to come up to me and say, 'You give me white pickaninny now?' I'd say, 'Shove off. You want the quartermaster for that.' This isn't quite conversation for the luncheon table but we had a Jewish doctor, Siegal. I quite liked old Siegal. Used to have his gonorrhea rounds every morning at seven. All these filthy people and not a stitch on. Siegal had them all bend over at once. We lived in these Nissen huts. Don't know why they called them that. Probably a chap named Nissen invented these tin-roofed huts. Four men to a Nissen. Siegal had all the wogs lined up outside his Nissen each morning at seven, backsides to the sun. Down he'd go with the needle, pop! pop! And give each one a slap. How you can do that just after breakfast every day, I'd say. Siegal. Great chap."

I don't always stir them up like this, but sometimes the devil invests me.

Dark news about Mary of Boston. Just had a word with the captain. Only an X ray will tell, but she is in a great lot of pain. The morphine on board, in a safe, is for the traumatic injuries. Mary is full of pills and they have her fairly stoned. We were due to come alongside in Suva at six on Sunday morning. To do this, we were slowing down to one engine. But since Mary slipped on the stairs, we've been at full steam. There will be an ambulance waiting at the quay. The captain has advised her if there is serious damage to her bones, get the repairs done back home in Boston. Now I feel more a jerk for not having gone another mile to be friendly. I hope she's only bruised.

At seventeen knots, our maximum, we'll be there in twenty hours. All I know of Suva is that there was a military coup there in 1987 and that the gents in charge have about as much regard for journalists as they do for any other strain of potentially harmful virus. If I were the old me, they would not let me in. It is said to be a censorious state. You are well advised to mind your manners and keep your seditious thoughts to yourself, especially in your faxes and your phone calls. Not many secrets. Good fishing, though. I am tempted to go fishing, and bring back whatever—tuna, mahimahi—and give it to Tuber the Root Crop Tsar. He'd probably char it, or beat it to death with a hammer.

Makes me sort of mad about Mary, that I wasn't nicer.

A most extraordinary exchange today. I was at the TraveLodge in town, where I had lost my mind and spent the night (if I am going to jump ship in every port and tear off to a hotel room, what's the point?), trying to hire a four-wheel-drive vehicle, which I aimed to take to the town of Lautoka, our next call. Lautoka is a twelve-hour sail from here. It is on the other side of this island. This island has good roads going around it, and bad ones going over it. And it is raining like the dickens. I wanted to take the bad roads overland, having had the lust to gander at something most people don't. I have also volunteered to take Little "Born to Be Wild" Peter with me. I *said* I had lost my mind. There were no muscular automobiles available. The young, smiley Fijian woman looking after me asked why I wanted such a car, anyway. While I wasn't paying attention, a woman who resembles the English actress Emma Thompson, except broader in the haunches, had slid into the seat beside me.

"Perhaps the gentleman desires an achievement," she said. Her accent was Australian. I didn't quite know how to respond to that. I looked her in her hazel eyes and said, "I just want to get off and see some different country."

But I did not get a car and so I went to breakfast at the hotel. I was squeezing limes onto a nicely grilled piece of local fish when this same Aussie woman slid into the booth with me. Smiled at me and addressed me by my full name (evidently she had heard me give it to the car rental girl). Ordered toast and tea. I thought: Does this woman just go around sliding into strangers' lives? She is not a prostitute, I thought. I mean, she's somebody's mother, I said to myself, from the look of what's gone on in her lower abdomen.

As it happens, she is from Brisbane and she has five children. Her oldest, a daughter, is thirty and her youngest, a son, is eleven. When that eldest child, who is now a doctor, was a second-year medical student, she delivered her mother's last baby. "There were some rounds bought at the rec club at university that night," this woman said, with pride. I said I reckon. I said you wouldn't catch me, the eldest of five children, going and delivering any of my mamma's babies.

I spent the whole day with her. I cannot explain the combustion. Whatever internal editor you put to work on what you say around people you've scarcely met—I gave mine the day off. Obviously I needed someone to talk to. Apparently, so did she. And talk is all we did, for it was a chaste encounter. The only time we touched was a firm handshake at the end of the day, under the words what a pleasure this has been. Then she went off to catch a flight to Australia.

Sometime during the hours we shared, I told her I thought I was in danger of becoming sad. She told me her husband, who is ten years her senior, has the most dynamic children a man could ask for—"most men would kill for these kids"—but "he can't seem to gather the threads." We went walking. In and out of rain showers, we trudged all over Suva. It is Sunday, and this morning there were believers, as the Russians call them, in the churches everywhere, singing at the top of some fairly formidable lungs. I saw Leicester of Devon sitting sweetly beneath a baobab, listening to the Methodists sing "The Old Rugged Cross."

We could identify things, we found. I know plants, some, but know them especially in these hothouse climates. She does, too. "That's a cassia," she says. "Looks suspiciously like a mimosa to me," I say. And tacky houses, for the most part, in Suva, for my taste. Hers too. Once, the sky poured down on us for two solid hours. She wore white cotton clothes, slacks, blouse, which became entirely transparent in the rain, but she was not in the least self-conscious. The water poured in sheets off her face, but dragged no cosmetics with it.

I told this woman about the people on my ship. Save this log of mine, she is the first to receive my uncensored impressions. She laughed at some, frowned at some—she didn't criticize. It wasn't long before she was asking, "So what does Toxic June feel about that?" Or, "Do you think it is wise to take Little 'Born to Be Wild' Peter along on your adventure?"

When the rain stopped she proposed a swim and lunch at the hotel. We walked to the ship to get my swimsuit. In my cabin she told me she had written a book about old people some years ago, but never published it. Essentially, her thesis was this: In Australia, one hundred years ago, the life expectancy of a male was forty-eight; of a female, fifty. Today it is nearly eighty for both. "This generation just now, the age of the people on your ship, are the first, actually, to have had a choice what to do with another twenty, thirty years of their lives—a whole second life they had that the people before them did not. But they did not realize they had that choice, to spend it productively, creatively, or perhaps indolently, and some come to bad thoughts. Your choice of this voyage: It was to work out what to do with those twenty, thirty years you have left."

I felt like saying I didn't just fall off the watermelon truck, but she only wanted to be of help.

The rain kept up until swimming was no longer an option. We decided to have the barbecue buffet beside the hotel pool. She went off to dry herself some clothes, to pack for home, and to change (actually, I went off to her room with her at first, but she was ironing her dress, and it felt awkward to me to be there). I stayed wet. She returned to my table a fifty-year-old, done-up woman, in silks. She looked new and fresh, and quite fetching.

Much of the time we talked children. Some intermittent times we talked about her work. She is a, for lack of a better description, marketing consultant. She planted the thought in my head of leaving my ship in Singapore so I could attend the birth, or nearly, of my first grandchild (as originally booked, before all the delays, that would have happened naturally). It's a long slog back from Singapore to Antwerp through the Suez, and no ports. Just a floating truck full of coconut bits headed home. I've never been through the Suez, but I've crawled all over that part of the world. Doing things just to say you did them doesn't have much appeal to me, but I'll tell you what has begun to appeal to me: my old life. The one that felt so lacking in promise last fall. At Singapore, I'll have been on this vessel more than three months . . . well, as I say, she got me started thinking.

We told one another personal things one does not tell close friends, much less some chatty oddball you bump into in Fiji. I feel I know her family. I know she's got my number. Chances are I'll never get to Brisbane. Never see her again. Remarkable experience, though. A woman, a mother of five, as is my own mother, a woman—three, four years older than I am—who looked at me from the back of my head, saw right through me to the front, and came alongside, all but saying, "Need a hand?"

January 29, 1996
Suva, Fiji

Nick the cadet says from here to Singapore it's one shithole after another. He says it's awful (which may mean it's wonderful; Nick's twenty; he could merely be saying there's no music, no hookers, no beer—well, sounds ghastly, come to think).

I didn't sleep at all last night for thinking of leaving the ship in Singapore. I kept telling myself the thirty days without a port of call from Singapore to Europe would be unhealthy for me. Even without booze, I beat myself up too much alone in this cell. The thought has been down there in the oil pan of my brain for days, perhaps weeks, but meeting that woman from Brisbane yesterday was what dredged it to the fore. She was the first person I've been easy with in three moons. She said, in so many words, leaving would be no mark of failure. Stop being stubborn. Go back to where you belong. I think she is psychic. That's all I needed, man: Australian juju.

I lay awake thinking I'm making a mockery of one purpose of this voyage: to learn my own mind.

"But the old oracle said, 'All things have two handles: beware of the wrong one.' "—Emerson. "Pursue, keep up with, circle round and round your life, as a dog does his master's chaise. Do what you love. Know your own bone; gnaw at it, bury it, unearth it, and gnaw it still."—Thoreau.

That stuff doesn't come off the top of my head. It's out of a repository, *The Practical Cogitator*. I've been dragging it around for years. I consult it, but I never come away from it saying: By God, Ralph Waldo, that's the ticket! A little J. Alfred Prufrock, that's about all I can recite a cappella. Naw, that's not entirely correct. A lot of Eliot sticks to me without crib sheet or cue. "Old men ought to be explorers / Here and there does not matter / We must be still and still moving / Into another intensity / For a further union, a deeper communion . . ." *That's* not in *The Practical Cogitator*.

Where was I?

Distressed and rambling.

If nothing else, from Singapore back to Antwerp would mean ninety more meals from Tuber the Root Crop Tsar. I'd rather suck a goat than eat one more meal than I have to here. Yesterday, for lunch Tuber served what he called "spaghetti with meat sauce." There was no meat in the sauce. It had a tomato base, but he had added orange juice, and chunks of oranges. You try that sometime on your pasta, Ralph Waldo.

I can feel myself tightening physically, resisting making a decision to leave. Perhaps I do not think it would be manly of me. On the contrary, remember Emerson's old oracle and his two handles: perhaps the cowardly thing to do would be to stay on this tub a needless month.

Fuck it. Walk out on it, like a man.

Easy now, big fella; let's think about this.

I walk Suva all day thinking about whether I really want to bail in Singapore. God, it's humid. In Memphis, we used to say: It's not the heat, it's the stupidity. Suva is a malodorous town, full of buildings named for Patels (if not the most ubiquitous, at least the world's most eponymous Asian family), and people signing the sidewalks with the contents of their nostrils. Just across the street is Fiji's *Daily Post* and Pawn Shop. It may sound like a spitball bucket to write for, but I'm intrigued by its possibilities. For example, on other newspapers, a man might find himself strapped between paychecks and ask for an advance against his salary, but on this one, theoretically, a man could hock his job. By my lights, such a perquisite would put the romance back in journalism.

A sign, with a rigid finger pointing at me like one of those old Uncle Sam Wants You! posters: "Jesus Christ, who loves you now, the same Jesus will judge you later!" That seems rather purple of Jesus.

I run into Leicester of Devon, who's looking for a haircut. The rest of the gummers have gone to a dress shop called Tickey Togs. Leicester says Toxic June went to see Mary in hospital. "A nice gesture, I suppose, but poor Mary: she hates June's guts." Mary flies out to America in two days, with nurse and gurney.

Lunch at a colossal Chinese palace run by Indians with a Fijian staff (not a Chinese in sight) and Merle Haggard singing American country music on the box. Ernie and May of Tennessee have joined me. We have learned that we have dropped a couple of scheduled ports, and picked up one unscheduled call: the island of Yap. Ernie starts talking about Yap back in his day, saying they wanted to close the port, and I interrupt him to comment, "You mean they tried to shut your Yap?" No appreciation from Ernie, who goes on to tell a story of terrible wartime bloodshed.

Run across Leicester of Devon at the foot of the gangway. We walk along the quay for a while.

He says, "I'm quite tired of this rain. Today I've brought along my jerkin."

I say, "There once was a man named McGerkin / Who insisted on jerkin his derkin. / His mum said, 'McGerkin, / Quit jerkin yer derkin. / Yer derkin's fer ferkin, not jerkin.' "

Leicester says, "Are you like this all the time?"

This does not look promising. There's a skid track down the toilet bowl and something just flew out of the bathroom. I'm slapping myself silly killing mosquitoes, and I only arrived at this hotel about five minutes ago. I blew in on a bus. The driver was a dead-serious reckless Indo-Fijian. It was an open bus, one of those cross-cultural adventures through miles of sugarcane a man of my resources could learn to live without.

About a five-hour journey along the coast, slowing down for speed humps in the villages. Everybody seems to have cinder blocks on their tin roofs to hold them down during typhoons. We also gave up forward locomotion, and occasionally yielded the entire road to bony-rumped cows that seemed poverty-stricken in every way but the right of.

Harry and Gerda were on the bus. About halfway here Harry said, "Here." And handed me a slice of cucumber and a square of Spam. He had gotten it from the galley. I ate it, even though there's no telling where Harry's hand has been. Harry's personality is mercurial, and I'm on the good side of whatever it is today.

So I get all the way here on the bus and find out my ship won't be along until late tonight. I had it in mind to kill an afternoon in a new town (the actor Raymond Burr grew orchids around these parts, I'm told), then get back to my cabin. Instead I'm in my third hotel room in ten days. Makes them nervous if you're from twelve or thirteen thousand miles away and you check in, hardly wearing any clothes to speak of, and without so much as a toothbrush on your person. They always ask me about my luggage, and I say, "I'm standing right in the middle of it."

Nothing for it but a traipse about. This municipality seems to be pretty near all Asians. Incense on the wind. Heavy Hare Krishna presence. Sparkie's General Electrical & Engineers says on his truck's windscreen: *Jesus Never Fails!* Of all the pissant places I've put in time, I can't remember one with such an impressive slew of secondhand shoe shops.

CNN in my hotel room! Wow! In the face, Newt Gingrich is the spitting image of a manatee. Wolf Blitzer is a really pale guy. The French have stopped blowing nuclear holes in the South Pacific. Well, that's jolly good, I think, since I happen to be in the neighborhood. Whoa! There's Bob Dole, looking mean as a snake. There's Pat Buchanan, talking a blue streak. Is Iowa over yet? CNN doesn't tell me. This man Forbes seems to be making a showing, though. Forbes, he could just buy the country, and give himself the job. Hold it! There he is, the Great Sweet Potater! Looks pretty presidential to me!

Five years ago today, CNN informs, the ground war began in the Persian Gulf. That was one of mine. Lousy war. But I desired a small achievement (do you hear that, Miss Brisbane?), and so it came to pass. I wrote a whole issue of *Life* magazine in six days. Only Ernest Hemingway and Norman Mailer have written entire issues of *Life* magazine, and neither of them in six days.

Of course, my blistering speed considerably lowered the quality of the prose. I'm tired of the news. I turn off the television.

January 31, 1996
Lautoka, Fiji

Up at dawn and see my ship in the harbor. Oxidation has got hold of her hull. She was gleaming back in Liverpool. Peruse the *Fiji Times* over a plate of papaya. Speaking of Jacques Chirac, the paper says in an editorial, "We should never forget what that arrogant French bastard did in the Pacific."

There's a piece on us in the paper, on the ship. The reporter misses the fact that we are an icebreaker, which is the only thing about us I find remarkable. Gives our tonnage, our size, says this is our maiden voyage to Fiji but the company has been trading here since 1973. Says there are eleven passengers on board paying, for the privilege, one hundred U.S. dollars a day. Make that ten passengers, and dropping.

I pay the woman at the front desk—"*Bula!*" she says (the Fijian greeting); a purple flower in her crow-black hair drops a petal on my receipt—and I pick my way along the seawall to my ship. Now and again a squadron of mosquitoes performs a flyby over the bay, reconnoitering.

Leicester of Devon is afoot and lighthearted. "Look who's home!" he halloos to me. He was just remembering how so he used to enjoy watching the women of Sierra Leone do their wash in the river. Every morning Leicester would go and have a look. "We called it Titty Creek."

"So," I say to Barry the Purser, "am I getting this drill right? Sailors go ashore and fuck their brains out with—shall we call them soiled birds of paradise?"

"Yes, except for the last thirty days. You want to be careful about not taking anything back with you. And you want to be able to put on quite a show for the missus."

"Thank you."

"You're welcome. Ya'll come back now, y'hear?"

Tolstoy, who has a word on everything, is now my god. Leo writes:

> The soldier in movement is as much shut in, surrounded, drawn along by his regiment, as the sailor is by his ship. However great a distance he traverses, however strange, unknown, and dangerous the regions to which he penetrates, all about him, as the sailor has the deck and masts and rigging of his ship, he has always everywhere the same comrades, the same ranks, the same sergeant Ivan Mitritch, the same regimental dog Zhutchka, the same officers. The sailor rarely cares to know into what region his ship has sailed; but on the day of battle—God knows how or whence it comes—there may be heard in the moral world of the troops a sterner note that sounds at the approach of something grave and solemn, and rouses them to a curiosity unusual in them. On days of battle, soldiers make strenuous efforts to escape from the routine of their regiment's interests, they listen, watch intently, and greedily inquire what is being done around them.

Tolstoy may have cut to the heart of my mood today; I'm in a vile temper. What I take from Leo's text is that he is telling me I am spoiling for a good fight. To that end, I am in training—not so much for a bout but to wear myself out, extinguish the directionless anger. I am back to exercising vigorously, and skipping meals when I can find some apples and oranges, and the only drink I take now I mix myself and consists entirely of club soda, one lime, and half a teaspoon of sugar—that and herbal teas in the mornings, and vitamins. If a man can sail the *Anti–Betty Ford* stone-cold sober, there's no telling what he can do when you turn him loose.

Been trying to think of a way to describe the blue of the ocean out here. Agatha of the Lakes says it is "dolly blue." She said when she was a little girl, there was a plant down the road, about half the size of this ship. The plant manufactured a laundry whitener, or bleach, called Dolly Blue. It was sold in a tiny bag with a ribbon yoked round it, and it cost threepence. When you added it to your wash water, Dolly Blue turned it the color of the Pacific Ocean. Dolly Blue has been out of business for more than half a century.

Bummer. We now drag an anchor off Lautoka. There's a ship, owned by this same line, a month behind schedule and just ahead of us at Vanuatu. It costs money to run this ship (ten to twelve thousand dollars a day), and it costs money to stay in port. So we live on the free sea, engines silent. We aren't dead in the water, but we're awful becalmed. The only good thing about it, if you live in my cabin, is that your balls stop humming.

February 1, 1996
Anchored off Fiji (Kong! Kong!)

The metal screws in the stainless steel fittings in my bathroom have begun to rust. There is a sour smell to my cabin (me?). I can remember when everything on this ship smelled new. I can remember lying in my bunk the night of the first of December, on new stiff sheets so fresh out of the box the creases in them pressed sharply into my skin, and smelling the new rubber mat in the shower. You could even smell the electricity then, everything was so new.

Rip the page of January off the calendar. Ettore says there was a guy he worked with in the engine room a few ships back who X'ed off the days. One day he was a little late reporting for his shift, and somebody else had crossed out the day for him. The engineer had a very emotional time of it, not being able to X out his own day. Ettore said he nearly fell to pieces.

Yesterday was Little Peter's birthday. Dick of the Lakes blew out two fluorescent light tubes with the champagne cork (amateurs always like to let 'em fly). His wife, Agatha, said, "You've never done that since we've been married," meaning it sexually.

The captain talked to Mary of Boston. It was 2 a.m. in Los Angeles. The New Zealand airline she flew there from Fiji had no problem taking out six or eight seats for her stretcher. But not a single American airline would do it to get her on to Boston. They have had to charter a plane, at a cost of eighteen thousand dollars. The sailors' insurance, which Mary subscribed to, as did we all, for the duration of this voyage, will cover the cost. "But we'll all make it up in our premiums over the next year or so," said the captain.

Mary's flight plight reminds me that much of the rest of the world has appealed to me all my adult life simply because I wanted to escape the United States' rigid rules and regulations. At the risk of sounding like a Republican (and therefore a fool), I have at times found America's legislative zeal for freedom suffocating. We are so free sometimes it seems to me there's a little man with a little piece of power everywhere whose job description reads: obstructionist. Signs everywhere saying danger, you can't walk on this cliff. Anywhere else, they don't care if you fall off and break your neck; go ahead, it's your life, you're a free man. And anywhere else, you bend the rules for need. Unbolt six seats from a plane and bung a crippled old woman on board? Yes sir, we can do that. In a jiffy.

You can walk into a bank, a bank with assets of about a dime, in one of these flimsily made countries, and get anything you want done for a smile. They'll take your money and give you theirs (and maybe not switch back with you in the end), they'll transfer funds, wire places for you, get cash to your aging Aunt Lulu in Iowa, and you all the time a total stranger and you can't even speak their language. You walk in an American bank, a foreigner with no account, and the only thing you'll get out of them is directions to the door. We've got rules in my country, and itty-bitty people to enforce them.

The news whipped through the cabins like lit black powder: New videos! A hot smell of rubber from the soles of my sandals as I screech off like a dragster down the stairs. Alas: more gummer movies. *April in Paris. Meet Me in St. Louis. Casablanca. The Importance of Being Earnest.* (Feels to me like something is missing here. Could it be *The Best Years of Our Lives?* Oh, for crying out loud, where the hell is *The Best Years of Our Lives?*) *Victory at Sea. Victory at Sea II. Victory at Sea III.* Two cassettes called *World War II With Walter Cronkite. Readers Digest's Pacific Frontiers.* I pick *Gorillas in the Mist*—for Sigourney Weaver's tits.

February 2, 1996
Anchored off Fiji

Leicester of Devon, ducking under the table: "Damn!"

Dick of the Lakes: "Was that your cheese jumped off the plate, Leicester?"

Leicester, his noble, eighty-three-year-old head coming up wearing an edge of the tablecloth like a tricorne: "No, it was my biscuit."

Dick: "Oh, I thought it was your cheese being lively."

Agatha of the Lakes: "Peter, in America do you say 'white rabbits' on the first of every month for good luck?"

Little Peter, chewing a piece of pork so tough all I could do with mine was masticate it for moisture, and put it back on the plate, points to his mouth and chews on.

Agatha: "We say 'white rabbits' first thing, before speaking to anyone else, for good luck all the month. Are you doing all right, Peter?"

Little Peter points to his mouth again. His eyes have begun to water.

Leicester of Devon will have none of this. He leans to me conspiratorially, a maneuver he has developed to communicate when he wants to shut out the rest of the crowd. "In Devon, it's taboo to say the word 'rabbit' on a boat."

"Why?"

"Don't know. Old sailors' superstition. Always been that way. Same as you can't take an umbrella on board. Sailors, particularly the old ones, take these things very seriously. I know one was an electrician, he'll hardly get out of bed on Friday the thirteenth. But this rabbit fear, my friend Horace, I used to go trawling with him, and one night he was drifting for herring. They were seven miles up the coast and he had brought this pie along, you see. They went into the cuddy to have some supper. One of the old mates with him, Glenn—oh, I've known him, had him crew— he says, 'Horace, what's in this pie?' This is just as true as I'm sitting here next to you. Horace says, 'Chicken.' His mate says, 'Tisn't. It's a four-legger.' Pulls in the skiff they were towing astern and rows himself seven miles back to Exmouth. Seven miles, mind you. Always been that way in Devon with rabbits. Can't say why."

Agatha: ". . . Of course it's just a silly expression from when I was a little girl. Everything all right now, Peter?"

Peter, dabbing away a tear: "My meat was a little tough, that's all."

Agatha: "Oh, I quite enjoyed mine."

My father has an expression for indiscriminate consumers. Perhaps he learned it as a boy, or perhaps he made it up. What my father says, when he encounters people enjoying what he considers inferior food, is "They'd eat a sack of nails."

Here is how it happens: You are in your tiny cabin reading *War and Peace* at five o'clock of a sultry afternoon. You could try to read *War and Peace* in the passengers' lounge, but sometimes the action picks up in there, and, as Tolstoy has described me in a previous life, in a similar situation: "As the hare, hemmed in by dogs, goes on lying with its ears back in sight of its foes, so he tried to go on reading."

You are a little annoyed by this big, thick, good-looking, hardcover edition of *War and Peace* you bought, because you think the English translator could have been a little more on your side.

For example: she's Princess Marya, no she's Marie, no she's Masha. He's Denisov, now he's Vassily Dmitritch, now he's Vaska. He's Rostov, no, he's Nikolay, now he's Nikolenka—but to his mother, sigh, a little tap-tap-tap on the breastbone, he will always be Kolya. Multiply *that* by about four hundred god-damned characters and you get some idea why people lie and claim to have read this book when, in the reality, they used it instead to anchor a garden wall.

(You'd think, by the way, I'd get some assistance from Third Officer Andrey on this, but not only is he acting testy lately, he couldn't even tell me the difference between a Cossack and a Hussar. And the last time I checked with Barry the Purser, who should be osmotically picking up the culture because he has to deal with the Russian stewardesses and the galley, all he could say in Russian was "hot pussy" and "thank you.")

Now, that's what you are thinking when the spoon on the saucer begins to tinkle against the teacup. Then the whiskey tumbler (filled with useless foreign coins, you inject defensively) strolls over for a dance with the water glass. Now, just now, if your privates were made of steel, would commence the music of an impressive pair of castanets. The big diesels are cranked. Your ship is leaving.

February 3, 1996
In the South Pacific

French toast on the breakfast menu. It came sprinkled with paprika.

Barry the Purser looked in on me later, bearing limes he had found in the galley. He knows what I use them for. He said he caught the cook making something that looked appalling yesterday. He said it was stale bread, yeast, sugar, and water he fer-ments in the refrigerator. Makes a vomitus-looking beer the Russians drink.

I told him about the oranges in the spaghetti—oh, I let fly with a full load. I said I had assumed he and his *Better Homes and Gardens Cookbook* had just given up trying to manage Tuber, defeated by frustration. Barry, sitting on my bunk, hung his head guiltily. When he raised it again, he said, sorrowfully, "They don't know about food. You know, he told me on the Russian ships they served the meal at eight-thirty each night. I said that's awful late. It takes two hours to clean the galley. He told me it was so they could sleep with a full stomach. They would have soup—more like a stew, really—and bread, as basically their only meal of the day. They'd go through the day hungry, but they could count on a full stomach at night to help them sleep." Though I seem to remember him telling me this story months ago, I swear when Barry looked at me now his eyes were moist.

"I'm not complaining," I wailed like a simp, my voice breaking.

And Barry slipped back out my door, drawing the cabin curtain closed on my impotent protest.

Fire drill day. Saturday always is unless we're in port. Suit up, stand by the lifeboat, stand down. Meantime a new schedule is posted of ports of call. Now we are due in Singapore the tenth of March. By my figuring, if we are on schedule—which is unlikely, but if we are—that puts it at one hundred days at sea. I only signed on for a hundred ten to a hundred fifteen around the world. This one, if we are on schedule—etc.—will take one hundred thirty, and change. Plus, we were a month late leaving, but such is the unreliable world of freighters, you could never be told you would be a month late leaving so you could make some alternative plans, like earning a living. You only got the tardy news every couple of days at the eleventh hour. It is one of the reasons you have to be very old and very retired to be able to do this. To go the distance, it means I will have been away from a wage for five months and stretching toward six (this is dire for a man who, rather than put much aside, OD'd in youth on carpe diem). I came along for solitude and self-examination, not self-sacrifice.

Still, I am indecisive. If this were a Hollywood movie, I would be leaving, but because I am so integral to the gummers' lives, I would be forced, at the last moment, out of compassion, to stay. The health of one of them, or all of them, would depend on it. Or their safety. Or well-being. Also in the scenario: the youngest passenger (me), who made all the elderly passengers feel young again, would be in hiding on this boat because the law was after him, and either he escapes now with his freedom, or he goes to jail but gets the geriatrics out of a jam. He elects to stay. Yeah, right—if this were a movie. Stick it in your ear.

On another Hollywood matter, I was unfair in my quick, sarcastic assessment of the new videos as gummer films. What happened, I suspect, is that the officers and crew got the pick of the litter when the boxes were opened, and the leavings were put out for us. Naturally, it meant the movies that appealed to a younger generation disappeared first. They are beginning to drift back onto the shelf now, and I check the shelf several times a day. It's Saturday night, and I am hoarding here in my sock drawer *The Commitments* (which I have seen three times already back home), and *The Name of the Rose* (which I have not seen). I feel good.

And a footnote: Sigourney Weaver did not expose her breasts in *Gorillas in the Mist*. Seeing the movie set me to reminiscing about going to Dian Fossey's mountain gorilla camp in Rwanda when she was still alive. But she was away, and I camped with two of her assistants and shared a tent with my friend Sandy Northrop, who was working for the *National Geographic*. We tracked gorillas and found them, there on the border with Zaire. Digit, her famous silverback, was dead, but Fossey remained, the terror of all who labored for her. She was put up to me as an egoistic, glory-hogging harridan. But I'll say this: she was a hard woman in a hard job. Tracking gorillas in the rain forests of those mountains was some of the most physically demanding work I've ever done. And when we found them—in the mist, yes—we sat there quietly, submissively, our heads down. The silverback, the great old male protector, sensed a threat and charged, but we did not move, as we were told, just as in the movie. It was extraordinarily difficult not to run. After he made a show of his courage, he backed off and reassumed his throne, as it were.

This was in 1980, in the rainy season.

We were just in and out—in last night at dusk, leaving this afternoon. I should like to have stayed longer. It's a lovely town, just as that American barkeep said back in New Caledonia. He said Port Vila was like Nouméa, sixty years ago. The harbor is pretty much unspoilt, as the Brits would spell it. There is a small green island in the center with a resort on it, but it is easy on the eyes. The lush vegetation conceals even the oil storage tanks scattered around. The water in the harbor is all the gradations of blue of the Pacific, and clean and clear to the coral bottom, even here at the wharf; you rarely find water this pure in harbors. You could swim here, right beside the ship. The town is small and manageable by foot, but buggy unless you find a breeze. And I don't mean to imply it's thatched huts, grass skirts, and coconut milk. It's poured concrete and leaded gas and expensive coconut milk, on a tropical back of the moon. It's sort of wonderful.

If I said any more, given the brevity of my visit, I'd be plagiarizing the information from somebody's book, a pointless exercise.

Restricting myself to something I know something about, then, well, that would be the tension/tedium aboard ship. The purser was telling me yesterday he has never felt such an undercurrent of tension—all attributable to Toxic June. Barry allows that my rebarbative shipmate has been insisting since we reached the islands that we have a barbecue. All the older ships do this sort of thing. But this ship does not have the hardware, and Barry could not get the dispensation from his superiors to purchase the sort of industrial-strength grill required for purposes of this scope. Now the chief engineer is having a barbecue grill built in the welding shop. June came up to Barry yesterday and, beating the deck with her stick to lend a drumbeat of emphasis to each syllable, chanted in a voice sharp enough to cut sheet metal, "Where . . . is . . . my . . . barbecue?"

I've become rather anthropologically fixated on my circumstances, ever since I began thinking the other day that, even if you have the constitution to live in a village with forty souls, that does not mean you possess the mettle to live in a freighter with them. In a village, you can walk out when you are displeased, frustrated. Throw tomahawks at trees. Lose yourself in the forest and cry. In this environment, take a hike and you take your life. Here, well, here . . . upon reflection, I find I am living in a preposterous community.

To begin with, you could say the Russians have flat-out seceded in their hearts. Many of them have stopped even the pretense of politeness. Many no longer respond to, say, Leicester of Devon's hale "good morning!"'s with so much as a grunt.

There are now ten passengers—eleven, counting the chief engineer's wife. All of the passengers and English-as-a-first-language officers know one another well enough now to know what they dislike about one another. There is something about every one of us, now that the voyage is in its third month, that gets on someone else's nerves. The trick is to manage it to your best advantage, to pull a winning hand from a full deck of garden-variety bores. In this game, Toxic June is the only card-sharp in our town, and even though she's slick, she has to compromise. According to Barry the Purser, who has studied June's modus operandi as assiduously as Bonnie studied bank robbing at the knee of Clyde, she buys her friends with booze. Last time out, the Poles were great ones to drink with her, Barry says, and every day she plied the chief engineer and the electrician with pitchers of bloody Marys. They became tight mates throughout the sail. "Wherever she is," Barry says, "she absolutely must be the center of attention." To my mind, June is much more com-

plicated than that, as are her needs. She is lame; thus she needs
people to come to her. Alcohol is her lure, but so is her biting,
sparkling conversation—to me—before she consumes too much
drink and begins to slur and dulls herself down. Another of her
requirements is youth. She wants some youth around her, to
stimulate her, to reenliven her, to take her into towns and sit in
restaurants and bars and tell her stories and listen to hers. None
of this strikes me as unreasonable. But you have to be shrewd to
have your needs met in our village.

Protocol and the English class system put the captain at the
top. He is our mayor and our most eligible man and he cannot
be brought down. He is a catch, and if he played favorites, the
man, woman, or couple on board who gained the preponderance
of his attention would attain the most prominent social standing.
Alas, our mayor is an impartial mayor. Next in line for social
plucking would be the first officer, but this first officer works like
a dog. He is socially skilled and graceful, but Ben barely takes a
moment from his duties to sit down for nourishment.

To digress: June came aboard in Antwerp, and immediately
scared the hell out of everybody, thereby establishing authority.
Fear bestows authority. She was born in China, she was in the
colonial service in India—she is accustomed to cushier accommodation, not to mention slavish attention. The older ships in
this line, to which June is also accustomed, were built with more
creature comforts. Outdoor swimming pool. Sunning deck. Ve-
randa. Awnings. Bar. Passenger lounge aft, and open, with views.
That was before cheap icebreakers came on the market. This
ship was built on the theory that a man was being punished if
he had to go out of doors. Swimming puddle belowdecks, a sump
in a cave. Passenger lounge with view of exhaust pipe housing.
No bar. June's heart, not overly large to begin with, shrank, and
she screamed. The home office did not want this grief, and immediately minions were dispatched to placate her. I was impressed. Things didn't change much on the surface, but within
hours after coming aboard June had a tight fistful of some very
short hairs.

Agatha of the Lakes, charging preferential treatment for Toxic June, demanded, back in Le Havre, that the company fly her and her Dick home. It brought her attention, and made the purser's life more miserable, which was her intention. A few stroke, stroke, now, now, dears, and she quieted.

Asail, then, June had her work cut out for her. She set about trying to do something with the foul food. The cook was made to attempt curries for us, but they weren't the sort of curries an aficionado (to say nothing of a health inspector) would allow past his nose. Soon even June was defeated by the food. She forgoes breakfast, she has an apple for lunch on her private sunning salon (a great noise went up in society over that!), and she picks at supper.

That left whiskey and companionship. She probed the Russians, to no great avail. She ran through the passengers, and was bored to tears. Oh, there was me (a fair raconteur on a good day), but I was unreliable because, except on a bender, I didn't drink. June doesn't want to kill me, and it is part of the reason I'm a non-player. I could see her scheming. She needed ambulatory mates. She didn't want to lie about with the crips. Of the women, only Mary and Priscilla could walk a country mile, but they were inane, card-playing chums from Liverpool on. Mary dominated Priscilla's days with stupid card games, but June worked the edges. June detested Mary; Mary loathed June. When Mary got drunk and fell down and broke her hip, June played it like a pool hall hustler calling the ball and the pocket. She piggybacked a ride with Priscilla to the hospital, brought a card, and caressed the injured old woman's drug-slackened cheek. She spoke sympathetically of Mary again and again. Leicester of Devon, a confidant of Mary's, was astonished by the hypocrisy.

The other day, June was trying to get up a fax from all of us to Mary. I've watched June's maneuvers with interest. These moves may seem petty and uninteresting in comparison to the scandals of your society, but in our town they comprise high drama. One among us has nefariously fulfilled her desires. June has won the devotion of the wife of the chief engineer, and with it the escort service of a couple with great standing on the ship, and, with that, access to their exalted circle in this maritime penal colony of forty dull souls. That her companion is a peasant woman with a brain about the size of a bottle cap is apparently a cross June is willing to bear. Stove up and old, she has beaten the game again: she is not stuck back with the gummers.

The Russians have a word for all this: *pissdubol.* Means "bullshit." The feminine is *pissdubolka.* Jane Austen had a line about it, too: "Three or four families in a country village is the very thing to work on."

So that's the soap opera in our town. That's the only story we have, as we beat on against the sea. It fills me with envy for a drifter's life on land, makes me yearn for a guitar, and a dust bowl.

Having a delicately grilled flounder by the bay today, I heard a Tennessee drawl behind me and Ernie and May took the next table. I looked along the shoreline and yonder came Dick of the Lakes at his silly lope (he walks like a man riding an imaginary bicycle). "Oh, please, Ernie, don't call him over," May implored. "He drives me crazy." I looked over my shoulder at her; we have never shared a confidence. "You weren't on that so-called tour the other day," May said to me. "That woman sat next to me and read out loud from the guidebook all day. She is going to drive me insane."

Not ten minutes later, Dick and Agatha appear at my table, inspect my fish, my green salad, my soda water, my two-week-old, six-dollar *Time* magazine, inquire of my every movement since breakfast (no bowel, so far), tell me they have seen Little Peter and Little Peter is joining Leicester for lunch and they have met a woman from California who runs a moderately priced snack bar down the way, and so they're off.

And speaking of my friend Leicester of Devon: we set off together on foot this morning, but Leicester didn't last long. He seems to have lost steam just since I've known him. For two months he always took the stairs with me, but for the last week he has taken the lift. A mile into it this morning, he hailed a taxi van. But we had a little chat first:

"I didn't know you were married again," he said out of the blue.

"Yeah, been married a pretty good while. Keeps me from getting married again, you see."

"Oh, I could never have married again after Olive. I'm afraid I would have made comparisons. Forty-four years. And it was a happy marriage. Not much fuss with Olive. She was pleasant—placid, you could say. She never wanted things we couldn't afford. We lived within our means. She was gone in ten minutes. A coronary. May 1984. What a shock. But oh, I could never have married again. My friend Silla is just that: my friend. That's when I started taking these freighters, when I lost Olive. If you have a wife, why are you here?"

"My reasons have left me, Leicester."

"I see. Then perhaps you should leave with them."

"It's in the cards."

February 7, 1996
In the South Pacific

While we sail to Papua New Guinea, which we will reach in two more dawns, I have withdrawn into videos, and a distracting bulk of Christmas mail that finally caught up with me in Vanuatu, and Tolstoy. I have passed my evenings with movie tripe (*Highlander*, *Batman Forever*), and December issues of *The New Yorker* (regarded, evidently, as tripe by my shipmates; when I finish a *New Yorker* and leave it out to share, it lies untouched for days until a stewardess chucks it in the rubbish bin). Significantly, my daughter has sent me a yo-yo, and I am good at it. The ceiling is not high enough for some of my tricks. She also sent me a two-pound bag of Hershey's Kisses, a whoopee cushion, a Santa hat with my name in glitter on the brow, and a plastic dart gun that fires a whirligig. I have left the toys out on the coffee table in the passengers' lounge, and from time to time when passing by I espy Dick of the Lakes, or Leicester of Devon or Little Peter, playing quietly by themselves with the things my daughter sent me. Evidently, they none of them ever mastered a yo-yo, for they let it hesitate and die at the bottom of the string. They never play with my toys in front of one another. Always alone. I don't disturb them, or let them know they've been observed, but the image stays in my mind.

I have spread out on my desk photographs of my dog, Willie, in a New York snowstorm of a month ago, various relations consuming great holiday feasts, an artsy, sunrise-over-driftwood shot of a piece of marshland I own on the coast of Georgia. And someone who loves me (Madeline Greenleaf, my wife, astonishingly enough) has sent me a newspaper clipping about drunks in January. "In a month of public resolutions and private revolutions, January is to sobering up as June is to weddings." The article says fifteen hundred Alcoholics Anonymous groups in New York City hold four thousand meetings a week.

The sea is blue and flat as a mirror out my porthole.

I have never been to an AA meeting. I have never consulted a physician who declared me an alcoholic. Denial? As I told the captain back during the holidays, I have never denied myself anything that I can think of. One day a few years ago I simply reckoned that I was an alcoholic and announced it. I didn't notice a queue forming to try and dissuade me. Today I am a self-made man, a reformed debauchee of the first water. And I trust I am over this drunken-sailor experiment. After years of exemplary behavior, the combination of my environment, Christmas, temptation, and the collapsing piece of rubber I call my backbone pulled the cork on a binge that lasted until New Year's, and then the joy and pure release of making landfall slid me into a bender from Samoa to Fiji. Given the circumstances, my hat is off to any rummy stronger than I who could have seen it through dry. I don't regret it. On the contrary, it has dispatched me, scared and scurrying, back into a sobriety that may see me out, if I'm lucky and strong. And it has revealed to me some new hairline fractures in my psyche. I should tell Madeline as much.

I've not been much of a hand at writing letters to America, but I've been sending self-censored sections of this diary home. My wife writes back that it sounds like I'm having a dreadful time, and I suppose I am. She says she looks forward to each installment, though, because she likes hearing about Toxic June and everybody. I called her once from the ship (it is ten dollars a minute and you have to holler in front of the radioman, Alexander, and I felt uncomfortable), and I've called from public phones in a couple of ports, and from a hotel room or two. They are having a bitterly cold season in New York. I reminded her of the winter she saved me from choking to death, when we had back-to-back blizzards and the morning paper sent me out to write a gay little feature about the snow, all the tots released from school, happy at play, and whatnot. It was brutal out and I found myself by myself in the elements. No New Yorker was stupid enough to brave that weather. Finally, in Central Park, far across the Sheep Meadow, I saw one dark figure, trudging my way. I thought: Whatever that maniac is doing out on a day like today, it has to be a story! We slogged toward one another in two feet of snow and a heavy shower of it continuing to fall all around, sycamore branches cracking under the weight. Three paces from the stranger, I whipped out my notebook and began to identify myself, just as he whipped out his notebook and identified himself and his employer, the *Daily News*. Silly-ass newspapers.

I was drunk twice when I called my wife. She told me to be careful. I told her Toxic June asks after her, too. She asked me what I said about her. I said I said only heartfelt, complimentary things, but that only led people to think I was lying or crazy, else why would I be here? I said I think people think we have a kinky marriage. She asked me what I said about my marriage. I said I said I just didn't have any interest in marriage anymore. She said too bad. We left it at that.

Of the many characters whose flaws I share or identify with in *War and Peace*, foremost is the grand dissolutionist Pierre. Pierre is drawn so finely, so comically, that I smile with admiration when I'm not laughing out loud. How come no one ever told me Tolstoy was funny, as funny as Waugh? Because no one till now ever read this book, that's why! Pierre is a lardy bastard who inherits a vast fortune and marries a beauty he imagines has cuckolded him with a friend (to telescope three or four hundred pages). He challenges the suspected thruster to a duel, picks up the first firearm he has ever held in his life, and wounds the man egregiously in the side. Dum-da-dum-dum: Remorse. Pierre splits for Petersburg.

At the stagecoach station at Torzhok, life's big, black questions expand inside Pierre's head like gas. " 'What is wrong? What is right? What must one love, what must one hate? What is life for, and what am I? What is life? What is death? What force controls it all?' he asked himself. And there was no answer to one of these questions, except one illogical reply that was in no way an answer to any of them. That reply was: 'One dies and it's all over. One dies and finds it all out or ceases asking.' "

Life's a bitch and then you die. Shit happens. Tolstoy had the good fortune to give up the ghost before aphorisms came stuck to the bumpers on the highway of life.

But then Pierre gets religion, natch. There at the station he encounters a freemason and converts, becomes a believer on the spot. Fifty pages on, Pierre has lost his mind and become a freemason himself. What's more, he's going around trying to free his serfs, thereby confusing his stewards, who can only read his actions as a reflection of his displeasure with their habitual embezzlement of his funds. Because Pierre, like me, is not a practical man, his stewards, the overseers of his holdings, are able to hear him out on his thoughts of liberating the peasants, and constructing for them schools and churches and asylums and infirmaries. The stewards nod and smile at his excellency, and rook him to the bone. Pierre then is able to return to Petersburg in a philanthropic and happy frame of mind, return to the pleasures of drink and rosy flesh, while the population of laborers he leaves behind are made to work until they collapse, trying to build his beneficent vision of schools and churches, infirmaries and asylums, while attending to the everyday obligations of his estates, chores in themselves enough to fell an ox.

"I beg you to disclose to me your chief temptation," a brother in freemasonry asks Pierre.

"I had so many," says Pierre.

"Wine? Gluttony? Frivolity? Laziness? Hasty temper? Anger? Women?"

"Women," says Pierre.

There is a fleeting period here during which Pierre feels cleansed, pure, a spanking new soul, when he's going around playing philanthropist and unintentionally wreaking misery on the multitudes, and if you come from where I do, you know Pierre's decline is just a matter of time. Where I come from, when you hear people have come through a cataclysmic or near-death experience and run off to God, you look for the peachiness to return to their color, and then you know they're feeling almost good enough to backslide.

A rap on my cabin door. Just now, as I was writing about my people backsliding (and thinking about my convalescing liver and how it is enjoying early retirement so). Barry the Purser. He wanted me to know I was invited to a party on board Friday night in Lae. It is for shippers, potential clients, coffee growers from the highlands of Papua New Guinea. Perhaps one hundred and thirty guests, in all. "We'll have three bars," said Barry, "two on the decks off the bridge and one on Monkey Island. It's just wine and beer and soft drinks. But I wanted you to know if you felt the need for spirits, I'll have a few bottles of whiskey strategically placed. Just give me a wink."

Sometimes I think the day is a loss leader for Satan if he can't find a way to trip me with temptation.

This morning, outside my door, I hear Little "Born to Be Wild" Peter trying to talk Galena into finding him some bleach.

"Bleek?"

"Bleach. For my shower. It smells. It smells very, very bad."

"No problem."

"Not perfume. Bleach."

"Perfume?"

"Perfume. Yes. Deodorant. Spray."

"Ah, spray."

"No!" roars Little Peter. "Perfume perfumes. Bleach kills. I . . . want . . . to . . . kill!"

You have to watch Peter. It's the little, fastidious fellows you can hear in a quiet room. They go: tick . . . tick . . . tick . . .

Been hunting wolves all day with Tolstoy. A hundred and thirty hounds and twenty sportsmen. A much more complicated business than wolf hunting with Cormac McCarthy.

It is raining and thundering as we approach Papua New Guinea. It is weather that makes a man welcome a lofty thought or two, but none visited. If it is any consolation, Tolstoy has principal characters with trifles in their head as well, and owns up to it. It is one of the reasons the book weighs five pounds. It takes a lot of dead trees to describe the emptiness in men's lives.

So these two chaps are sitting at a bar and one says t'other, "Where are you from?"

"Smithsonia."

"Get out of here. What part?"

"East side."

"I don't believe this. Where'd you go to high school?"

"Kingsbury."

"This is incredible! Me too! What year did you graduate?"

"Sixty-five."

"My God in heaven, this astounds me!"

The telephone rings. The bartender answers. After a couple of grunts, the bartender says into the receiver, "Naw, it's pretty quiet so far tonight. Nobody here but the Barlow twins, and they're shit-faced again."

It's a tale that's long in the tooth, and I think of it each time I toddle through the passengers' lounge and hear the gummers telling one another stories they have told and retold these last months, not that it offends anyone, since no one remembers hearing the business the first time. Tonight, at table, for example, Agatha of the Lakes said to Tennessee Ernie, "I don't like getting old." She has said this many times. She was born in 1923.

"Oh, I s'pect everyone would stay young if they had the choice," Ernie (1925) said. He has said this many times in response to Agatha's oft-put declaration, but if he remembers, he doesn't let on. "But I think it's a privilege gettin' old. I think it's a privilege gettin' as far as I have. I'd of hated to die ten years ago and miss all this."

"Well, I suppose you're right," Agatha said.

Once or twice I've thought of asking them how old they are in their dreams, but I don't get around to it. I would assume, like me, in their dreams they are about twenty-five. I am always twenty-five. Everyone who was old when I was twenty-five is old in my dreams. Everyone who was young continues to be. The dreams can take place in the past, present, or future, but no one's age advances or reverses in my dreams, no matter the time. In my dreams, I am always fleet, and brighter than I am. If I die in my sleep, even if it is thirty or forty years on, it will be the passing of a mustang. That is why they call them dreams.

In the stairwell after supper Leicester of Devon (1912) had it in for Toxic June (1918). "Did you hear her ladyship in there? I don't know what kind of dragging up she's had," he said, disgusted. "Saying 'bloody' at table in the dining room!" He fairly harrumphed. In fact, I'm certain. Leicester harrumphed.

Into the muddy harbor at sunrise. A river runs through it, dragging the topsoil down from the mountains. Just another one of those thick-aired, poured-concrete port towns, but this one comes with a reputation for violence. All the literature harps on seven hundred fifty tribes, seven hundred fifty languages—seven hundred fifty nations, practically, up until about eighty years ago. Governments come and go, the strongest of them capable of mustering little more self-defense than a corner cobweb against a kitchen broom. Strangers get rocked, out in the settlements. Vehicles come with steel mesh, like chicken wire with substance, over all the windows. War wagons. They call the thugs here rascals. I like that. I like it better than hooligans, the term for brigands in so many places. Everybody smiles at me, I don't know.

Little "Hang the Expense: Give the Cat a Goldfish" Peter set off for "an ethnic adventure" and the purchase of a wood carving, I'm told. He was back in the middle of the afternoon, empty-handed, having been bushwhacked by missionaries.

I spent the day at the post office and at the town hotel, at long length successful in getting a ten-minute call through to New York City. All is fairly well. I am missed, after a fashion. And just how exotic is it where I am? "Well," I say, "there's a butterfly from here in the British Museum. It's pretty big. The lepidopterist who collected it brought it down with a shotgun."

People think I'm kidding about these things.

The crew and the shipping agent, the captain and caterers spent the day tarting up the boat. There're palm fronds and potted plants all over Monkey Island and the two decks off the bridge. Three bars. A reservoir of wine and beer. The party starts at half-past five. Close to two hundred people are expected. Shippers. Potential shippers. Friends of the line.

By gloaming there's an offshore breeze and a world of boozy expats aboard. Perhaps six dark nationals in all, the rest honkies and most of them Australian. The expats talk about what expats talk about in bongo countries everywhere: how long they've been in country, when they're leaving. The cook made off with the silver, the gardener made off with the weed eater, the maid is in the tank, and the cow jumped over the moon. Corruption, tsk, tsk . . . The expats' is a blasé society. In West Africa, for about a century now, when something bureaucratic and asinine causes a wheel under your life to fall off, they say "WAWA." It stands for "West Africa Wins Again." Here on Monkey Island I keep hearing "TANGFU," which stands for "Typical Air New Guinea Fuck-Up," which means, I guess, the national carrier has a way to go to be recognized for on-time performance. The cynics will tell you this is one of those places where people don't know how to blow their noses without ruining the wallpaper.

Only one cocktail story lifts my own ennui (and I just got here). A village in the highlands, fed up with making unanswered entreaties to the government for assistance in filling the potholes that made the road from the village to anywhere nearly impassable, planted mature palms in the craters, thereby making the road from anywhere to the village impossible.

A large, gracious young woman who puts out a fishing magazine invites me to spend the next thirteen days with her while my ship goes a-calling around this island (the second largest non-continent island in the world, after Greenland, I am told three times). "You'd enjoy yourself." I decline, graciously, I think. Or perhaps cowardly. I decline because I have a quick flash of myself in harness on the stern of some great killing machine, hooked to a record-book marlin, a vein throbbing in my temple and the blood from my bare feet, braced against the gunwale, collecting in pools on the deck as the serious piscators in my party douse my flagging upper body with cool water. In my vision my companions, like my hostess, are a little on the dumpity side, and the backs of their necks are crosshatched from all that sun. No, I tell this friendly lady, I'm not the type who'll wet a line on the first date. I accept a cold beer and move on, as people are wont to do at drinking parties.

But while I'm thinking about fishing with fat people for a fortnight, Leicester of Devon sidles over and asks me what I think Gerda and May of Tennessee weigh. I say I don't know, but both are much bigger than I am. Sixteen stone [224 pounds], Leicester says he'd bet. I think Leicester's sense of the way nature wants things is offended by fat women. He says his sister, who is ninety-two, is in a lovely home, "but she has one moan. She says the only snag is the meal portions are too small."

Vast beer guts on the Australian men, and the slenderest hips and legs. Barrels on sticks.

Toxic June is slurring in a corner, holding court. She has managed to drag her broken body up here, but she won't last long. The Russians she has assembled, Andrey, and Alexander the radioman, are showing signs of restlessness.

One bored wife after another engages me. There's only one stunner in the crowd, and she knows it. She has planted herself dead center of Monkey Island, in an arrangement of lesser beauties, like the black eye in a Susan. Blond and buttery. About thirty, thirty-three. Athletic. Sleeveless white blouse, midnight slacks. We catch each other's glances about three dozen times before she asks someone I know—John the Scot—who I am and he beckons me over. She is the daughter of missionaries from Middle America. She was born here. Teaches school. She landed a blue marlin after a three-hour fight (isn't that marvelous? A fisherwoman, my, my . . .). She makes a muscle for me. She flirts. I hike my foot up on a chair, rest my elbow on my knee. She does the same. Our thighs brush. She is either terribly attractive or I have lost all critical acumen (a possibility), and she is seductive. After about an hour and a half, I learn her husband is standing ten feet away.

I console myself that it's a fitting end for me and all the other shallow men like me who were let loose this Friday night from their vibrating cabins to prowl among the innocents on the roofs of Russian freighters in fair harbors off exotic islands throughout the tropical world.

On my way to my cabin to retire, I dawdle twice to tell the Russians I do not know whether the captain will allow the whores on board in the Philippines. Some skippers do, some don't. Davao, where we will be for three days, is aswarm with hookers. The Russians have been hearing about it for months from the mates who have been serviced there before. Even though the Philippines are still three weeks off, they are anxious. They don't want any more snatch in the bush. They want some softness all night long.

~~~~~

February 10, 1996
Lae, Papua New Guinea

Sharon, a lawyer here and the wife of Charles, the shipping agent, told me last night she would show me around this morning if I didn't mind three kids. At a lush patch called a rain forest natural habitat on the rim of the local university campus, I saw a blue pigeon big as a turkey. Queen Victoria's crowned pigeon. Also Papuan king parrot, Raggiana bird of paradise, dusky lory, black-capped lory, Papuan lorikeet. Glorious birds with red and blue down like velvet. And two crocodiles.

At the central market, I bought some red peppers and an avocado, which is ripening right now in the sun beneath my porthole. Between the bananas and the cabbages, Charles said hello to a white woman, and after she had passed he told me she is called Lead Lips. I asked why. He said her husband, who works in the steel division of a large British corporation, is called Tin Dick. "The lads just had to come up with a name for her, I guess."

I valiantly defended Toxic June before the shipping agent and his wife yesterday, saying for all her bother she is the only fresh air I have; without T. J., I said, I'd break into a swivet and die like a coal mine canary. Someone in the one-good-deed-deserves-another department must have had an ear out. Last night, June foisted upon me a copy of a fortnightly journal published on her Channel Island, Alderney. I am a sucker for little hometown newspapers, the littler the better. This one was, for me, an El Dorado.

I did not know until I read it that Alderney was evacuated during the War, and occupied by the Germans. On December 15, the citizenry celebrated the fiftieth anniversary of their return. From Her Majesty the Queen:

> To my most loyal people in Alderney I send greetings on this fiftieth anniversary of the islanders' return to Alderney.
>
> The decision to evacuate Alderney just before the occupation in 1940 must have been a most difficult one to make and the return to your Island after five long years to find the devastation that existed must have been heartbreaking.
>
> During my visits to the Island in 1957, 1978 and 1989 I have been proud to see how you have put those sad times behind you. With your traditional courage, loyalty and devotion you have worked hard to build a better and happier future whilst maintaining your ancient privileges and very unique institutions.

Not much of a stylist, the Queen. I like the word "whilst," though. Elsewhere in the journal:

> The most poignant moment came when Charlie Greenslade gave a heart-rending performance of "Home Sweet Home" played on the

silver cornet which belonged to Deputy Bandmaster John McCarthy. It was Mr. McCarthy who played "Home Sweet Home" on the same instrument as the Autocarrier sailed into Braye Harbour on that morning fifty years ago . . .

. . . The grand finale was a 'piece de resistance' which almost brought down the house—a rendering of the Andrews Sisters' forties hit "Don't Sit under the Apple Tree." This was performed by three rather nice young girls dressed in matching khaki shirts, skirts and forage caps; the audience loved them and they performed an encore. On closer inspection, word went round that the three beautifully be-wigged "birds" were in fact none other than Tom Neill, Louis Dupont and Billy Bohan. Their superb act would justify inclusion in any television variety show and be funnier than much of the so-called comedy of today!

In the birds-of-a-feather report, I learned that "several Chiff-chaffs were feeding on insects around the sewage plant near the nunnery." Also: "Two Snipe were feeding in a garden at Platte Saline on the seventh." And my horny old heart leaped at this news: "Great Tits are back."

Tonight in the officers' dining saloon, I invited Toxic June for after-dinner drinks in my cabin. I keep a bottle of the Famous Grouse around as a test, a torment, or a teddy bear. June declined. She said she was having a party. She gave me the guest list. My name wasn't on it.

February 12, 1996
Rabaul, Papua New Guinea

In at dawn, as is our habit. A volcano working off steam on our starboard. Belching. Erupting. "Belching" and "erupting" aren't words I normally fling about. We sail one of the world's most seismically active regions.

And sharks. Sharks all around (two swimmers devoured yesterday in the harbor at Madang, our next stop).

That pretty woman at the party a couple nights ago said it breaks her heart to go fishing with her husband. You hook into something, she said, and it's looking at you and looking over its shoulder because there's a shark fast behind about to swallow it. "You're going to kill the fish, or the shark is," said this creamy issue of missionaries. "Poor thing is fucked either way."

I'm worried about Leicester of Devon. Very concerned. He says he is feeling "muzzy." Been three days. He hasn't been to breakfast, and the other meals he is fussy with. Leicester has the most even disposition of anyone on the ship. I looked in on him after we gained the quay. It's the first time on the voyage Leicester hasn't been on deck to see in a new piece of geography. He was sitting shirtless on his settee, having his second cup of tea, he said. He said he would be all right. And he thanked me for my inquiry. Although I like him greatly, we aren't close enough for him to tell me what is wrong, but something is wrong.

A few years ago, I was in Romania, in a ghastly industrial town called Copsa-Mica. There was no protection from the pollution, and so everything, everybody, every scrap of clothes on the line, every bite of food, was covered with soot. People presented themselves to you with sooty faces. It is surprising how easily you can put a hellish place like Copsa-Mica entirely out of your mind, until you come across a place like Rabaul.

I was warned not to leave the ship and go to town, so of course I left the ship and walked to town. The configuration of the gangway is such—it is not our gangway, it belongs to Rabaul—that the gummers can't negotiate it. It is basically a fifty-yard-long vertical board, with slats for traction. I slid down it like a fugitive.

Everybody in town but me was wearing a mask. Volcanic ash settles on you all the while you are outside. The particles collect at the bottom of your lungs and make you feel tubercular. People cough along.

The central market was stocked mostly with green bananas, and every now and again I peered into a shop selling crappy clothes and chicken parts. Citizens pad about their business in this gray world, just as they did in the cinders of Copsa-Mica. It astonishes me. It's like people eating the food on my ship without comment. Where has consciousness gone? Where have all the angry men gone? I am eating badly, to be sure, and I am swallowing ash, but I do not take these insults without raising a stink. These people hereabouts, though, they seem to carry on as you would if there were no grit in the air—I mean, they fornicate, have babies here, and your white shirt turns black in half an hour. Day of the living dead.

Tennessee Ernie and Okinawa. War and peace. *War and Peace.* He is obsessed. He says people remember Pearl Harbor. He says people remember the shot that took Hitler. But no one remembers Okinawa, the worst maritime war moment in history. Ernie will not let it go. Ernie saw a war like nothing I've ever seen. The way Ernie talks about Okinawa, I can't sleep. I think this is why May goes around shushing Ernie so much. She knows it serves little purpose to keep terrifying us all fifty years after the horror.

Leicester of Devon is all right. He says he doesn't know what it was, but he's over it. His color is back. His broad face glows. I'm very relieved.

February 14, 1996
Rabaul, Papua New Guinea

Went to the market in the town of Kokopo today with the captain and Barry the Purser. Kokopo is about twenty miles south-east of here. We had a truck and an extremely polite driver named Anton. We drove through a countryside of terrible devastation wrought by the volcano and a tidal wave that followed the blow. No vegetation, just ash and pumice, the old road buried six, seven meters down. Anton said it was dark here for seven days when the volcano went, and without roads, and without light, it was questionable where to run. Only five old people died, he said, but there has been an enormous psychic cost. When you look at that monster smoking on the horizon over there—everywhere you are you see it, you smell it, you breathe it—you think evil. I wouldn't live under a volcano for any price.

On the way, the captain said he could not sleep last night, for he received word from the home office he is being relieved in the Philippines. So is Ettore, the chief engineer. A Scot is coming on to sail us the rest of the way.

This shipping line has a queer system. In return for being sacked en masse a few years ago, and then rehired with no benefits the next day, its mariners are paid slightly higher wages for their time at sea than they were paid before. However, where once the sailors received paid leave between voyages, now they earn nothing while ashore. But at the end of two months' leave, a man is entitled to a berth. If the company fails to find the fellow work, it must then start paying him a daily wage, even if the man is home in the Andy Capp position on the sofa. As it happens, a ship's master and a chief engineer are coming up on that rotation in which the company either has to find something for them to do or pay them for doing nothing. So my captain and the first engineer are being furloughed. The skipper seems pretty upset.

We changed some money in a tumbledown bank. You could put your hand through the pressed wood walls; and all the bank's cash seemed to be kept in a two-drawer, sheet-metal file cabinet in the center of the room. And we set off to buy stores for the ship. Mangoes. Papaya. Spring onions. Great melons. Avocados. Corn on the cob. Now this is more like it. Lemons, limes, bananas—all right! We flirted with all the young women vendors, their mouths red as fire from betel nuts. They giggled at us, and made eyes. We let the juices of various fruits run down our chins. We told bawdy tales. Sailors on the beach.

Noontime we found a place that knew how to fry a chicken.

After lunch, I discovered a new plant, a nelimosa, a touch-me-not, or, in the local argot, a *mat-mat* (which means "die"). It's a fernlike green thing, grows around here like crabgrass. If you touch it, it completely withers, folds in on itself and goes stone dead. Remove your finger and it returns to life. The captain and I spent half an hour playing with the plants. I think, though I wasn't conscious of it, a certain degree of the stranger called happiness crept up my spine.

We sail this afternoon for Madang.

~~~~~~~

February 15, 1996
At sea

It is one in the morning and even Tolstoy can't rock me to sleep. I continue to be impressed by this man's freshness, his relevance. Even when he mentions a barbarity such as bleeding someone, I half expect him to say parenthetically it was an ill-conceived medical practice no longer in favor today.

Has your grinding toil gone overlooked in the workaday world of the nineties? Here's Tolstoy on how suck-ups pulled ahead over a century ago.

> He had completely assimilated . . . that code in virtue of which a lieu-tenant may stand infinitely higher than a general, and all that is needed for success in the service is not effort, not work, not gallantry, not perseverance, but simply the art of getting on with those who have the bestowal of promotion, and he often himself marvelled at the ra-pidity of his own progress, and that others failed to grasp the secret of it. His whole manner of life, all his relations with his old friends, all his plans for the future were completely transformed in conse-quence of this discovery . . . He sought the acquaintance and cultivated

the friendship only of persons who were in a higher position, and could consequently be of use to him.

The closest Tolstoy comes to graphic sex is to say a rake visited a house "on a footing of the closest intimacy."

I see I'm rambling here.

I wonder if the breakup of that old gang of mine has anything to do with my restlessness tonight. The captain and the chief engineer will be gone when we reach the Philippines, and Toxic June says she will bail in Singapore. I seem to have lost the knack of listening carefully to Ernie of Tennessee, for one, and in the dining room tonight the look on people's faces seemed to be the look of fatigue with one another. A feeling of dreariness has crept in. Whine flu is going around.

I have the ash of an active volcano in my mouth and still I am restive. What does it take to settle a man these days?

I watched *Lawrence of Arabia* tonight. I was an usher in a movie theater when I was fourteen years old, and *Lawrence of Arabia* played my palace. It seems so quaint now that people had assigned seats in the cinema then, reserved seats for the big road shows. *Cleopatra* was another one; Elizabeth Taylor was paid a million dollars; it seemed as if you could buy the earth for a million dollars then. I wore a white tuxedo, carried a flashlight, and assisted the theatergoers to their places. The smell of popcorn was perpetually in my hair. And I could talk along with the dialogue of *Lawrence of Arabia* for three solid hours. I think I made a hundred dollars a week—more, incidentally, than I am earning now.

"What nonsense does sometimes come into one's mind," thought Prince Andrey in *War and Peace*.

That's Tolstoy for you, always ready with a quip.

Barry, my friend the dirty old Irish purser, lent me a nasty video called *Tusch Push Vol. X.* The cast affected Zorro masks, and tended, at the least provocative times, to gasp without conviction, "Oh yeah! Oh yeah!" It was revolting, and so I've watched it twice and may again soon.

~~~~~~~~~

I was walking a potholed lane lined with eucalyptus bearded with fruit bats when a Land Cruiser passed me with a tape blasting Little Stevie Wonder (they don't still call him that, do they? "Little Stevie" must run two, two hundred twenty-five pounds, and be about forty-six years old now) singing about how as long as he had love he could make it.

It occurs to me I am going down a flat, depressed, more-homesick-than-usual road. Look at the niggardly jottings in my journal of late. I can hardly be bothered. And once again I am tipping the Famous Grouse bottle back till it's dry, as if *that* were an answer. My guess is I'm going for some personal endurance best by obliterating my days. Whole calendar pages have a way of falling off the wall if you're hammered and then . . . *voilà!* Time to brush your teeth, comb your hair, and go home.

I am also so lonesome I could cry.

And now I think on it, one of the worst things wrong with me is that I am at last certifiably in denial. I have made a mistake coming out here, and instead of admitting it, if only to myself and my God—I HATE THIS SHIT!—I have been gutting out my days unconsciously. I don't think I ever knew denial could derange a man so.

~~~~~

A shark ate a man in the harbor yesterday, the fourth victim of a great white in these parts in a fortnight. Today there are primitive, dugout vessels and ancient rusted tubs all over the port, looking for the shark. A special Australian shark-hunting team flew in this morning. The man who died yesterday was a fisherman, who was standing in water up to his waist, casting a net. The shark took his left leg, and was gone. The community has to be rid of predators like this quickly, for Madang not only feeds from the sea, it bathes in the sea, washes its possessions in the sea, travels—well, the sea is all. A violent loss of life to sharks is indeed a fact of life on this island. People aren't exactly nonchalant about it, but an obligation that goes along with citizenship is to band together every few years and go and slay a sea monster. It's not as everyday a responsibility as, say, being a member of a volunteer fire department, but more like living in a hamlet imperiled by a dragon.

At the moment, I am the only passenger on a public bus, and as I travel toward the wharf I am trying to piece my night back together. Blackouts are hard to throw light on, but I am aware I have done something reprehensible. I woke in the dark to the sound of rain but it wasn't, it was just palm fronds raking together in the wind. The door to my hotel room was wide open. First memory: some sort of black simian face with a red mouth dripping blood; must have been a nightmare. Second memory:

so you got snockered and you feel remorse, so what? Third memory: an old white colonial in the bar; his empire-builder shorts encircled his pipe-cleaner legs like lampshades. I asked him about a woman, and he took the matter to a friend with the establishment.

—The bus driver just spoke to me over a microphone. I'm his sole passenger and I'm sitting not three feet from his left shoulder (it's right-hand drive in these parts), and he just picked up his microphone and looked into my rheumy eyes, and he said, "On our right is the new wing of Madang General Hospital." As if he were in the business of referrals for reprobates . . .

By Miss Universe standards, the woman was hideous. I was in bed on my back, and I came up on my elbows out of unconsciousness to see her grin at me from between my knees, and her mouth was full of blood. I panicked, shouted, frantically dug my heels into the mattress to scoot myself away. I gave her a bad fright because I thought the poor thing had chewed through my johnson. I reached for my shorts, flung the bills and coins of America and five islands at her. She made a hobo's purse of her pitifully thin sundress, scooped the money into it, and streaked out naked into the wind that made the palm fronds sound like rain.

It was not blood in her mouth. It was betel nut juice.

An awful night in the dining saloon. Priscilla and Toxic June, the woman who is (by galactic agreement) pure-dee evil, ganged up on Agatha of the Lakes. Priscilla was shouting across the room, "Shut up, Agatha, shut up!"

At this point, Ben the first officer, John the Scot, and Leicester of Devon tore off the premises like chickens. Chickens may be too birdbrained to get out of the rain, but they know when the shadow of a hawk crosses the yard.

I kept my seat because I was hungry, half-loaded, and rubbernecking.

The nut of the thing seems to be that June, Priscilla, and Priscilla's husband, Ettore the chief engineer, spend the lion's share of their days denigrating the ship, and the ship's owners. Ettore's legitimate petition, I feel, is that, in stripping all these men of their benefits a few years ago, the company forfeited its right to expect jack-all for loyalty. Ettore also is concerned about cutting corners at the expense of safety. As for Priscilla and June, why, they're just hard to please.

Today the issue was over the petty fact that the captain and the purser took the three Russian stewardesses to lunch. "You'd never see the captain taking the Afghani stewards to lunch," Toxic June went on, introducing a sexist point and acutely aware of it. Priscilla's complaint was the lowly Russian stewardesses got lunch ashore with the captain while her husband the officer had to stay on the job back here in hell (Priscilla is always imagining disrespect to her husband's station and, by extension, insult to the woman behind the man). Perhaps I should mention that all the characters in this drama were inebriated.

I did not know she possessed a ventriloquist's skills, but from her table across the way Agatha of the Lakes, full of gin, threw her unctuous voice and it dropped like bat shit on June's and Priscilla's *plats du jour* (fillet of knotty pine, or so it tasted). Now my two dining companions' brows knitted into black thunderclouds as Agatha trilled on inanely about "some people" and "company loyalty."

This from Priscilla at the top of her lungs: "Shut up, Agatha, shut up!"

Agatha got to her unsteady feet, purchased some equilibrium with her blackthorn walking stick, and lunged toward us, shouting she had had just about enough. My eyes fixed on a tinned string bean I had pronged with a moody fork, and stayed there.

Agatha said she had had enough of June's carping, of her spoiling her holiday, her once-in-a-lifetime voyage around the world on her "dreamboat" with her new husband, Dick (perhaps I am misplacing the "dreamboat" here; it is possible Dick was the "dreamboat," not the ship, though you'd have a hard time getting up a plurality for either one).

June began to cackle. Agatha was quaking as she spoke the last of her (this noun coming up is open to challenge) mind. She turned with a glower and broke Dick from a trance-like examination of his cuticles. Then Agatha hobbled out on the arm of her husband, a thoroughly pussy-whipped human being, one of four men aboard who suffer subservience for earth's oldest, all-too-fleeting pleasure.

Silence in the dining saloon. I eased my chair back and stole away. Then I came up here to the fifth deck, where I live. In the companionway I saw Agatha, Dick, and the captain. I came into my cabin and then thought I should try to assist. So I went back out and stood beside the captain.

It does not suit me being the occasional man of nominal authority (the few times I have had people working for me, secretaries, researchers, and such, I have felt somewhat awkward). The captain seemed to think I might play a part in putting things right, as did Agatha, as did Dick. A number of people on this ship seem to hold the wrong impression that I possess some sort of intellectual magic. Agatha was crying in the hall. Exhausted, I said, "Agatha, the captain cares about you, and I care about you. Go to bed and know that you are loved." For whatever it was worth, there were no more tears in the companionway. Soon enough, things were quiet in the cabin next door.

And I am up in the middle of the night and fit to be tied. As if denial weren't enough, living outside my generation appears to be driving me quite mad. Already I'm as curmudgeonly as them. I'm only lagging chronologically, physically. The disparity in our ages seems to put them off as well. I think sometimes if I don't crip up a little, if I'm too agile, I make them feel decrepit. They deserve respect and deference, I know, I know, but patience is finite.

I was thinking just now: What is it about even an ordinary day around here that gets me down? And I answered myself: Here is the way an ordinary day gets me down:

I am in my cabin reading. My curtain is drawn across my door. Etiquette in this neighborhood dictates a drawn curtain means I

am open to disturbance; a closed door means it should be important. Only Olga the stewardess and the captain have carte
blanche.

Voices beyond the curtain: "So go and find Barry, Dick—he'll put it right." A mumble. Thirty seconds pass. "Oh, Dick! Richaaaaaard! Do you want to take some loo paper? Wait! Gregory! Gregory! Are you there?"

"Here."

"Does your toilet flush?"

"Don't know."

"Would you check it?"

I check it. Doesn't flush. No sweat. Happens all the time. It will flush again in a little while.

"No."

"Doesn't flush?"

"I said no."

"Richaaaaaard! Tell him Gregory's doesn't flush either."

As if I had joined them in a bill of complaint.

Evening of the same ordinary day: supper. On the menu, I swear, is "julienne of root vegetables." The julienne is just beets. The captain enters, all dash and tan. "Evenin', all!" And takes his seat at the head of the next table.

"Oh, Captain," trills Agatha of the Lakes. "A crisis was averted."

"Pardon?"

"We returned to our cabin from a lovely summer's afternoon sunning, and Dick had to, well, I shouldn't say at table, he had to go—but the toilet wouldn't flush." She's calling this across the dining saloon, at supper. "Wasn't just ours. Young Gregory's was knackered as well."

The captain looks at me. I give him a big shrug, and mouth, silently but exaggeratedly, "Who . . . gives . . . a . . . shit?"

"Anyway, it's all right now."

"I'm glad, Agatha."

Take your pick: a day like this, a day like any other? Or a day you wake up screaming because you think you hired some heathen who bit off your dick?

February 18, 1996
Madang, Papua New Guinea

Trouble. I suspect I may have had a mini nervous breakdown this morning. I rose with every intention of stealing a march on denial, and packed my bags—my bags are here beside me now, packed—and went in to see the captain to say I was leaving—no, actually the captain caught me wrestling my bags out of my cabin, and once I got into his office with him I was speaking rationally for a second, and suddenly I began to cry. I couldn't stop the tears. I sobbed, able to choke it off only for a second when Dick, answering his wife's command, burst into the office to tell the skipper the blockage in Agatha's shitter was cleared. Then Dick left and I cried and apologized, cried and apologized. The captain said I couldn't leave, that I would regret it. He came back in here to my cabin with me. He sat down. And he stayed all day. At one point, I'd swear he cried with me.

I have never had a nervous breakdown before, that I know of, but I now know what to look for. You break . . . down. You lose control. You say, I'm sorry, I can't think what's become of me, and you cry. Great awful painful crying. Well, come on now, really, it's not like losing a loved one. But to me, it was so novel, I'm sure I exaggerate. Let's just classify this temporary (was it?) instability as considerably more consequential than a case of the sniffles.

The captain said I was the last person in the world he would expect to see in such sorry shape. He didn't say it critically. I said this is rather embarrassing. He said, "You're a strong personality. I mean that. I am not patronizing. You show your other feelings with no restraint. People know it when you're angry.

Everyone knows when you're happy. Why not sadness? There's nothing wrong with showing you are low. You have nothing to be embarrassed about."

I apologized, and continued to feel raw, though I managed a loose rein on the sobs. Then I think I got it: the skipper was saying this unnecessary gusher of apologies was the only weakness I was putting on show; the hell with saying you're sorry—stand up and cry like a man! He said, "If I could get that haircutter from Nouméa with the tattoo on her tummy in here, I would. I mean that, I would."

Who could ask for more in a ship's master?

Obviously the whole mess overtook me before I could jump ship. Isolation. Loneliness. Numbing boredom. Dread of another meal with the most stimulating stretch of conversation running along one of Agatha's metronomic lines: "The potatoes are usually lovely." Tick. Tock. "Are you enjoying yours?" The generational thing; being segregated with some people who seem to have outlived their wits. The thought of all the nautical miles that lie ahead, and the jetsam of dead brain cells I'd leave in their wake. The confines of my cabin. Past mistakes. Lost loves. Various failures. Innumerable reasons to panic. Pressures building over time. Simply too long, for an old daily newspaperman, spent on a single theme (self). Self-pity. Without question, booze was the detonator on the charge that finally breached the dam.

The captain just sat through it calmly, reassuringly, as though men seek him out for a whacking good cry on a regular basis. We didn't talk about me, or any of my personal problems as such, for all that long, as it turned out. He seemed to recognize innately I had no business being in this marine nursing home, and so we just talked like friends, which he kept insisting we were. The man is such a nice human being, such an impartial, evenhanded Libra. If you were to ask him his assessment of Adolf Hitler, he would say, "Well, the finest in his field." I genuinely like this captain.

And I appreciate his indulgence more than I can say. But it's not a point of honor with me to stick around. I mean, manly? I fucking broke down today. I'm a man without a woman on a ship without a country in a harbor called home sweet home by a shark on a winning streak.

Spent the morning unpacking, putting books back on the shelf, trembling slightly and feeling a complete fool and a crybaby (although the tears seem to have disappeared). Depression—I can speak from greater experience now—is almost always worth avoiding if you ever have the option.

Any shrink will tell you alcohol only exacerbates a dog like this, so a side effect, or should I call it a healthy by-product, of my predicament is there's no happy way out but up and there's no way up but sober.

I have a history of resilience in most matters. I think I will be able to pick myself up directly. It's just not going to be today. The test today is to respect the gravity of my situation, and not monkey with it. Still, I wish I didn't feel so goddamned tender.

They caught a twelve-foot great white in the harbor last night. Cut it open. Found a turtle inside. No human parts. Wrong shark, evidently.

Smart asses shouldn't get the blues.

In an effort to lift my spirits I have been trying to recollect some of the more irreverent acts I have been associated with in my life. Once during a murder trial in Crittenden County, Arkansas, I was kicked out of court by a judge. The prosecutor was pointing out to the jury that not only would the state prove the defendant guilty of killing this poor woman, the state would prove the pagan committed the unnatural act of cunnilingus on the victim. Something seized me and before I could check it I said, from my reporter's perch in the front pew, and entirely too loudly, "Aw pattooooooooey!"

In a flash, a bailiff had me by the back of my belt, hitching up my trousers into the crack of my buttocks, marching me out the county courthouse on my tippytoes.

Truly now, smart asses shouldn't get the blues. I'm far too much of an aleck for this to happen to me.

I slog on with Tolstoy. Sport doesn't seem to like his women all that much. Good men get cuckolded and torn up by low women all through *War and Peace*. In real life, he seems to have traveled the great arc from loving to loathing and detesting his own wife. Crazy old fart went from being a real rounder to an advocate of celibacy, in or out of marriage. "Until the day I die she will be a stone around my neck," he wrote. "I must learn not to drown with this stone around my neck." He married this woman, Sofya, on September 23, 1862, when he was thirty-four and she was eighteen. According to a brief bio in the edition of *War and Peace* I'm using for a pillow, on October 28, 1910, he walked out on her, looking for some peace of mind, and caught a train. Then he caught a fever. Ten days later, in a stationmaster's house, he died. They fetched his body back to the very home he had finally mustered the nerve to flee. He is buried in the woods at the family estate, Yasnaya Polyana (Bright Glade), about one hundred thirty miles southwest of Moscow.

Not everybody was nuts about *War and Peace* when it was first published in 1869. According to the jacket copy of my edition, Turgenev and Flaubert were among the heavy hitters who disparaged its formlessness. "A wonderful mass of life," Henry James called it. Virginia Woolf admired it. "There is something proud and superb in the attack of such a mind and such a body upon life." The trouble for me here is, I've never been all that keen on Virginia Woolf.

I'm in some very dense geography with *War and Peace* now. Tolstoy is giving us history lessons on the causes and curses of the Napoleonic Wars and the evil in men's minds. He's gone to preaching, which can be an aggravation. And different names for everybody continue to confuse. Here, lately, the old, dueling, cuckolded debauchee I've come to know and love as Pierre has been answering to the name Count Pyotr Kirillitch. To me that's like changing my name to Prince Ballcock Vladivostok overnight. And Natasha—God, Natasha's names are all over the block. Natalya, Countess Rostov, Natalya Ilyinitchna. Keeping track of this stuff wears me out while I'm trying to get on with the yarn.

And then, out of the thicket rides the true gift of genius. Makes you want to press it like some memory-soaked boutonniere between the leaves of your journal:

> He had only just finished dressing for his ride. He was wearing a blue uniform, open over a white waistcoat, that came low down over his round belly, riding-boots, and white doeskin breeches, fitting tightly over his fat, short legs. His short hair had evidently just been brushed, but one lock hung down in the middle of his broad forehead. His plump, white neck stood out in sharp contrast to the black collar of his uniform; he smelt of eau-de-cologne. His still young-looking, full face, with its prominent chin, wore an expression of imperial graciousness and majestically condescending welcome.
>
> He walked out with a quivering strut, his head thrown a little back. His whole stout, short figure, with his broad, fat shoulders and his prominent stomach and chest, had that imposing air of dignity common in men of forty who live in comfort.

That stretch of text gives me the impression Leo Tolstoy detected something of the slimeball in the character of Napoleon Bonaparte.

The captain is still looking after me, telling me all the backstage word. I guess when you cry in front of your captain, you bond. John the Scot has the theory the skipper finds something of a big brother in me. I know he has a mother and a sister and his father died two years ago. He tears up when he speaks of his father.

Anyway, he has to pick his way between mines on this sailing, says there has never been a voyage as bitter and tendentious and full of bad blood as this. In twenty-five years of sailing. He said after he spent so much time with me yesterday, Toxic June cornered him. She demanded to know where he had been. He said he had been occupied. She said she had been frantic to find him, and demanded again he account for his absence. He said he had been occupied. Well, she required a fax to be sent to England. She is looking into the possibility of serving Agatha of the Lakes with a writ for slander. When they all get back. She said, to her horror, in front of all her friends, Agatha had called her "a worm." I didn't recall the word "worm," but then I got snagged somewhere in the gin-soaked fray, as you would in a thornbush, and as I was trying to free my trouser cuff, much was said outside my attention.

So now there's two, three, maybe ten warring factions among the passengers alone. I don't feel like a fight with anybody. I'm locked in hand-to-hand combat with myself. Tonight there's a barbecue on the afterdeck, using the grill they made in the welding shop to pacify June. I don't look forward to it, but a man's got to eat. As it is, I already skip two meals out of three around here to avoid these people. And I'm spending a fortune on hotels I can't afford, and hotel rates on long-distance calls.

The captain and all the senior officers are agreed that this shipping line will never allow June back on one of its vessels. *Touché!* That certainly trumps my getting tossed out of a measly cunnilingus trial once.

February 20, 1996
Madang, Papua New Guinea

Three a.m. Spent the last few sleeping hours alert, in a cold sweat, unspeakably melancholic, intermittently turning on the bulkhead light above my bunk and taking up Tolstoy. Eight hundred pages behind him and Leo still has a full tank of gas (and for all I know two jerry cans in the boot). In *War and Peace*, in Prince Andrey's house, where once dwelt domestic bliss, we have seen the last of smiley faces; in this unpleasant period the house is split into hostile camps. People are glaring daggers at one another over the supper table. Sounds to me much like life here on the *Anti–Betty Ford*. And the Russian army is rent by half a dozen or better opposing factions, from the strict military tacticians who want a campaign by the book, to the men who think it's preposterous that Tsar Alexander is playing general. The word "contumely" entered my mind as I sweated my sheets; I don't think it has ever been a part of my vocabulary.

Last night, I went down for the barbecue. Barry the Purser greeted me with a wonderful smile and a great grip of a hand, saying, "Welcome home, lad." Everyone on board thinks I've been ashore for the last two days, when I've just been quietly passing time in my cabin. Apparently, my collapse is not yet shipwide knowledge. The captain is a discreet friend. I've never seen any information that has remained confidential in this environment.

"Nice night," I said to Barry, "but what a pity about the company."

He convulsed with laughter, an easy audience. June once called him "simple." I couldn't disagree more.

For once it wasn't so humid. You could breathe. There was a breeze, and swifts rode the air taking mosquitoes. I was hanging off the stern, watching a fisherman in the bay hurl a crude spear off a rusted vessel that vaguely resembled the *African Queen*, when Leicester of Devon took hold of my arm. "My friend, have you heard about the deplorable old bag and her writ against Agatha?"

See what I mean about information having legs here?

I was offered ice-cold South Pacific beer about a hundred times. Finally found a warm soda water. The food—pork sausages, lamb chops, sheep livers, beefsteaks—was black and brown. There were a lot of people having nothing to do with one another. Only the captain moved easily between opposing sides, showing no partiality.

The killer shark had been spotted from a government helicopter, I learned, but it still eludes the hunters.

I ate quickly and slipped off back to my cabin, to brood.

My predecessor in a job I once held, corresponding from Africa, was a fellow named Carey Winfrey. I've spoken of Carey before. Carey had one wearying Third World experience of brutality, criminality, slaughter, and hardship after another until he found himself in Lagos, Nigeria, which was the hellhole then that it remains today. After a smelly period without water at his hotel, he grew tired of feeling soiled, and complained.

We have water, the manager said brusquely. You just aren't paying attention. You sleep all night; you're out all day. You should be more flexible, and more sensitive to the rhythms of the plumbing.

By and by there was a rumble in a pipe and a gurgling sound in the loo and Carey Winfrey roused himself quickly sometime after midnight and drew a bath, a brown-water bath but a bath all the same. Being bright, Carey thought: Why waste this bonanza now, only to lay me down on dirty sheets again? This cold, auburn water will keep. And so cheered he fell into the soundest and sweetest repose he had yet attained in the sorry country, relaxed in the promise of the cleansing relief that lay ahead.

When the correspondent awoke between seven and eight, uncharacteristically refreshed, he found a chambermaid had entered while he slumbered, crossing the dirty tile softly on crusty feet, and unstoppered his bath. Worse, an expensive watch—of irreplaceable sentimental value to him as well—was missing from the nightstand by the bed. The two events combined to crush him, and he broke into great, racking sobs. You could hear him as far as the other side of the dual carriageway, he would go on to say. Not long after, I was called in to replace Carey, who would be returning to America after an African tour of six months.

It behooves me to look up Carey, once I regain my own shores. I have something to tell him.

Such an eventful morning! It is only noon as I sit in my cabin, chompers sunk in an apple, impelled by said events to catch the ledger up.

Two sharks caught in the harbor at first light. Neither thought to be big enough to be the killer, but both big enough for me. Yesterday two three-quarter-inch-thick stainless steel hooks baited with two bloody briskets the size of blue-ribbon calves were swallowed by a shark that snapped the thousand-pound-test line (with steel leaders) as though it were dental floss, and shot away to digest a free lunch undisturbed. That's the fish we're looking for. By comparison, these first two today—nine-footers, I'd say—were reeled in conventionally, like mackerel. Dropped them off at the dock of the maritime fisheries icehouse across the bay from us. Hearing the news, I rounded up Leicester of Devon to join me in some ichthyological investigation, and we set off on foot.

We trudged a muddy path that ran down the shoulder of the main road, the harbor on one side, leaded fumes on the other. We were the only two pedestrians wearing shoes. Leicester passed the time regurgitating the whole Saturday night feud, and I scarcely listened. It was ninety-six degrees Fahrenheit, one hundred percent humidity, and Leicester's clothes soon soaked through. His breathing was fast and irregular, too, and I was beginning to think we should turn back just as providence lent a hand. Someone hooted at us. It was Tom, the young, likable representative of the shipping line. We got in his air-conditioned car and he agreed to go shark-hunting with us.

The harbor was out of sight, on our right, and the icehouse where they took the sharks was somewhere in that direction in a tangle of dirt roads. Tom hailed a barefoot boy. "Mi sharki go to!" he hollered, as one truant to another, and the boy gave back instructions in a pidgin tongue that sounded playful and fun. Soon enough, we were in a long queue that wound through the icehouse to view the monsters. The last time I was in something like this, I filed past Vladimir Lenin, whose corpse lay flat as a Mississippi sailcat (that's the state bird, a dead cat that's been run over in the road so many times you toss it for sport, as you would a Frisbee), except for his stuffed head.

There they were, snout to tail fin. Massive shoulders, massive heads, just nothing but muscle, tip to tip, on the concrete floor. Mindless eating machines, according to the most famous shark book ever written. All Madang, it seemed, had heard the rumor (ding-dong! the devil is dead!), got dressed, and padded on down to the shore. The sharks hadn't been gutted, and both looked full or pregnant, but upon seeing them no one mistook either for the fiend. Still, the citizenry crept past softly, with shuddering respect, the way they do in capitals where the dictator has been executed and the corpse displayed on the square so people can feel safe again. Tom took my picture with a foot on the spine of the largest creature, while the smaller—though no less toothy— remained in focus in the arch between my legs.

Back in town, posters had been nailed up; they bore an illustration of a shark, all teeth. *"Tok save. No ken was was long salwara tripela kila sark istap."* Danger. Do Not Swim in Sea. Dangerous Killer Shark.

In the bank to change money, I encountered the infamous Toxic June and Priscilla. T. J. and I haven't shared a word in days. Priscilla hasn't spoken to me in six weeks. T. J. greeted me as a mother would a lost son. After pleasantries, a squeeze of the hand, and an air kiss, she asked me, "Did you hear that torrent of abuse that was heaped on me the other night?"

I said, and it came out, to my embarrassment, in a squeak (like an unarmed man backing out of a saloon full of .45s pointed at his pecker), "No, not really."

The battle was replayed. For my part, I said I'd never seen so many grown men turn yellow-bellied so fast, and fly from a dining table. T.J. allowed she has faxed her son to consult her nephew—"who is a barrister"—about serving Agatha of the Lakes with a writ for verbal abuse.

"Did you hear her call us scum and rubbish?" Priscilla asked.

"Did you hear her call me a worm?" T.J. asked.

My right hand involuntarily reached for the sky, and the fingers on my left hand stretched forward to touch a Bible, as I caught the scent of a subpoena to testify for the plaintiff. Recovering, I stammered that I really didn't follow the exchange all that closely. I declined an offer of a lift to the hotel, came back here, cored my apples, and set to bringing my accounts in line. Lawsy; mercy.

I went to the post office this afternoon. I prepaid for a six-minute telephone call to New York City, and it cost me about twenty American dollars. Three times, I got a connection, enough to say, "Hello," and hear a responding "Hello," and then the line went down. The fourth time, I said, "Hello," and the voice on the other end, shot through now with impatience and frustration, screamed out, "Greeeeeg!" All of a sudden there rose in my ear such a baying, howling, barking, yelping, yipping, and thrashing as to be a din that could only be associated with Judgment Day.

"Forgive the noise," my wife said evenly. "Until a moment ago, your dog thought you were dead."

A quiet, uneasy truce between the tables at supper, as fragile as the cease-fire between a newly reformed smoker and the nearest open pack of Marlboros.

So it comes down to this: you make work to keep the battery from going dead, even if it's an exercise in cynicism. For example, we aren't there yet, and I've never seen photographs of it, but let me describe Kimbe:

A single wharf, a one-boat town. A string of dark, sparsely stocked shops along the rim road that hugs the harbor. In the unlit shops you can purchase a box of detergent, or a six-month-old copy of *Parents Magazine*, or a T-shirt that says "Chicago Bulls," or any of a number of Christian missionary books written in pidgin English on the subject of living life the way God would like to see you play it out. Two or three churches and one that looks as though it's been a-building for a decade. Poinciana, frangipani, oleander, baobab—the usual floral suspects, along with eucalyptus and Australian pines wearing black tiaras made of live, squealing fruit bats.

Beneath a pavilion with a rusted, corrugated tin roof, the central market. Women, old and toothless, with cheeks so concave the Japanese used to hide in them during the war, squat, or sit cross-legged, behind reed mats upon which are piled tomatoes or peppers or limes or coconuts, papaya, mango, sugarcane, or various hairy roots that grow across the land. The women wear floral, shapeless frocks of a cotton worn so thin an infant pitching a fit could rip it with tiny fists. When the women bend over to scoop up your fruit or make your change, you see they wear nothing underneath, and even the young ones are old; they have fed so many babies their breasts look like empty wineskins suspended from a tack.

Men with sharp ass bones pad about barefooted or wearing flip-flops, great green stalks of bananas on their bent, black backs.

Everybody's mouth is red from the betel nut.

We've started the engines. The sun is just rising on Madang. We'll reach Kimbe late today or early tomorrow. Seeing it for the first time, I'll mark my own words.

Barry the Irish purser came into the sanitarium that used to be known as my cabin this morning for a coffee and a gossip. We trashed the lot of them. I inquired why Barry never took a meal with the rest of us in the dining room, preferring to dine alone in his quarters on the third deck. He said for thirty years he has taken his meals aboard ships in the dining room, including this one. However, because of Her Highness the Toxic One, he ceased eating with us three days out of Le Havre. France seems to me moons ago, so far in the past I hadn't remembered Barry ever supping with us.

The captain has taken to staggering his mealtimes, something he's never done before. According to Barry, he's probing to find a formula that allows him to enjoy a meal now and then, but no success so far. Ben the first officer, on the bridge this dawn, said of the dining experience, "It's getting downright painful down there."

I asked Barry to solve a mystery for me, and he did. There are three fat women passengers, and three fat women stewardesses on this ship. The stewardesses stay fat because they eat all the time. But the three fat women passengers eat sensibly in the dining room, often picking at their food, decrying the large portions, offering to share. So, then, how come they're getting fatter before my eyes? (Here I have to remove T. J. from the formula; it's my guess her size is sustained by the booze and her inescapably sedentary life.) "You should see the load going up to their cabins every day," Barry said. He sends each woman two large packages of cookies, plus various sandwiches, cheeses, fruits, all of which are free. They have to pay for the chocolates, and Barry sends them an arm or two of chocolate on a regular basis as well.

Learning they were closet gorgers made me feel sad, and sorry I had sought out the answer.

Barry said the last writer he had on a ship was a woman named Shannon who was working on the television series they made of John Jakes's Civil War fiction *North and South*. She was only on for two months. "She told me, she said, 'I don't see how anyone in their right mind could stand something like this for four months.' You should have seen her eyes sparkling as she left us. She skipped down the gangway like a little girl."

~~~~~~

February 23, 1996
Kimbe, Papua New Guinea

Strike the tent! After eighty-some-odd days at sea, I have just passed a night in a bed that did not vibrate. Professional inquiries lead me to believe it has to do with the placement, or rearrangement, of the cargo. Evidently, the 3,500 tons of copra we took on in Madang have stilled the rib of the ship my cabin straddles, transformed the movement of my mattress to nothing so much as the soothing rock of a berth on the Crescent out of Birmingham bound for New Orleans. Perpetual tumescence is a thing of the past. Of course, none but a blockhead would fail to use the experience inventively in the future.

Now it's dawn and we approach Kimbe. Ernie of Tennessee asks me, as he does at every port, whether I could live here. I say, as I do in every port, not enough action for me. I say I saw four lights shining ashore.

"I reckon the population here is about minus fifty," Ernie says.

"Actually," I say, "I think the sun sets between here and the nearest town."

"That's a good one," Ernie says.

After breakfast, I'm sitting here in my sanitarium getting collected to walk to town to see whether anything I wrote yesterday was prescient, and Leicester of Devon pokes his head through my curtain and asks me to accompany him to the market. It's just across the road and I agree and we walk. Leicester is a little unsteady lately and I don't like him off by himself. Sure enough, at the market (which is as I described it, except this one is under two tin-roofed pavilions) he takes a nasty spill maneuvering a steep step, and lands on his side in the mud. It's embarrassing for him, and he gives every assurance he is unhurt, but now he is really wobbly. So we're back at the ship, and I haven't been to what there is of town, and I can hear through my curtain the gummers are at odds over just when a coach should come to collect them to take them to some resort for lunch.

I am being very still at the moment, assessing my feelings, and planning a move. For one thing, I believe I may have exaggerated my fall from composure a few days ago. I have suffered such good health most of my life that when I get a headache I tend to ascribe it to a brain tumor. A case of athlete's foot one time I made to be the beginnings of something indescribably horrible, with amputation a certainty. I do not mean to diminish or trivialize any of the reasons I have already listed leading up to my good cry, and the extraordinary release I felt, and the tenderness afterward. However, upon reflection, I think I've got to a big part of the bottom of the bottom that sucked me down.

Can anyone—anyone!—imagine living in the same house with the same people—make it any taxonomy you want: kissing cousins, hired killers, philandering plumbers—for three months, sharing three meals a day, many days no one even leaving the house or able to? Put that together. Table habits. Toilet complaints. Old women's sickly perfumes. Is there any wonder that for a single day after all this time I became a sniveling idiot?

I don't believe people with a serious degree of mental instability snap back in a day or two. I mean, there's manic-depression, but that's way out of my league. As it happens, I feel fine, balanced, untender (which is not the same as tough), sober. Right now this minute I'm going to do some stretches, and then go out and run through what there is of the town, run on for an hour.

With the exception of a Toyota dealership and a Kmart, I pretty much nailed Kimbe in my imagination yesterday. It's not a real Kmart, as people know them. But the dealership is real—not glitzy, but the genuine article (fifteen new trucks on the lot).

I was too self-conscious to run along the road. The shoulders were thick with shoeless people. A thirty-minute walk away I came upon a white people's golf club, a dirt road leading down to the links by the bay and all manner of pidgin English signs warning us darkies to stay off the fairways and greens and, if we weren't members and we didn't work there, just stay out in general. But since I'm a white guy I reckoned no one would object to me running down their dirt entrance road to the bay, past the clubhouse and back out the exit, maybe do it twice, get the heart up. With three short-haired, slick, purebred guard dogs at my heels, I got my heart up, all right. (I can't identify the breed, and I did not stop to ask; guard dogs, fast ones.) I don't suspect I ran more than one half to three quarters of a mile, but the second half of it I ran like a man one step ahead of a coffin trying to claim him. The sons of bitches stopped just before the main road, at the last sign that warned no trespassing, as though they could read.

At any given moment, I've found that Tolstoy, like the Bible, can be as relevant as your circumstances and interpretation. For example, as I prepared to go into supper tonight, I was reading that, in 1812, as Bonaparte threatened Moscow, posters began to appear in the capital saying the French "would be blown out with Russian cabbage, that Russian porridge would rip their guts open, and cabbage soup would finish them off."

You'll get no argument from the non-Russian diners on this ship.

It is some men's nature to aggravate their suffering. To that end, I have changed my dining venue tonight to the Russian mess. At least I will have no knowledge of whatever intrigue is going on in there. Only a couple of them speak a limited English. Third Officer Andrey is on watch, so I may get through much of the meal in blessed silence. The food and the yellow clouds of cigarette smoke—well, the bitter with the sweet. If I live, I shall account. Otherwise, adieu.

Fifteen minutes, I ate in fifteen minutes—the Russians, in less. Their mess is opposite the galley from the officers' dining saloon, where I have been taking meals for three months. When I walked in, Tuber the Root Crop Tsar saw me from the stove and thought it was a joke. I ladled myself a bowl of soup (ham bits and turnip greens) from the common pot and took a seat at one of the two Formica tables the crew uses. Also got a glass of what looked like dishwater but turned out to be that ersatz beer they make out of stale bread. It didn't give me a buzz and it didn't give me a sense of failure for falling off the wagon—a lapse of taste, perhaps, but no other guilt association. The Russians only grunted at me, and slurped. They all know who I am. They know me as the madman who tears around the main deck in the noonday and climbs to Monkey Island and back once for every revolution. It's a culture that gives a madman his head.

Walter Cronkite's narration of the war in the South Pacific was the video they were playing on the television in the corner. It was the only English spoken. It then struck me that all the Russians I know who speak English are officers, who eat in the officers' dining saloon. These guys were just looking at the pictures. So it was me and the deckhands, grunts and slurps and Walter Cronkite. Tuber came out with bowls of eggplant and hamburger meat. He set them down two at a time by the common soup pot. You took your soup bowl back to the scullery, put it in the sink, and came back and got some meat. There was sliced white bread on the table and a box of salt. Directly, Tuber brought out a sponge cake with some orange slices on top of it. If you wanted some, you got a slice and slapped it down on the grease left in your meat bowl. Seemed a fair way to fuel up.

You don't like it, starve.

No one spoke to me. A couple of grunts, as I say, but not even a nod. I'm going back tomorrow night, and the night after.

I may have stumbled onto something that works for me.

A half hour before supper, having not used my voice all day, I went into the passengers' lounge, knowing Peter and Harry and Gerda would be there. They are always there. They talk about anything and nothing—they natter. They are never at a loss for a topic, and every topic engrosses them. I call it the American Nerd Corner.

When I reached the lounge, Peter was saying, "One of the reasons I wanted as many acres as I could buy was so that I would never have to smell someone else's septic tank."

They had been talking about waste disposal. Peter could not understand why he had not smelled shit in these primitive port communities. Gerda and Harry talked about what they did with their shit on Guam, and what they did with their shit in Wyoming. Peter talked about efforts to use human shit as fertilizer in Brazil. They talked about short drops and long drops and honey bucket trucks. They talked about how you'd smell shit all over Manila if it weren't for the burning garbage. From half-past five, when I walked into the lounge, until six, when I left for supper, they talked about shit.

In the dark beginning of a new day I heard the spoon tinkle against the teacup, then my very bones picked up the bass, the rumble below, and like bow strings my every sinew began to resonate. They had started the diesels before sunrise. On my back, I gave in to my mattress completely. From my heels, up my calves, thighs, from my coccyx up my spinal cord to my cranium, I began to vibrate. The three thousand tons of palm oil we had taken on in Kimbe had brought back the imbalance that shakes the ship's rib I live upon. Aquiver, atremble, out of sweet repose, once more rose the mighty obelisk of the night.

In again with the lads for supper. Not one of them acknowledges me. The soup seems to have the shoulders of some gray fish in it. There are meatballs and a tough slice of beef and a boiled potato. Coarse brown bread. Tuber comes in from the galley from time to time and gives me a bemused look. In my paranoia I think the Russians think that I am patronizing them, that I am slumming and that I will go back to my rich chums and speak of them contemptuously. If only we could speak one another's language, I would talk contemptuously of my vapid companions on the other side of the galley.

I know we cannot communicate with words because on the television in the corner they are watching an old episode of "Fawlty Towers." The Russians laugh only at the slapstick, as when John Cleese, playing Basil Fawlty, pokes his Spanish servant, Manuel, in the eye. On the other hand, I'm the only one in the mess who laughs when Basil Fawlty, perusing some drawings of nudes at the reception desk, loses himself when the telephone rings and answers, "Fawlty Titties."

It is basic peasant food and I appreciate it. This is what Tuber was born to do. The man's task has always been to keep other men running on meat and root crops. Nobody told him he would wind up being made by twits to produce beef Wellington. My heart has softened considerably toward Tuber. If he put oranges in the spaghetti sauce in the officers' dining saloon, it was because he was under pressure and got above himself. If he put green beans and ravioli alongside your poached egg at breakfast, it was because he thought his mandate was to give the swells not a plate so much as a palette. Over here in the mess he is not challenged, but then he is not so likely to lose himself in a frenzy to please. Tuber is a man who belongs in a mess. For dessert, he has put out a platter of thick cookies and some apples. They aren't oatmeal cookies, but close. And they aren't sweet. It's as though Tuber learned out of necessity how to ration his sugar; just a pinch. The Russians love them, I notice. Leaving the mess, they stuff their pockets full of cookies. Each cookie is the size of an American backyard hamburger pattie. I take four and come back to my sanitarium.

~~~~~
~~~~~

February 26, 1996
Oro Bay, Papua New Guinea

We came alongside the stingy, short quay of Oro Bay about nine this morning. About ten I accompanied Leicester of Devon on a walk to the little stick village nearby, on a shopping trip for bananas. The jungle leaned in close along the road, and now and again a pig squealed out of the bush, demanding we give way. Cocks crowed left and right. Our conversation was nothing worth recording for the first half hour, but then, at a sawgrass bend, Leicester suddenly said, "I'm going to tell you a story I have never told anyone else. That's the truth, so help me. I have never told this to another soul."

I said, "Why, Leicester, I'm flattered."

Leicester said, "You don't know when these things will come

to you, but this one came to me this morning and I thought, 'I shall tell old Greg this one, yes, I shall, old Greg's one for a story like this.' After the war I was covered in divorces for a while. This would have been in forty-six, forty-seven, forty-eight, along in there. I had one woman who had had a colostomy, is that right?"

"You mean a bowel thing? A bowel, uh, well, you know, re-arrangement of things?"

"Yes, a colostomy, something ghastly like you say having to do with that bit of the anatomy. Her husband had something to do with a fire engine company. We went before old Judge Pratt, who looked like he wasn't paying attention, the way he always did. This woman said, 'May I tell the court something my husband told me one night?'

"Judge Pratt said, 'Madam, you can tell this court anything you believe will help your cause.'

"This woman said, 'One night my husband told me my cunt was so big he could drive his fire engine and trailer through without touching either side.' "

I won't deny I laughed in the middle of the road.

I asked, "Well, Leicester, did she get her divorce?"

"The judge awarded her a decree nisi."

"What's that Latin for?"

"It means her divorce was final in six weeks."

"And you have never told anyone else this story?"

"No, sir, not a soul. No one but you in fifty years. It's not the sort of tale you'll catch me passing round. I couldn't imagine telling my wife, Olive. I couldn't tell my partner, Jack. Jack would have been disgusted. The woman didn't tell me she was going to say this, just came right out with it in open court. In those days two policemen stood right beside the judge. I don't know how they kept their composure, nor how Judge Pratt, nor I, for that matter, controlled ourselves. Can you imagine? And not touching either side?

"I said, old Greg will appreciate this one, yes I did, directly it came to me."

We left Oro Bay at one o'clock this morning, full of palm oil. We'll be back in Lae at one this afternoon, picking up empty containers. Tomorrow, we leave Papua New Guinea altogether for Yap, where we will discharge a bulldozer, and then it's the Philippines for five days, and then Singapore, where I jump ship. I think that is why I am sleeping so soundly: my compass is pointed home. I wake up three or four times, but then I sink back into a slumber so profound it takes an act of Congress to bring me out. Last night, I remember being roused momentarily by three long pulls on the ship's horn (three octaves below an A flat), signifying we were leaving port. I joked this morning that no one consulted me about departure, that I had an appointment for breakfast with the first family of Oro Bay, people whose genealogy is a direct arrow marker back to the tree.

I did not say this with any intention to provoke or shock. It is true: Charles Darwin could have saved himself some time by putting in here. If all man is descended from the ape, as all intelligent men should believe, why should it come as an insult that some men sport a stronger family resemblance than others? If the faces don't give you a clue in Papua New Guinea, have a look at the feet. Go to the Congo and watch people peel bananas with their lower lips. This is not provocative stuff. This is science based sheerly on observation.

If you want xenophobic travel writing, or just offensive nationalistic generalizations, turn to Tolstoy. Why, there's not a German in *War and Peace* who isn't referred to as a "sausage stuffer." Tolstoy, just on conceit:

The Frenchman is conceited from supposing himself mentally and physically to be inordinately fascinating both to men and to women. An Englishman is conceited on the ground of being a citizen of the best-constituted state in the world, and also because he as an Englishman always knows what is the correct thing to do, and knows that everything that he, as an Englishman, does do is indisputably the correct thing. An Italian is conceited from being excitable and easily forgetting himself and other people. A Russian is conceited precisely because he knows nothing and cares to know nothing, since he does not believe it possible to know anything fully. A conceited German is the worst of them all, and the most hardened of all, and the most repulsive of all; for he imagines that he possesses the truth in a science of his own invention, which is to him absolute truth.

In Lae this afternoon I will go to the post office and buy some boxes. I will fetch those boxes back here to my cabin and pack them with books and the heavy winter clothes I wore and brought with me to Europe last November. Tomorrow morning I will mail them home. This act toward homecoming lifts my heart like none other in three months. It is true that no man is an island, but I have taken a good old Yankee run at living like one for nigh on a hundred days now. I have driven down deep inside myself and come up with nothing much you couldn't find with a stethoscope and a fair guess (a proctoscope might yield more, but if you read me even casually, that's on the surface, too). I am impatient for the end of my voyage, but this impatience, I notice, does not interfere with sleep. Nor is it the sleep of depression. I feel it is the sleep of release.

Nor is it the withdrawal of depression. I dine with the Russians, who do not speak to me. I live with Tolstoy, who speaks to me only in abstract ways. It is the withdrawal of survival.

A factory-like frenzy of arc welding and pipe removal has cut loose on deck topside of me. The captain is having the hands dismantle a radiation flushing system installed by the Soviets. He is concerned someone will accidentally set off the thing, and we'll be flooded.

And one more note from the end of the Cold War: the crew is selectively thinning the forest of antennae this ship found necessary when it supplied Soviet military installations in the icy far north (as though some law of the sea required every innocuous little old supply ship to be wired for Mars). Already the electronics harvest has seriously denuded Monkey Island, where I once counted seventeen aerials before it occurred to me I was obsessively counting just to be counting something, like Pedantic Peter, and I became self-conscious and stopped.

I'm still here, only quieter, more calloused. My realm is a contemplative, carpeted, ten-by-twelve cell a hundred feet above the blue Pacific. Where once I was a trigger-happy diarist, possessed with the zeal of a jailhouse lawyer filing appeals for every cellmate in the joint, lately I pick up a pen with a moan.

I have all but abandoned the gummers, with the exception of Leicester of Devon. The gummers have not noticed I have abandoned them. So much the better. What presumption I had, what gall, to think I could get them to play my game. They have been at theirs for decades (the Brits would say for donkeys' years, or donks, or, in some cases, yonks) longer than I have been at mine. They have, if only subconsciously, embraced the great futility and now advance numbly toward the mystery.

It does not bother the gummers if the conversation never climbs. They are unaware that they talk about the quality of the potatoes every day. (Am I wrong in thinking a potato is a potato, not a wine grape? You either get a good potato or a rotten potato—oh, maybe the odd mealy potato. There is no such thing as a *great* year for potatoes, is there? Even the vodka guzzlers on board never chug-a-lug and holler, "Now, *that* was a *great* year for taters!")

Other than breakfast (bran and shredded wheat for me, and several of the gummers do not attend breakfast), it has been yonks since I have taken a meal with my fellow passengers in the officers' dining saloon. The next to last supper I had in there, Agatha of the Lakes, who was at my left, noticed "beetroot salad" on the menu and commented, as she has, oh, eight or nine times before, "Does it seem to you the Russians eat a lot of beetroot?" I remarked, as I have for three months and tomorrow entering the fourth, that the Russians, owing to climate and impoverishment, exist largely on foodstocks that grow beneath the earth, not above it. My last supper in the officers' dining saloon, the following night, Agatha of the Lakes noticed "beetroot salad" on the menu, turned to Little Peter, and commented, "Does it seem to you the Russians eat a lot of beetroot?"

I understand old age bestowing on one the right not to give a damn, but does it mean not bothering to rise to even an infinitesimal challenge? Why do I let it annoy me that they won't, for example, make the smallest attempt at pronouncing an unfamiliar word? We have a stewardess, Nadezhda (Nah-dee-ezh-da). Not one of the gummers has attempted to wrap his tongue around this woman's given name. You think that throws them, you ought to get them to try ratatouille (it's on the menu from time to time; Tuber is an eggplant man). We are headed, after we drop off two generators on the island of Yap, for a port in the Philippines called Davao (Da-VOW), and on this deck they pronounce that Davey-O, and will not countenance any other pronunciation.

They go on marking the days in their meaningless ways and I grow weary of trying to shake up the complacency. In *War and Peace*, Pierre, the character I identify with most, feels petty and false in comparison with the force and simplicity of the Russian infantryman. I expected to feel more humility around my companions, and more respect. Instead they just mostly make me mad. I stupidly bash my head again and again thinking I might get them to intellectually *engage* more, but if it does not bother them that they are not living consciously, why should it gnaw at me? Tonight will be the sixth or seventh night I have not dined with them, and only the captain is on to me. Could it be this insults my sense of my own importance? Indeed, didn't I book this ride to begin with because I was in the throes of losing my sense of my own importance? Now we're getting somewhere. If that is what's eating me, why take this inclement interior weather out on the gummers?

Do men in penitentiaries struggle with themselves and rant like this all the time?

My guess is they do when they are cherry. And then without taking any special note of it they begin counting—steps to the yard, train whistles at night, personal urinations in the course of a day. Then one supper they begin to consider the quality of the potatoes . . .

Silence. I cannot loftily say that nihilism reigns in the Russian mess, but gloom does—even with *Some Like It Hot* (from the library) playing on the VCR in the corner. Tony Curtis and Jack Lemmon in drag, bookends to the pendulous Marilyn Monroe. Vegetable soup. Roast chicken. French fries/baked potato/mashed potato (the Russians will eat all three). Lettuce and green pepper salad. White bread. An apple. Silence. My companions are surprisingly clean and well mannered at table, but gruff. I may be misreading them, but I continue to think I put them off. Other than the sound of knives scraping their plates, silence.

Tolstoy says there is a "vague and exclusively Russian feeling of contempt for everything conventional, artificial, human, for everything that is regarded by the majority of men as the highest good in the world."

Like civilized discourse at the evening meal. Or a rudimentary smile. Or mere recognition that you live upon the earth and breathe the air.

I take my dirty dishes back to the galley, pick up an apple, and prepare to go.

"Gregory!" It is Veniamin (I have just recently learned his Russian name; he first introduced himself as Benjamin), the Russian A.B. who used to speak to me back in Europe, donkeys' years ago. "Tomorrow night, you sit here!" He pats the empty chair beside him at the table.

First words. It took one full week. A breakthrough. I feel like Dian Fossey, with the silverback.

~~~~~

March 1, 1996
Bound for Yap

Great day in the maundering!

Today is my son's birthday. Today my daughter is expecting a son. I search the larder of a father's experience for wisdom to impart, and find a leftover drumstick, a quarter-wheel of Brie, and an old, flat Schlitz. Only in the movies do men of vast experience give useful advice. Well, there was Conrad Hilton. Asked what he had learned after fifty years in the hotel business, he said, "When you take a shower, always put the curtain inside the tub."

I could no more be extemporaneously wise . . . well, hell, I couldn't even do it with a lifetime of planning. I remember reading once that on his deathbed, on the Fourth of July, American Independence Day, in 1826, John Adams remarked that at least Thomas Jefferson (down the road and only moments from death himself) still breathed. And when I read that, the old rocker in me thought: Comes my moment to shout or forever hold it, I could rasp, "At least Joe Cocker lives!"

In any event, all we have for communications on board is a telex. My daughter doesn't have a telex. My son doesn't have a telex. I used to file newspaper stories by telex, in the Stone Age. Nobody has had a telex since facsimiles went large. We don't have a fax on this ship. We used to have a satellite phone (I used it Christmas; ten dollars a minute), but it broke. The phone requires Russian parts. It has not worked since New Year's.

But what would I tell my children anyway? What have I learned? I crawled out of my bunk at half-past two this morning, fished my pencil and my notebook out of the pocket of my shorts, and scribbled this:

> love
> liberty
> security
> you're done for without all three

I think I would tell them I have come to believe the key elements of an agreeable life are love and liberty and security. I think I would tell my daughter that a satisfying life is making that baby feel free and safe in her arms—and feeling free and safe herself, in someone else's.

If it is a love that nourishes and comforts, and warms against cold winds, yet poses no threat of asphyxiation, only the intellectually damaged would risk an hour without it. Sons never speak disparagingly of mothers who love like that. Nor, if they have found someone who offers this blessing unconditionally, do husbands, wives, daughters—nor the searching heart lucky enough to have caught the eye of one who shows this kind of promise.

Ten years ago, my daughter won a beauty contest. She cringes when I call it a beauty contest. She insists it was peer pressure got her into the thing, but for all the urging of her friends, she wouldn't have capitulated and gone through with it if it had not involved as much poise and reasoning as drop-dead looks. Whatever you want to call it, then (it was a beauty contest, I say), I was in the audience when the judges asked my daughter what she considered the most important element in any relationship.

She stepped to the microphone, fixed them with a defiant honesty every human being manages to misplace sooner or later, and said:

"Trust."

Then she stepped back. And they crowned her.

> love
> liberty
> security
> trust
> you're done for without all four

~~~~~~

March 2, 1996
Bound for Yap

It was just an unclaimed chair in the mess. I thought I was being invited to sit between Veniamin the A.B. and Pyotr the Bosun and chat amiably while we fed ourselves. In truth, it was a directive from the only English speaker in the mess.

Now I have my own chair, at least. Passed the meal (beet soup—not borscht, I should be so lucky, just beet soup—and white fish, mashed potatoes, coleslaw, leftover sausages from the officers' lunch, and an orange) in silence, again.

But outside the mess, Veniamin asked me to his cabin. He has come a long way with his English since December, when I first met him on the bridge, where he was taking inventory of flags.

As it turned out, the reason he invited me to his cabin was to practice his English. He said Andrey, the third officer, will not help him with his English (the Russian philosophy being: zealously protect what you've got; don't share a skill, or the competition might gain on you), and the passengers were out of the question because "they have their own collective."

Veniamin offered me vodka. I declined. In a few minutes, he offered me vodka again. I declined.

After a while, he poured me a cup of vodka.

I handed it back.

"Please, why?"

"If I am going to help you with your English, you have to accept that I cannot drink with you."

"Yes, maybe later, no?"

"No."

He showed me his dictionaries, his lesson book, and the vocabulary cards he made himself. Reading one of his cards, he said solemnly, "Decease—it means sick."

"No," I said, "it means dead."

"Dead, not sick?"

"Stone dead."

"Decease—not sick?"

"Let me see the card. Oh, no, disease. You are right. Disease. You were not pronouncing correctly. Zee . . . zee . . . zee . . . disease. See . . . see . . . see . . . decease. You understand? It's a hard language."

"Yes, I understand. I was lazy with my pronounce. It is not so hard for me. I must endure. It is the word for this learning for me, no? I must endure to learn the English."

For a Russian, I could see the attraction in a word like "endure," but I couldn't let it pass, if only because Veniamin was beginning to sound like Faulkner with a bourbon in one hand and a Nobel in the other.

"Give me your English–Russian dictionary," I said. I looked up what he needed. "There," I said, pointing. "That's the word you want."

"Per-se-vere," he said, sounding the syllables. And then he read the definition in Russian. "Persevere! Oh yes. Is much different."

"A great difference," I said. " 'Endure' and 'persevere' aren't two to be confused, in my book."

"Yes, this is good. You will teach me your English all the way to Europe, no?"

"Well, I'll try to help as far as Singapore. I'm leaving in two weeks, at Singapore."

"No! No! But what about our friendship? We have made a friendship."

Ah, Lord—the innocence and immaturity of isolation, like army buck privates at a hardship post. Big old open thirty-one-year-old face. An openness, once you are in, that would be so easy to exploit. And here I was suffering the beginnings of a terrible attack of indifference.

This morning at ten o'clock, I finished *War and Peace*. I had written my name in it on the opening page and dated it the first of December, 1995, Liverpool. This morning I wrote my name on the last page and dated it, and, after a swift, fact-finding mission to the bridge, fixed the spot where I read the last word at 2 degrees north, 131 east. I don't know how I feel, reaching the end of Tolstoy's great thunder mountain of humanity (even Leo's Epilogue comes in two parts and runs over a hundred pages). I respect him for the courage it required to make a run at understanding the essence of this life. In the end he gave Pierre God, as you would the dog a bone, but heroically took on the inexplicable himself, only to emerge from the battle, like all who went before and all who have gone after him, demolished by the effort. Still, it was good to see Pierre pitch up at peace with himself, a man content with his God and his freemasonry and his family, especially since his wenching wife Ellen had gone to the grave and been replaced by the good Natasha, earth woman, angel, and sitting-room chanteuse. "What had worried him in old days, what he had always been seeking to solve, the question of the object of life, did not exist for him now . . . And it was just the absence of an object that gave him that complete and joyful sense of freedom that at this time made his happiness."

I can't touch this. I don't possess the tools and may never.

This afternoon, as the weather came in sideways and fat drops of rain blew horizontally out of gray, equatorial skies (we're headed north again), and beat against my porthole, I put on a video, *Monty Python's The Meaning of Life*, and watched the lads boil it down to Eric Idle asking: "Isn't it awfully nice to have a penis? Isn't it simply swell to have a dong?"

Unlike Pierre, I continue to search for answers, and, whether it is Monty Python or Leo Tolstoy, in my shape, a man can't risk disregarding a source, any source.

Strange night, last. We were to have another one of those bar-
becues astern, our second, and probably last. At six o'clock the
captain announced on the public address system that the squalls
that were presently raking us had altered the plans. A couple of
the Russians would go on and man the grill under umbrellas aft,
but we were to dine in the Russian mess. This titillated my fellow
passengers, none of whom had been in there before. I think they
expected *Hustler* centerfolds on the walls, and inflatable women
on the settees.

The mess is plain, not tasteless. The captain chose it for the
barbecue venue because it is impervious, like the Russians—it
rejects exterior influences, to say nothing of grease stains. There
is no carpeting on the linoleum floor. There is no cloth on the
tables. It is so casual it is a natural indoor picnicking environment, and there isn't a chance of anyone embarrassing himself
by selecting the wrong eating utensil. It's a knife-and-fork room,
but your hands are all right, too.

When I walked in I found Toxic June, Ettore, Priscilla, Andrey, and Alex the radioman at the first table inside the door.
Also Ernie and May of Tennessee, who were inebriated and stupid.

"Darling!" June beckoned. "We would be delighted if you
would join us." I sat down, leaving one vacant chair to my left.
"Please guard that chair against an imbecilic occupant," T. J.
commanded, just as Pedantic Peter slid into it.

June, the Russians, and Ettore were knocking back three-
fingered vodka shooters, the Russian way, and chasing them with

beer. "You can have a baby vodka, can't you, darling?" June said. I declined. Tennessee Ernie had a beer and a vodka; then so did Little Peter, surprisingly. June was going flat out, slamming her glass on the table each time she finished a shot. "Bloody hell I could be Russian!" she declared (lustily—yes, I believe "lustily" is the word).

Meanwhile the other table filled up with the enemy camp, and leery Russians roved the edges.

Na zdorovye! Wham! T. J.'s glass hit the table. Watching this action, the captain at the next table was thinking (he would tell me later): She's just like an infant throwing toys out of her crib.

Again a carnivore's dream was laid on—lamb chops, steak, liver, sausages—and the diners chased the meat with cases of beers.

The captain, whose relations with Ettore are strained, and who is trying to be polite to the T. J. faction while offering no encouragement, did not circulate impartially, as is his custom. He kept himself tethered to his chosen table, manned a corner eating station, spoke when spoken to, consumed his chop, and left.

At my table, I was a chary gourmand. I ate while feeling a certain jumpiness, as though I suspected someone dining with me carried a concealed weapon. These people had all but shunned me for weeks. Now Priscilla was speaking to me warmly, and rolling her eyes in mock exasperation whenever T. J. said something provocative, or simply outrageous (I can only guess June was being provocative and outrageous; she had reached that level of intoxication where her aristocratic intonations descend so far back down her nasal passage I cannot understand her). Ettore was telling me stories, which I appreciated. Last year, he told me, bringing another one of these Russian ships back from Bombay, he drank some of their homemade vodka with the crew and went blind for an hour. I have missed Ettore. I lost him when he came under the tyranny of what Tolstoy calls the "petticoat government."

I let them be nice to me, but I did not give much in return. I do not know what brought about this change of heart, but I know they want something from me. This is not groundless suspicion. I know Ettore's career with this line is in jeopardy; I know that for a fact. The more he has groused, the more he has joined his wife and T. J. in running down the firm, the more the three of them have haughtily alienated themselves—entering the officers' dining saloon fashionably late each evening "like the three graces," as Leicester of Devon puts it—the more paragraphs have been added to certain letters to home office. Perhaps Ettore thinks a good word from me might assist his case, even turn a tide. That would be a wrong assumption. If he thinks he can expiate through me, or, conversely, buttress his cause, it is a poor draftee he has selected for the resistance.

Or maybe Ettore just misses me. I know he finds a kinsman in the malcontent in me. While I have never been fired, a constitutional failure to hold my tongue has moved more than one of my employers to dispatch me to some very mean exiles. Yes, perhaps that is the deal with Ettore: one hotspur can always spot another.

Off in a corner, the guileless Veniamin gave me a wave. Today, we worked on "outbreak" and "break out." War breaks out, and yet AIDS is an outbreak (and yet—they say—herpes breaks out on your pink parts, just when you had other uses in mind). I'm glad I'm not just starting out in this confusing language.

Tennessee Ernie was talking to Pedantic Peter: "And so you watch it snow and the temperature falls down below zero and that's your winter wonderland from this God who's supposed to be the God of love, but these little birds starve to death and lots of creatures can't get food and they all die, too. Is that your God of love? Cattle have feelings, too, you know."

Love of warm-blooded creatures has not made a vegetarian of Ernie, I've noticed. He believes in the food chain, all right—he just also believes in being kind until the dinner bell rings. Love of science, on the other hand, has made Ernie an atheist. He gets on this subject when he gets drunk. After a fundamental Tennessee Christian upbringing, one of the things that first drove Ernie nuts was the realization that it could rain for forty days and forty nights and it wouldn't raise the level of the ocean an inch.

This is my fourth month on this ark. I've heard all this, and heard all this.

My mind had begun to leave my surroundings when, out of the blue, Tennessee Ernie turned his besotted face to me and guessed my age at six years higher than its chronological fact. There was no transition here. I cannot say how my age got on the table. I corrected his guess.

"I'm a pretty good guesser," Ernie said. "I'm hardly ever as far off as six years, don't think I ever once been that far off. So I guess you'd just better start looking out. The miles are starting to show on you."

It can be a vicious crowd on Saturday night, if you're clean and sober.

The foe at the other table rose to leave, en masse. Agatha of the Lakes pinched me under my arm, goosed me, as she passed behind my back. It is an old pattern with Agatha. She always practices her coquetry during her Saturday night toots.

I waited till the doorway was cleared, then made my own clear-headed dash. Everyone who had not spoken to me in days called to me a warm good night.

It will all come out in the wash, but this morning I don't believe any of last night's revelers wanted anything from me. They were just drunk. There was no subtext. Only an asshole teetotaler like me would try to read something sinister into it. Loquacious Ernie gets a little antagonistic toward me when he's in the bag, but the rest of them are pretty sweet drunks. They were just trying to have a good time, that's all. If I could be a classic Saturday-night drunk I would be a Saturday-night drunk. Blow it out, look at yourself in the mirror Sunday morning, exhale, "Mercy!" and throw up and go to church. That's the life. Me, just after about an hour, maybe two, of bibulous euphoria, I slip into a brooding zone. It could be worse. Some drunks get violent. I just grow dark, and fade to black.

Would it be of any geographical help if I said, with calipers in the chart room, I have determined it is four hundred and fifty miles southwest of Guam?

We are half again as long as the longest ship that has ever called here, so we had to come in backwards, in order to get out later. There is not room in the harbor to turn around. We came in the slender channel astern, as I say, through a gauntlet of the grounded skeletons of ships that couldn't even make it coming in sailing forward—some that entered the bay flying the Rising Sun. The captain was very much on edge, and the stress showed. He said in his dreams he sees coral reefs port and starboard, and here they were. "Some nice bits of coral down there," he said to me on the wing of the bridge as we backed in. It was a bitter joke, and he didn't mean for it to evoke a laugh, and so I only nodded. Ain't my fifty-million-dollar boat.

Finding the air too tense on the bridge, I went up to Monkey Island, where Leicester of Devon was viewing Yap through his binoculars. I had a look, making out a couple of dozen modest structures and a sewage treatment plant out on a peninsula. Pretty primitive. Below us, we heard the unmistakable mellifluity of Toxic June hallooing Harry: "Good morning, darling."

"Her ladyship," said Leicester. "She didn't come to dinner last night. The word was she was seasick. I reckon she was pissed." Leicester sighed. "The coarsest piece of humanity I've ever come across. God help me, I can't save myself getting a bit shirty with her."

Once here, I was first ashore. On the quay, I declined an interview. There was a television crew from Guam on the wharf. We were bringing new power to Yap, two seventy-five-ton generators. To come alongside, we had had to hire a tug from

Guam, and it cost twenty thousand dollars. We were a big deal. "I'm just a tourist," I said at the foot of the gangway, and waved the camera off.

I found Yap a little, friendly, simple place. The Spanish had it (the Spanish knocked it up in 1686; premature ejaculators, they peaked early everywhere, the Spaniards), then lost it to the Germans, then the Germans lost it to the Japanese, and then the Americans became Yap's stewards until independence ten years ago. But there's still Budweiser on tap, and the fragrance of cheeseburgers sails on the tropical wind through the palms. No matter where I walked, people knew I came from the ship. These generators mark a banner day for Yap (Yap-pee!). When the Yapese get them plugged in, you won't be able to give away a candle in Yap.

Once I became accustomed to large, brown, stunning, inviting, bare breasts every which way I turned (in a blueball situation, this is a harder adjustment than it sounds), I looked for a phone. This being an American-influenced island, the post office did not offer telephone service. Anyplace else in the world, it is still the PTT (post, telephone, and telegraph), but if America has anything to do with it, any recognition there is a world outside (international telephone service, money-changing facilities) is nonexistent. At the post office, a woman with a bloody-red mouth from betel nuts directed me up a pig trail to the TeleCom building.

I learned I am not a grandfather yet. My grandson weighs eight pounds, but isn't much interested in the dark journey out into our dubious light. From this earliest sign of his inclinations, I know I'll love him dearly. But he can't win against my daughter: if he does not choose to join us out here in the struggle in five days, my daughter, with the blessing of her physician, is going to insist.

I will now try, for at least forty-five minutes of every hour, not to think of my daughter.

When she was five years old, I had a farm in Georgia. On

the farm was a barn, and beyond the barn there was a dirt road that snaked over a ridge through a ruined apple orchard, and white oak, tulip poplar, and loblolly pine, and on the back side of the ridge lived a playmate of my daughter's named Lisa Ryder. One day, I was sitting on the front porch of my house, trying to write a piece of fiction about a very old couple who still found each other enthralling (when you are young, you do not know the definition of the word "pretension"), and I saw my daughter coming back from Lisa Ryder's. She was skipping—five-year-old girls skipped then and I suspect they do still—over the ridge behind the barn and down toward home. I saw her when she lost her balance and pitched forward, dredging down the corduroy road (it had rained in the morning) with the heels of her palms cutting through the muck before her like a double-bladed plow, and her bare knees digging two more furrows behind. I saw her stand up and stamp her foot in anger at herself, and then begin picking out the pebbles embedded in her palms and her knees. Cleaned up but abraded red, she began skipping down the hill again, and was lost to my view behind the barn.

But when she emerged back in my vision on the near side, and saw me on the porch, she ceased her song (a child's jump-rope chant) and fairly collapsed in pain and tears. I couldn't do enough to ease her trauma.

If I could think of some smart way to dovetail these two considerations—my daughter having my grandson, and my daughter taking a flying spill behind the barn twenty years ago—I would pull the nose up in time to avoid crashing this plane.

But I'm just a father, fourteen thousand miles from a daughter, who is having a baby, or trying.

Yesterday on my walkabout I passed a tan, low-slung, poured-concrete building with a silver tin roof and the legend above the front door: Yap State Legislature. In the parking lot were five reserved spaces:

Speaker
Vice-Speaker
Senator
Senator
Senator

Old newspapermen are suckers for a statehouse. I let myself in. A secretary at my immediate left asked if she could assist me. I asked if the legislature were in session. She said, "No, they are in session for forty days starting in January."

I said, "What do they do with their time when they are not in session?"

She said, "They rest."

Barry my friend the Irish purser, who managed to find the one Irishwoman on Yap, a woman whose father played the publican in the John Wayne movie *The Quiet Man*, no less, told me this morning he spent an hour with our three gargantuan stewardesses the other night. It was Galena's forty-fifth birthday, and they were celebrating.

"I was fortunate to get out with me life. To watch the three of them dancing—oooooh, I tell you, Gregory, it was horrifying."

The captain dropped in for a long visit this morning. Two days to Davao, and he is history. He will fly back to England from Manila. I am tempted to go with him, but I think I would regret not sticking it out to Singapore, the last port on this run. After all, it was the captain who told me just that (don't jump ship) the day I was overtaken by the crying jag.

The skipper said there was a nasty scene yesterday involving the chief engineer, the shipping line's representative in the Pacific, and himself. They just turned ground in the same old played-out field. Personalities. Toxic June. The engineer's wife's ceaseless bitching. The engineer lost his temper. There is fresh hostility in the companionway today.

A whiff of Yardley's brilliantine in the accommodation ladder this morning as I descended to breakfast, alerting my nostrils to the eggs-and-bangers trailblazer ahead of me below, Leicester of Devon. I entered the officers' dining saloon hot on his heels.

Leicester told me T. J. swept into the saloon for dinner last night "with her entourage [the chief engineer and his wife]," as is her custom, and her two companions promptly secured the only unoccupied seats at the captain's table. That left T. J. with the table where sat her archenemy, Agatha, with her second husband, Dick, and my Leicester.

June would have none of this. There is a tiny, unused table over near the door to the galley, there to absorb the spillover in case we draw a crowd in some port. "Her ladyship came over here," Leicester recalled for me, tapping the tablecloth with a forefinger, "and collected a load of cutlery and went over there and sat by herself. I know you would have found it a delicious scene. As long as you insist on avoiding us at supper, I suppose I'll have to keep supplying you with these titbits."

The captain told me that on her way to her lone table, T. J. muttered, "I simply can't eat with that bloody woman."

Cahn't.

It doesn't seem to matter where I sup on this bucket, there's a constant struggle for status and position. In the Russian mess, the oilers do not sit with the deckers. In the officers' saloon— well, now, there's June establishing her own separate satrapy.

(Still no word on the impending writ from Basil, T. J.'s nephew and barrister. T. J. faxed him from the shipping agent's office in Madang. She awaits a telex from him on board, or a fax at one port or another.)

At midday I was sweating through my regime when T. J. motioned me to stop as I tore through her fourth-deck tanning salon. "Darling, do you know where I had dinner last night?"

"Leicester told me. I love it. I just love it."

"Wasn't that divine?" She nickered like a racehorse.

Go on, I say to myself, rage, June, go on. The others are just crossing off days. You've got more sand than the rest of them combined.

Watched *Out of Africa* last night. Makes me overwhelmingly nostalgic. Even the sappy music melts my heart. We lived not far from Karen Blixen's place, used to prowl the Ngong Hills once or twice a week. My wife gave the screenwriter, Kurt Luedtke, names, contacts, phone numbers, directions, road maps, advice, and a whopping load of her time and energy as he set off to conduct his research in Kenya. It always rubs me badly when the credits roll and I don't see Madeline's name. They should have given her some acknowledgment, "best boy" or something.

March 7, 1996
Davao, Philippines

Last night, pacing the deck—like an expectant father—under a silver moon, I found a magazine on a coil of heaving line astern. FOR MEN. THE ULTIMATE COLLECTION. IT JUST GETS HOTTER IN HERE! 164 BABE-PACKED PAGES. Good grief, Alena, Jodie, Roslyn, Carla, Robyn, Rachel, Jenny, Fawn, Jessie, Kelly, Melinda, Bobbie, Julia, Solange (Solange?), Annette, Katherine, and Roxy, what would Daddy think? In the back of the book an advertisement directed readers to telephone 010 852 172 42 743 (if calling from USA, replace 010 with 011) and "eat smelly knickers." Like a drinking Muslim (or a wenching Baptist spewing hypocrisy from the pulpit of a Sunday, for that matter), I was instantly ashamed of the polar forces at work within me. Here I was a panicky, perambulating grandfather-to-be, a picture of head-of-the-family compassion. And here I was ecstatic that Jodie, Roslyn, Carla, Robyn, and the rest would expose themselves to such photographic inspection for a sailor such as me, a randy old goat who would like nothing better than to wake up next to a woman who smelled like low tide.

Yes.

A star fell and my sense of shame burned out about as quickly. A man is a host country to contradictions. Innocent but possessive parental love and unbridled lust for someone else's children (Solange!) aren't the half of them. I put the magazine back on the pile of rope for the next tramp passing in the moonlight.

March 8, 1996
Davao, the Philippines

A boy, and they call him Andy. Eight pounds, four ounces, everything normal, mother doing fine. A two-day labor, but she stuck it out, declining the alternative as the sissy way to go. The fax says she loves me and the baby has my nose. I find myself thinking about my nose, a thing on my face I've never given any thought at all.

I was tempted to bail. I could see planes taking off across the highway from the wharf. Commuter to Manila, connection to Los Angeles, Delta (they're ready when you are, they say) to Atlanta—better get steady here, and sleep on it. It's an emotional day. Wide-bodied jets and stewards and galleys full of champagne and emotions—and me!—do not mix.

We had to drop the anchor in the harbor last night. Inept pilots. The captain was cross. Twenty-seven Filipinos boarded us, all in the name of customs. Barry the Purser gave them fourteen cartons of cigarettes and ten liters of whiskey. They took the bribes with alacrity, would have accepted more, but did not let us move. We could, however, sail in at first light on a high tide. At four this morning, Ben the first officer commenced trying to raise a pilot on the radio. Nobody home.

We came alongside at noon.

The captain is being relieved here, and, as I said, he was an unhappy man until half-past noon, when he rapped at my cabin door with the fax the shipping agent had brought on board. "Congratulations, Granddad," he said. Great smile.

I didn't tarry. I just stuck a clean shirt, a razor, and a toothbrush in my backpack, tore off down the gangway, outwalked a posse of whores to the highway (I thought of dragging a foot, I did), flagged a taxi, and stopped at the first resort hotel we came across. I'm still in the lobby. Can't get a room for four more hours. But they're letting me use the phone. Nothing like a new baby to lend you the opportunity to wake the world up with a bawl.

Andy. I hadn't heard that one. No one ran it past me. When the sun rises in Georgia, in another couple of hours, I will call Andy's mother and tell her what an exceptional human being I believe she is.

Andy! Let's go fishin'! Shoot marbles! In seven or eight years we'll sneak out behind the barn and share an unfiltered Camel, turn green, and puke. We will speak ill of girls together until your head begins to be turned by them, and then we will speak of yearning and we'll hear our hearts beat in our ears (the truth is, I'm better at this than fishing).

You'll be bright. I'd better keep sharp if I am to tell you anything of value about the common enterprise of man.

By my watch, Andy, you are twenty-seven hours and four minutes old. For the first twenty-five hours of your life, your grandfather was confined to a ship in a harbor of the Philippines, dying to get ashore to see how you turned out. For the twenty-sixth and twenty-seventh hours of your life, your grandfather has, in addition to nobly declining the services of three Asian prostitutes (this is another subject we'll get into behind the barn,

Andy), been watching the clock, waiting for a civil moment to phone and hear you cry.

And now a high sign from my sloe-eyed Filipina friend behind the plaque that says "Reception." I am to be received in forty-five minutes, when the chambermaid is finished. Room two-o-one, left, through the palms.

Meanwhile, I occupy an airy lobby. I sit on a bamboo sofa, sunk into deep floral pillows, thinking about my grandson. I hear you asking, Andy, from down the years (I picture you reading this in, say, the year 2006—it's just an arbitrary guess, based loosely on the age when my own curiosity pointed my nose [your nose, too, boy, according to your ma] toward books)—I say I hear you asking, why was I here?

To gain some perspective is the short answer. On the television across the lobby from me just now, an American politician said on CNN that the rationale behind a certain policy was "strategic ambiguity." Some world, huh? That's what we need, all right, more men of backbone, leaders with a keen sense of strategic ambiguity.

Sorry. Why was I here? I had it in mind to pick up some perspective. I thought I'd run off and work out what I might do with the rest of my life and the first, oh, say, thirty years of yours. As it happened, I became engaged in a demoralizing idleness trying to find my way home, while my life remained its same old inconclusive tangle. Let that be my first lesson to you, boy: When in doubt, stand your ground!

I'll be done with my ship in ten days. I'll be back in America in a fortnight. I'll see you when the dogwoods bloom on that red clay hill outside your window. From the North, where your vagabond grandfather hangs his hat, if only for the nonce, I will cross into vernal Dixie, your birthplace and mine, about the time the border is described in purple and formed of sweet wisteria.

Except for one dawn approaching Singapore, I pretty much quit writing on the day I learned I was a grandfather. I had no interest in mewling in a journal anymore. From Davao, I flew on up to Manila, where I knew a couple of Americans, and celebrated for the weekend. No great wassail, just a spell of happiness and release. I began drinking moderately. I told myself there's a difference between drinking to celebrate and drinking because you are miserable. The difference is you can manage drinking to celebrate. It's an old lie, but I bought into it for the duration. I told myself I would give up drinking in Singapore, and that was not a lie.

On Monday, the eleventh of March, when I got back to the ship—hoping down deep she had sailed without me—I went first to the purser's office to suss the situation. Barry was not in, but there were two notes on his desk. From Little Peter: "As of twelve-thirty today, my toilet does not flush." From Agatha: "Dear Barry, Loo does not flush!!!" Life aboard ship: same old shit. Thus it was not necessary to keep looking for the purser.

Soon after my return I was insulted by Toxic June, and the following morning I was insulted by Ernie of Tennessee. In the same breath June called me a terrible drunk and called me a sponger for never having bought her a drink. I said I *was* a terrible drunk. I said I never bought her a drink because, as she may have noticed, I was trying my goddamnest not ever to accept a drink from anyone, much less encourage poor conduct in others by stocking my cabin with booze, clanking bottles together, and hollering down the hall, "Bar's open!"

Glutton for guilt that I am, I went and found Barry the Purser this time, and had him dispatch a bottle of whiskey, a bottle of gin, and a bottle of vodka to both T. J. and the chief engineer. Then for good measure I had two cases of Heineken delivered to John the Scot, the second engineer, who has less bullshit in him than anyone else on this ship. I figured that was about everybody who had given me a drink in the last four months. Cost me a hundred pounds sterling. Sponger my ass.

So I go in for breakfast next morning and Tennessee Ernie says, "You know, I can read people pretty well, and I think I know what you've been doin' off by yoreself in all these ports. The young girls find you real magnetic, don't they?"

I said, man, I believe in humanity, and one day somebody in this crowd will cut me some slack. Young girls my ass.

So then I go see John the Scot, who has in the past called me paranoid, and I say these people are insulting me again. He says if that is so, he says he thinks he has it figured out. He says it's envy. I say envious of what? He says youth, mobility, the whole rig. This I suddenly believe is not casuistry on John's part; this is penetrating analysis. Forgetting I had confided as much to my journal, probably while drunk, some time ago, I congratulate John on his perception and step away, paranoidal no more.

A couple of mornings later, I wake up fairly palpitating with promise.

～～～～

First light. A Vermont cheddar moon off the bow, and a gold doubloon of a sun astern, a cargo ship with a black hull and a superstructure the color of English mustard, and all of this crossing stage left over the Dolly Blue. I feel solid and balanced as the dark pulls away the firmament, retreating west overhead like a spangled drape drawn back to reveal ceiling art, a reliable gyroscope keeping me steady somewhere in my soul. Well-being; I breathe through pink sacs, the lungs of Pheidippides (early in the run, I mean, before he finished and died). Nearing journey's end and glad, I suppose. As this day breaks I hold in my breast nothing so much as goodwill toward men. I forgive all past slights against me, real and imagined. I repair every busted affair so that fair ones everywhere place me tenderly once again into the forget-me-not drawers of their hearts. My head is filled with sound counsel for my children, and their children, sagacity I will parcel to them only when beseeched. I stand on the roof of the wheelhouse, one man alone on top of twenty thousand tons of steel shouldering on at ten knots to the hour to touch the ancient ground of Asia beyond this sea. And the world all of a sudden is a place I never want to leave.

From the sound of it, I believe on that morning I was happy nearly to the point of hallucination. Didn't last; never does.

It was a four-day sail to Singapore and I just kept my head down. I was anxious, sipping beer steadily, late in the day, quietly; no big scenes. We had a new captain, an even-tempered Scot who seemed to have things well in hand. He had been briefed on the personalities and let me know he knew what I was up to, including this journal. The old captain and I never did manage our night on the town in the Philippines, but we did catch the same plane to Manila and we said our goodbyes there. We said we'd keep in touch, but I doubt we will. People don't.

Everybody on board seemed fairly preoccupied, more somber than usual—not that I had ever witnessed a cartwheel. I suspect it had something to do with the interesting bits of the voyage being behind them. At Singapore, the ship would lay off shore and bunker. Then the long, single-pause (Suez) ride to Europe, marooned at sea in the village of the unamusing.

June was packing to leave at Singapore, and to join some relative in Kuala Lumpur until it warmed up in the Channel Islands. She thanked me for the booze, kissed me on both cheeks, we exchanged addresses and never spoke again. Leicester of Devon came to me with his address and that of his son. He had agreed to write once he reached England to tell me how the final leg had gone. With June and the chief engineer and his wife absent since Singapore—and me, for that matter—we figured Leicester could capture the last leg in three words: Peace broke out. "I won't let you down," Leicester said. "I'm a reliable man."

I continued to boycott the officers' dining saloon. On my last night aboard I ate in the Russian mess as usual, and when I was through I shook hands goodbye all around. They looked at me quizzically, as you would at a stuffed tick that attempted to say thanks and so long. Surly peckerwoods.

Dawn of the day I was to leave the ship, I had been up and packed for two hours. I had gone to the bridge in the dark and when I stepped into the dim light of the chart room Ben the first officer started and exclaimed, "You scared the shit out of me!" Over the months I had come to admire Ben, for all his workaholic ways. We had a little something in common: Ben was a forty-one-year-old grandfather. We had exchanged a confidence or two. Once, when I pressed him for details of his accident two years ago, when a container broke free and crushed his head (I may have neglected to mention this gruesomeness: his helmet saved his life, but a plastic surgeon had to reconstruct his face from a passport photograph), he laid them out for me in no more dramatic a fashion than one would expect in a tale of a sprained ankle. His memory of that awful business gets him exercised only when he recalls that the penny-pinching company refused to fly his wife to Fiji, where he lay in hospital three weeks.

In the dark on the bridge I told Ben I had a rather embarrassing problem. I said I could not find the clothes I had on the evening before. This would be small potatoes were not my passport in the left front pocket of my trousers.

"Were you drunk?"

"In a purely technical sense—that is, from the point of view of an Alabama state trooper—you might say that."

"Perhaps you packed them."

"That's a good suggestion. It's something I would do absent-mindedly, with or without a drink. I once found a pair of my dirty socks in the freezer."

I had indeed packed them.

Later that morning, as I dragged my bags out of my cabin, I saw Olga down the companionway. She had looked after me all these months. What an intimate association, cleaning a man's toilet every day. "Gregory," she called out, "you are so beautiful!"

"No, Olga," I cried, "it is you who are beautiful!"

"I know," she said, and her Hoover gave a great roar.

As I struggled with my gear I passed the new captain. "Well," he said, offering a firm hand, "short but sweet."

I had left Leicester of Devon in good humor the night before, and a fine thing, because I could not find him when the hour came to say goodbye. I suspect farewells disagree with Leicester. As I handed him off to the sandman one last time, I had said, "Leicester, do you know what you get when you cross an onion with a mule?"

"I can't say that I do, dear boy. Would you help me to the answer?"

"Well, mostly you get a lot of stubborn onions. But every once in a while you get a piece of ass that'll bring tears to your eyes."

Ben helped me with my bags down the gangway and into the launch. Toxic June was already aboard. Gerda and Harry were going to town for the day while the ship bunkered. Ernie and May of Tennessee were going in to see a doctor about Ernie's health (he had lost energy and appetite and had been feeling poorly in general). Agatha and Dick of the Lakes were going in for a tour. Little Peter was nowhere about. The chief engineer and his wife would be along later, when his successor came on board. Ettore and Priscilla and Toxic June were going to spend a little time together in Singapore, before Ettore and Priscilla headed back to Liverpool.

We beat across the harbor with no one saying anything for an hour. At the pier, we simply dispersed. Agatha of the Lakes kissed me (no tongue this time) and said, "Goodbye, dear." The deckhands assisted the aged with their bags, got them down the quay, and hailed them public transportation. By the time I had wrangled my luggage off the launch and the considerable distance to an empty taxi queue, I was alone. They were all gone without a single gesture of something shared, or a word of remembrance. We were rid of one another, and it was good.

So I had a Saturday night and a Sunday in Singapore to myself. I managed to find a little mischief Saturday night, and Sunday morning I was at the Long Bar at Raffles Hotel. Everyone around me was drinking a Singapore Sling, a brain-busting concoction of multicolored spirits blue-haired people seem to favor. I was having beer and peanuts, having just watched the courtyard wedding of Tetsuya Tsukamoto and Kaori Takahashi. The couple left in a Rolls. A tall, dark bartender from Bombay told me that Raffles' most famous habitués, Conrad and Kipling, Hesse and Maugham and Noël Coward, actually drank Singapore Slings, thereby diminishing my admiration for these dead men. Maugham took up the opium pipe in Singapore, I read somewhere. I used to smoke opium in Tehran. It got me wondering if entering the Kingdom of Heaven would be anticlimatic. I ordered a smoked salmon sandwich, borrowed a pencil, and committed some disjointed observations to postcards.

Singapore was all I had heard. Hot, oppressively sticky, and clean to the point of being antiseptic. Nevertheless, I had been giddy since Davao, when I got the word of Andy's birth. That news, and being a short-timer on my ship, reduced me to an almost comic gratitude for all things. I was moved by any kindness, however small. In Manila I was all but blowing kisses, effusively grateful to any stranger who merely refrained from frowning. By the time I reached Singapore the world was a grand old place. I imagine my feelings were the same feelings anyone has coming from some long form of deprivation into sunlight and a reason for rejoicing. Suddenly you see the mortar between the bricks. People are lovely. Someone gives you a smile and you vow to name your next child after them. Every time I was served a meal or a drink or received directions from a cop on a corner in Singapore, I wanted to sit right down and write this generous new friend a bread-and-butter note.

I flew from Singapore to Frankfurt to New York City. Twenty-six hours. The flight attendants showed eight movies. I saw *GoldenEye*. In *The New York Times*, Janet Maslin said, on the evidence of this film, the James Bond series now "suffers the blahs." I raved and cheered at *GoldenEye*. I saw *Powder*. The *Times* reviewer, Caryn James, called *Powder* "nearly unwatchable." I watched it all, touched by it, moved to trickling eyes by the story, gushing down the aisle what a movie, what a movie!

And then I returned to the life and people and stuff I had left behind. My dog all but tore my clothes off at the door. My wife was more reserved. She was glad to see me, though, and I was delighted to see her. When it came time to account, I told her what I had done. She said, "Nothing lasting?"

I said, "I never knew their names."

She asked me whether I had gotten what I went looking for. I couldn't answer that straight. Certainly at that moment I *appreciated* what I had more than when I left. That heightened sense of gratitude that started in the Philippines, making me want to drop to my knees and kiss the ground, Pope-like, was with me on the day I got home and would stay with me for about a month. During that time I would go to Georgia and be a grandfather in the flesh and take glory in it. I had forgotten what a melting experience it is to have your finger squeezed by a pink hand as tiny as a possum's.

But had I gotten what I went looking for?

Provided I went looking *for* something, no. No epiphanies. No catharsis. No key to the universal. No hard-learned lesson, really, to pass along. On second thought, I said, I had written in my diary on the day Andy was born that if I had any advice for him it would be: Stand your ground.

"Does that apply to marriage?"

"My interest in marriage has not come back," I said. "But I'm not going anywhere."

My wife said, "Then neither am I."

I had a letter from Leicester of Devon, mailed from Exmouth the twenty-fourth of April:

I am enclosing a few notes about the voyage from Singapore which I hope you will find interesting. Mostly gossip I'm afraid but there was not a lot to report. The voyage was very peaceful and the atmosphere at meals was great. You wouldn't think that one person could have such an unsettling presence.

Leicester's journal:

16th March: Saw Barry and he told me that June went to see him before she left ship. She was in quite a race and used all the "F" words to describe the ship, food, Russians and Barry. She had some unused spirits in her cabin which Barry took back and refunded her the money. She also complained that Barry hadn't booked her a hotel. How could he when she said she was staying on the ship? She didn't even say goodbye to [Nadezhda] who had worked hand and foot to please her and who she had reduced to tears on more than one occasion nor did she give her a tip. Goodbye to a really nasty type!

17th March: The atmosphere in the saloon at dinner now has completely changed. Barry has resumed having meals in the saloon . . .

18th–23rd March: . . . The two American lady passengers so far as I can see are still eating as much and getting steadily fatter. Harry is supposed to be cutting down on his food intake. He now puts sweetener in his tea then shovels three or four teaspoons full of sugar on his cereals. He is still drinking many tins of beer each day. Peter is still recording sunrise and sunset each day. I asked him what he is going to do with all the statistics he is recording, but apparently it is to keep his brain active!

When we reached Antwerp Lord . . . and two of his fellow directors came aboard on a fact-finding mission. They saw Agatha and Dick and myself and we told them we had thoroughly enjoyed the trip and that we had no complaints. I said there was only one exception and they replied, "We know all about her and she will never travel on another one of our ships."

We docked at Hull at 0400 HRS on Sunday 14th April and I was able to get home at 1900 the same day. It has taken me quite a while to get into my old routine but I am winning slowly! The distance steamed on the voyage was 29,587 miles. Your friend from Devon!

I got a letter from Gerda from Wyoming, dated May 11, 1996:

For all of two days, all of us, including Airhead [Agatha of the Lakes] seemed to have a genuine desire to get along. The chance to play the Queen was overpowering for Airhead, however, and her voice grew louder and louder. It became more and more difficult to get away from either her or the voice. Poor Leicester got caught in her web. She wouldn't let him out of her sight, dragging him to Barry the P. or the Captain over any little thing that must have appeared a threat to her queenship.

Gerda said Airhead gave herself a birthday cocktail party, but didn't invite Gerda or her husband, Harry. "She told Harry she didn't invite him because she didn't want to buy any beer." Gerda wrote:

After Singapore the senior British officers were expected to be at dinner. Barry the P came plastered one evening and sat next to the Capt. Barry the P got up after ordering ice cream (not on the menu) and sang *Cockles & Mussels Alive Alive O!* The captain took it in good humor but Barry the P was henceforth banished from the captain's table . . .

I got a letter from Barry the Purser, mailed from Antwerp on the tenth of April:

The morning you left had its own small amount of drama. Toxic June called me to say that she might not now leave the ship till Europe. I concentrated, in my usual heroic manner, to stop myself from what seemed an inevitable bout of vomiting. Actually, our six-foot-three-inch, two-hundred-and-thirty-eight-pound Captain, who happened to be standing in the alleyway, trembled perceptibly . . . Anyway, our worst fears were shortly allayed. The fucker left the ship!

I again started to take my meals in the saloon. The dining room environment took on a new atmosphere—a sort of nervous jocularity. Almost as if T. J. might, if we were not good, suddenly walk in again . . .

We had a lottery to determine which was the most non-existing human on board. Dick of the Lakes won.

Hope to see you in 1997.

On my desk in my apartment on a roof over Broadway in New York City is the journal (how I wish I could say truthfully it was briny!) containing my diary of the voyage. The last notes were made at the Long Bar of Raffles Hotel, in Singapore, on that sticky Sunday morning several months ago. They say:

It looks now as though I will leave at midnight tomorrow, Monday, and I will have to fly through Europe. So round the world it turns out to be.

Is there anything left to say?

Yes.

I am not a gerontophobe. There will come a day when I will start to miss those funny old people, and wonder what has become of them. The advantage they have over me—all of them save Toxic June—is that each has come to a peace with, and has accepted, what there is. June hasn't; won't ever—it's why I liked her best. June and I will put up a fight until we go down into the earth.

Another thing: When I got up this morning, I could only think of one loose end left to tie. I rang the shipping agent in Madang with my question.

The shark is still out there.

Acknowledgments

Patricia Ryan midwifed this memoir, one embryonic installment after another. My debt to Pat, who has been editing me now for twenty-five years, may never be squared. Mark Warren put dibs on eighty-five hundred words for publication in *Esquire* before passing along the manuscript to Philippa Brophy, a literary agent who was a stranger to me then. Flip called and declared, "I love your book." Sight unseen, I blurted, "And I love you!" She asked John Glusman at Farrar, Straus and Giroux to read the work, and here I am. Without these friends, I wouldn't be.